JALLIKATTU

New Symbol of Tamil Angst

an analytical narrative

JALLIKATTU

New Symbol of Tamil Angst

an analytical narrative

N Sathiya Moorthy

Vitasta
LET KNOWLEDGE SPREAD
www.vitastapublishing.com

Published by
Renu Kaul Verma
Vitasta Publishing Pvt Ltd
2/15, Ansari Road, Daryaganj
New Delhi - 110 002
info@vitastapublishing.com

ISBN 978-93-86473-19-6

Cover and layout by Vits Press
Printed by Vikas Computer and Printers

Contents

To

Lakshmi

Friend, Companion—and Wife

Acknowledgements

This book would not have become possible but for Renu Kaul Verma, Managing Director of Vitasta Publishing, sounding me out even as the Jallikattu protests were unfolding in Chennai and elsewhere across Tamil Nadu. She was personally caught in the midst, touching and feeling it all. With mutual introduction from our common friend A Ganesh Nadar, Renu also persisted with my elaborating on the history of Jallikattu and the context of the unfolding angst, as witnessed by a frequent visitor to the State.

Of course, my thanks are even more due to Papri Sri Raman, my Editor at Vitasta, who has done a great job. This is not to leave out Team Vitasta, including their printers and binders, and their sales and marketing desk.

The title, *Jallikattu: New Symbol of Tamil Angst*, chose itself even as Renu was talking to me the first time on the phone with her wonderful idea. Yet the contents owe to the lengthy conversations on this and other issues of contemporary relevance to Tamil Nadu and the rest of India, with friends like Ramasubbu Krishnamurthy, Deputy Editor, *Dinamalar* and M Kasinathan, journalist and political analyst, and a host of other knowledgeable persons who are happy in anonymity.

This is also not to leave out the every-day nameless commoners that one comes across in the towns and villages of Tamil Nadu, whose perspectives are as sharp as their feel, understanding and knowledge—all are deep.

I thank them all.

N Sathiya Moorthy

Chennai, December 2017

Prologue

Taking the bull by the horns! There is no Tamil equivalent for this English idiom. But when in mid-January 2017, Tamil Nadu erupted in angst as never before, barring of course the anti-Hindi agitation of the mid-Sixties, a forgotten piece of identity-logo spread across the social media. It was of a man holding a bull by the horns and trying to tame it—or, taming it. The legend around the circular logo in Tamil read: *Veezhvadhu naamaha iruppinum, vaazhvathu Tamizha-ga irukkattum.* Loosely translated into English, it says that as a people, Tamils should not think twice about giving up their lives and whatever else they possessed in the cause of Tamil.

The picture with the legend was a straight lift from the logo of the nearly-forgotten DMK mouthpiece, *Murasoli*, or the 'Sound of Drum', founded by party supremo and former Chief Minister, M Karunanidhi, in his teens. As coincidence would have it, the newspaper celebrated its 75th anniversary only months after the Jallikattu protests, which in turn happened when Karunanidhi, 93, was slipping into memory-loss and other age-related health problems.

Originally, the logo found its way into the mast-head of the newspaper in the Sixties, followed by the legend around it in 2006, penned by Karunanidhi into one of his daily *Murasoli* letters to the '*Udan-pirappaye*', or 'Dear Sibling', much earlier. Most Jallikattu protestors were apolitical and some self-styled coordinators of the agitations from a later stage could be perceived as either being non-conformist or as belonging to peripheral pan-Tamil and other ideology-driven 'radical/ extremist' outfits not inclined to be supportive of either the DMK or the ruling AIADMK in the State. Some of them were also perceived as having problems with the Indian State structure. By one count, pro-Jallikattu protests, or pan-Tamil protests in the name of Jallikattu were staged in 50 countries, most of them just symbolic but some of them as vigorous as in Tamil Nadu, though with fewer participants but with equal vigour.

The legend around the 'Bull Fight' logo referred to only the cause of the Tamil language, but in the context of the mid-January protests seeking an instantaneous reversal of the ban on the annual bull-taming sport of *Jallikattu,* it also extended the cause to cover all that was Tamil—customs, traditions and practices from the distant past, to the present day aspirations of irrigation waters, development and jobs, but synchronised with Nature and environment. The slogan had been used earlier at the time of the anti-Hindi agitation, too, with a direct reference to the protection of Tamil language, so to say. This time there was another, equally important difference, too.

The anti-Hindi agitation had a visible, if not declared, political purpose, of targeting the then Congress Party government in the State, then going by the name Madras. Violence was in the air almost from the start. In a way, the over-heated violence caused a re-think in the student-participants, their parents, and possibly the Opposition DMK organisers, too, contributing to an early end to the anti-Hindi agitation than possibly planned for.

Anyway, which organiser of protests of the kind plan for the end, and more so for the day-after—whether in India or elsewhere? What more, with demands fully or mostly met, the issue is lost and lost for good. Re-inventing an issue from the pre-Independence past (1937-40), re-energising a protest and re-capturing minds were all not an easy task—not within living memory, yet precisely that was also the conceptual achievement of the anti-Hindi movement of the Sixties.

In comparison, the Jallikattu protests were peaceful to begin with, there was no violence either at the beginning or at the peak, in the middle—though at the end, there was enough of it at the main Marina venue in the State capital of Chennai. More importantly, there were no identifiable organisers for the 2017 protests. There were also no mood-setting preparatory rallies, conferences, or any other propaganda initiative of any major kind, which is typical of those called by political parties. For the same reason than as an element of surprise, at no venue was any formal police permission for the rally, sought or obtained.

The limited publicity campaign was through the social media, from man to man, woman to woman. The propaganda part, in justification of the protests and also the sport of Jallikattu, followed again through the social media, as if it were an after-thought. Then came the time when the traditional media could not overlook or ignore the protest. Soon, the Jallikattu protests were all over the nation and elsewhere, too. That way, even an equally quick-fix 'trial balloon' of a rally a week earlier did not show up what was in store as much or even much less. The rest, as they say, was/is history.

The January 2017 protests were to press the nebulous demand for lifting the ban on *Jallikattu*, a martial sport, mostly localised to south-central Tamil Nadu and even more identified with the martial community of Mukkulathores with its three identifiable sub-sects in particular. The Supreme Court of India had successively banned the sport for two previous years. Though the Central and State governments had alternated in trying to lift the ban through legal means and through Executive orders, or both, and try and restore the sport—the Judiciary would have none of it.

Yet, the competitive 'Dravidian politics' of the State, with an element of coalition spirit at the national-level up to 2014, ensured that the people always remained unconvinced and suspicious about the party or parties in power. So, when the ban stayed and no one seemed to be wiser as to which way the pendulum would swing in the Jallikattu season of 2017, the call for the protests came. It suddenly caught the imagination of the people.

But it was still not about Jallikattu, and Jallikattu alone.

The protests, and the readiness with which the Tamils in the State first, and those across the world, embraced the call without a second thought, said a lot. It was an expression of the Tamils' sense of denial and alienation, for which they had repeatedly targeted the Centre, the State government (whichever party or ruler was in power), and neighbouring States—and at times a neighbouring nation, southern Sri Lanka in particular.

Of course, the issues too went beyond a game or sport of Jallikattu, with its divine cause flowing from Hindu religious texts, both in Tamil and Sanskrit, and cultural moorings in Tamil legends of valour and literature, among other sources. There were water-sharing issues with neighbouring States, which when became violent, saw fellow-Tamils in those States being physically assaulted by the 'locals'. Issues of the kind were numerous and almost repetitive, evolving into a pattern, but with no end or solution in sight. At least, the Tamils of Tamil Nadu felt that they had been wronged, not just as a State in the Union, but as a community—and as an ethnicity, and always so. The sense of 'ethnic unity' was not exactly there earlier despite the 'Dravidian political identity' to the extent that the later-day Sri Lankan Tamil issue revived and re-kindled it ever more.

To the defence of them all, it should be said that judicial verdicts of the nation's highest body, namely, the Supreme Court, were seldom enforced, in matters where the Tamils' (*read*: Tamil Nadu's) interests purportedly suffered. Nor has been any serious and conclusive political initiative taken (especially by the Union of India) to find a negotiated settlement to the pressing problem(s) of Tamil Nadu, which at least were real.

The 'Cauvery water dispute' with Karnataka and the 'Mullaperiyar storage issue' with Kerala, both neighbours of the constitutionally-mandated political entity called 'Tamil Nadu', are prime examples. Every such issue and every such initiative ran into a predictable stone-wall, only to bounce back with greater momentum with even more predictable periodicity. But when it came to 'anti-Tamil' (?) verdicts of courts, they were enforced without fail. Or, the governments at the Centre and in the State would cite the court verdicts and the propriety to abide by such court verdicts, as the *sine qua non* for the continuing constitutionality of the Indian state and the States within the Indian Union. The 'Jallikattu ban' was/is a prime and near-permanent example in recent years.

Towards the end of days of protests, a sudden awakening to the immediate Tamil cause across the nation, a workable—though not wholly satisfactory—solution was found for restoring Jallikattu for 2017, with the season's events in multiple venues commencing a week or so later than usual. Rather, the workable solution, though interim, was the one that facilitated the early end of the protests, which had otherwise threatened to drag on longer.

It was known that people could not be expected to stay on and on without tending to their daily chores and other priorities, including day-jobs and other income-generating enterprises to support their families. But there seemed to be a possibility that if left with no alternative, members of the dis-organised 'core group(s)' would take turns during week days, calling upon the rest to come back during evening hours and week-end. With the fact that many members of the core group(s) and also many of the equally youthful participants were doing shift duties in 24x7 IT and ITE firms, the possibility of maintaining a decent turnout was not entirely ruled out.

The Court Position

Though Jallikattu came to be staged later in the season, the real issues in the overall context remain. One relates to the pending Supreme Court case against a facilitating Tamil Nadu legislation that made Jallikattu possible in Season 2017, and an earlier one, challenging the Centre's lifting of the court-ordered ban.

With little time left for the 2018 Season in mid-January, the First Bench, headed by Chief Justice of India, Justice Dipak Misra, took up the pending petition from PETA (People for the Ethical Treatment of Animals), the international animal rights NGO, on 6 November 2017, and issued notice to the Tamil Nadu government, returnable in four weeks. When the matter comes up before the court in or after the first week of December, the court in the normal course is expected to give reasonable time for the petitioners to respond.

In ordering notice on the new PETA petition, the Bench has also clubbed this case with the pending cases on Jallikattu, in one of which the court had declared that it was finalising the verdict in the midst of the protests that broke out in January 2017. Either the First Bench or another Bench may then hear the case, on a pre-scheduled date. It is hoped that the Supreme Court will either pass its final verdict well before the traditional mid-January start-off date, or pass an interim order, either banning or permitting Jallikattu for the five-week Season-2018.

Not a Reluctant Partner

Unlike propagated by some, Tamil Nadu was not a reluctant partner in the post-Independence Indian political and constitutional schemes. If anything, it was the first of the unified political entities on whose foundations British India was founded. So, it was also natural that it should be the first one to be counted in for merger, both in terms of political preparedness to join the new nation and also the administrative set-up prepared to make the transition smooth and effective.

Rather, there were no big kings or rulers wanting to go 'independent' or join Pakistan as was the case with the erstwhile princely States of Travancore and Hyderabad in the immediate vicinity, other than the enclaves of French-ruled Puducherry, then Pondicherry, in the immediate neighbourhood, Pudukottai was the only officially-recognised kingdom embedded in the larger Tamil-speaking territory in British-India at Independence, and the ruler signed up for merger without protest. But there were social elements of the Dravidar Kazhagam (DK), who took a politically conscious decision, to observe Independence Day as a 'black day'. In the end, the Indian democratic scheme embraced them, too, and provided for the constitutional political accommodation and elevation of DK's political off-shoots in the DMK first and the AIADMK, later—an elevation that has remained unbroken for 50 long years, as never ever elsewhere across the Union.

The change of political identities, from DMK to AIADMK, and personalities, involving DMK Chief Ministers C N Annadurai and Karunanidhi, and AIADMK's M G Ramachandran (MGR) and Jayalalithaa, have only strengthened the Dravidian political scheme and structure, not weakened the same—at least, not so far. Many have tried and failed. Others have dreamt and worked out some strategies. Some continue to do both.

Yet, travelling away from the days of yore, the Dravidian polity too has been compelled to re-invent itself, in the face of non-competition threatening them with inner-most fears of extinction. This has meant that peripheral political parties and groups, which alone remain to challenge them on their turf and on the causes that they had once held dear to the Tamils and their 'Tamil identity', have been able to do enough to stir them into competitive political action.

After the periphery too had failed them and also compromised the cause, so to say, a faceless, non-existent leadership and its messages through the social media was enough to stir up the people into taking pro-active positions, even if it meant that only a limited goal had been achieved in the end!

Layer after layer

The Jallikattu protests have ended, at least for now but not the protest-mode that had gripped Tamil Nadu.

If anything, like everything else that is synthesised at the bottom and travels upwards, the Jallikattu protests too peaked out, and have begun travelling back to the grass-roots, with more and localised protests, and some like the post-January Tamil Nadu farmers' agitation reaching up to the national capital of New Delhi, with all its shades unfolding, layer after layer with each passing day.

Peaking again in what otherwise should be unthinkable in such a short span was the 'anti-NEET protests' across the State after the Supreme Court upheld its order for nation-wide common entrance examination for medical college admissions, with no relief or exemption for Tamil Nadu, over the short, medium or long-terms. If the post-NEET suicide of S Anitha, a 17-year-old girl who had just completed her Plus-Two examinations with high marks under the State scheme, but could not make it to medical education of her dreams owing to low NEET scores at the entrance examinations, triggered the State-wide protests, the fear of the law possibly coming in the way of the current crop of high school kids otherwise, became a dampener after a point.

Yet, the underlying 'Tamil angst' remains to be fully understood, appreciated and addressed. But in seeking to educate the 'blind' elsewhere, the protestors too have begun leaving their angst behind and bringing 'action' to the forefront. These angst-mongers' methods militate against the conventional understanding of the Tamil psyche, of theirs being a peaceful and peace-loving people. Suddenly, the Tamils are re-discovering someone within, but from the outside. Not many of them like what they see of themselves. Or, what they are made to see of themselves, by some from among themselves.

Everything in the name of youth, student groups and as an expression of unexpressed Tamil angst has suddenly become passé. The new-generation peripheral groups—and they are still peripheral groups, and nothing more—has replaced the jaded, older ones with a clear political identity and acknowledged leaderships. They have also replaced the latter's rhetoric with direct action, which is both imaginary and eye-catching. The forms of protests and calls for protests that they have initiated at times border on violence. At least, they had potential for whipping up violence, if not directed along the right path, over a rightful cause, all the time. The Jallikattu protests, especially in the central theatre of Chennai's Marina sands, was/is a case in point.

The question then arises. Was the hidden agenda of the faceless leadership of a just and timely cause aimed at creating confusion, leading up to chaos in the politico-administrative structure of Tamil Nadu? After the relatively localised 'Kudankulam protests' against the Russia-funded nuclear power project in southern, coastal Tamil Nadu, which did however capture national and at times international headlines the Jallikattu agitation, soon followed by other micro and mini-protests across the State, the question arises: Is the 'Tamil angst' the effect of what has not happened over years and decades—or, is it also the cause for the indeterminable more that may follow? A trial-balloon of sorts!

Introduction

ACROSS THE Tamil-speaking world in India and elsewhere, the community's centuries-old annual harvest festival of *Pongal* in mid-January 2017 will be remembered for a long, long time to come—and for all the wrong reasons. What should have passed off as three days of community-centred festivities across Tamil Nadu, and wherever Tamil-speaking people lived, turned out to be a mass movement of protest unknown to any regional/ sub-regional part, party or sect of India, which is even otherwise diverse, and at times divided.

True, the 'Team Anna' protests across the country against corruption and more especially the Congress-led government of the day at the Centre did draw huge crowds not very long ago. The 'Nirbhaya protests', following the gruesome gang-rape and murder of a young girl on a moving bus closer to midnight, aimed at underscoring women's rights and security, also began in the national capital of Delhi, which was the scene of crime, and had similarly drawn massive crowds. But both carried the hidden blessings and/or participation of political leaders/forces (however invisible—or visible—their symbols and/or symbolism were) and their politico-electoral motive too was all-pervasive.

Like the 'Nirbhaya protests', the '*Jallikattu* rallies' in the Tamil Nadu capital of Chennai and elsewhere, was a student/youth movement that grew into a mass agitation cutting across gender and age, caste, class and religion. At least in the early days of the Tamil Nadu protests, too, no speeches were made, or no condemnation heaped upon any political party. If anything, the protest-leaders, or whoever claimed to be one before the cameras, assiduously kept politicians of every hue far and away. For students and youth protests of the kind, both were as quiet and peaceful as they were efficiently organised, whether you give credit to the faceless, non-existent student and youth leaders or some hidden hand, as you desire!

The 'Team Anna' rallies were an expression of the average Indian's helplessness against the system, particularly focussed on large-scale corruption. They sought to highlight the political and administrative ills that the inherited pattern of post-Independence governance across the country had been reduced to. So, when a call came, the people responded. Truth to be acknowledged, Anna Hazare was not known outside of a select circle of activists, confined mostly to Maharashtra and lesser to Delhi. His chief lieutenant of the time, present-day Delhi Chief Minister, Arvind Kejriwal and later-day Puducherry Lt-Governor, Kiran Bedi (whom Anna soon disowned) was known lesser, even in Delhi, when Team Anna took shape. Anna Hazare was not another Jayaprakash Narayan of Independence era vintage and later-day 'anti-Emergency fame', to be known to very many people in the country at the time, but the cause that he espoused had become dear to every Indian's heart. In context, Tamil Nadu's Jallikattu protests too were a symbol of the pent-up Tamil sentiments, emotions and expression of anger, against the neglect and worse, by the rest of India. Or, so did the protestors and the protesting State believe.

Whatever the impression outside of the State, and outside of the country, the Tamil angst of the times flowed from deep-seated perception of the abject insensitivity and consequent failure of successive governments at the Centre and in the State, to measure up to the unexpressed expressions of the expressionless (people) on varied counts on various occasions.

The irony is that especially over the past two or three decades, one or the other of the two Dravidian majors, namely, the ruling All-India Anna Dravida Munnetra Kazhagam (AIADMK) or the parent Dravida Munnetra Kazhagam (DMK), had alternated as partners in and to power at the Centre. The situation changed only after Elections-2014, when the National Democratic Alliance (NDA) came to power on the steam of a rediscovered Bharatiya Janata Party (BJP) under the leadership of Narendra Damodardas Modi. As may be recalled, Modi became Prime Minister, without having to look up to any Dravidian political partner to ensure parliamentary majority.

One of the two 'Dravidian majors' have been in power alternately in Tamil Nadu over the past 50 long years, ever since the undivided DMK dethroned in 1967, the then ruling, unified Congress Party, once and for all—as it would seem now in retrospect. To be fair, the Tamil Nadu voter too acknowledged the 'national mood', especially in the Nineties. Like others of their ilk, they too had tested sub-regional parties from within as alternatives to the 'Dravidian strangle-hold', if it could be called so, for nearly two decades. Rather, a new-generation of voters had emerged, and they wanted change, just as their predecessors had wanted in their time—in the Sixties.

In doing so, the Tamil Nadu votes also went along with the national sentiments, and were ready to vote with whichever alliance that was identified with the BJP alternative to the shrinking Congress behemoth at the national-level, too. They were the first ones to sense trouble for the BJP-NDA ahead of the 2004 polls, and they were together at it, in crossing over to the refurbished Congress—or, what they and the rest of the nation had thought it would be. It was an enriching experience may be, but the Tamil Nadu voter was not enamoured of the Congress.

When the rest of India thus voted the BJP and Modi in, the State went back to its regional ways in the historic Elections-2014. In doing so, it also let the tried and tested Dravidian majors to subsume the political space that they had given sub-regional parties and leaders, though only in stages and paces. The latter did not measure up, as their political performance and poll figures showed.

Pongal and the Protests

The Jallikattu bull-fight, as it is loosely translated, dates back to centuries and millennia, unlike what is commonly (mis-) understood. There are references toJallikattu in ancient Tamil literature, and relatively recently in Tamil films, too, as it readily captures the mass-imagination of a brave youth's rural instinct to join the sport and win—and win a beautiful maiden's hand with it, at times.

Even in the North, Hindu/Indian mythology has references to bull-fights, where Lord Krishna was the tamer. Needless to point out, Krishna too won a princess' hand with it. Ancient Tamil history, mythology and literature are all replete with such instances, too. So have been recent Tamil works of fiction, non-fiction and semi-fictional narratives, until urbanisation and urban sport like cricket, and later on, video games, began capturing the imagination of the local youth, from the childhood on.

The Jallikattu protests have their origins in the more recent past. It began with a notification of the Centre, followed by the orders of the Supreme Court of India. Both banned the traditional bull-fights, or bull-taming to be precise, held either on the Pongal day or the day after, celebrated as *Mattu Pongal*, dedicated to *maadu*, or cow—and other cattle-heads. For the uninitiated, Pongal festivities in Tamil Nadu run through three days.

The first day is called *Bhogi*, when people discard the old, ready to welcome the new. If the term is pronounced as *Poki*, which it is not, there is some etymological link to Tamil. The term *Po-ki* can be a derivative of '*po*', or 'go', telling the past to go away as one gets ready for the new—new harvest and the prosperity that comes with it. Better still, *Pok-ki*, as differently spelt, could mean 'to remove'. It then implies the 'removing of difficulties of the past year of poor rains and crop in a new one'.

Pronounced as such, the term *Bhogi* might have also been derived from the word *Bhogam*, which refers to a crop season. That is to say, in most parts of Tamil Nadu, farmers raise two crops of paddy each year. In some parts as in the Cauvery delta, they also raise three crops in the year. This is called *Bhogam* in Tamil, and hence extends to include harvest and the harvest season.

In many other languages and regions in the country, the word *Bhog* means 'offering', offering to sun god in this context. On the day of *Bhogi*, people clean their houses, give a good coat of white-wash or paint, and also paint the outer walls with the auspicious 'kavi' or saffron—and also burn the rubbish that has collected in the home through the previous year, all in preparation for the post-harvest prosperity. They also burn the stumps left behind in their paddy fields after the harvest is completed. The ash of the burnt stumps is good manure. It also makes ploughing of the paddy fields that much easier.

The Pongal is celebrated the day after Bhogi, on the very day the rest of much of India observes *Makar Sankranti.* The term 'Pongal' refers to the overflowing of the cooking pot on the oven. The pot contains rice and milk, and when it boils and overflows, the whole family and the community celebrates.

It is an expression of hope and cheer, for eternal prosperity for the individual, village, and the nation at large. Jallikattu forms a part and parcel of the Pongal festivities in regions wherever it used to be conducted traditionally.

The Jallikattu sporting event is conducted in some places in the afternoon of the Pongal day, in many others the very next day, called the *Kaanum Pongal*. That day, people also visit family elders and friends, to seek their blessings. There are also other local practices in different places, the Jallikattu gathering being one of them. But the Jallikattu part of the festivities extends over a few weeks, held in different villages on different days. So, for these people—and by extension, for others—to accept the Supreme Court ruling of 2014 was an impossible task, however much they tried. They felt miserable when the 2014 verdict said that Jallikattu was not a part of 'Tamil culture'—and was also dismissive about the findings in this regard.

In the end, as the protests showed, the Tamil angst was not just against the Establishment, be it at the Centre or in the State, or both. It was not even against the Judiciary, if at all. For, even when slogans were shouted during the five/six-day long protests in Chennai and elsewhere against the 'Jallikattu ban', no one shouted any slogans against the Judiciary. At least, there has not been any report to the effect, either in the media or otherwise.

In between too, court battles had been fought and lost. The Centre and the State government were seen or at least shown as doing their best to restore Jallikattu. However, there was no clear idea until after the last minute, why either the Centre or the State could not have intervened as effectively earlier, for the conduct of Jallikattu, as a martial sport of Tamil Nadu, this past Pongal season, January 2017.

The average Tamil had some, and at times selective, knowledge of the law. He has had past experience(s) with court cases, orders and the Centre's disposition. It is the same in the case of other people, wherein property ownership and related issues have a knack of ending up in courts, at times only civil but otherwise with an add-on criminal element, in terms of knife-cuts, if not gun-shot wounds. Such experiences have been compounded by daily evening doses of local TV channel talk-shows, where self-styled experts vie with one another and also with the self-possessed anchors to mislead the viewer-voter.

In between all these, the voter had been made aware that between the two, either the Centre or the State could and should promulgate an ordinance, to make Jallikattu happen this year. That's if it had to be unlike other years since 2014, when the Supreme Court had intervened decisively again, after a gap.

Virtual Stand-still

Adding to the Jallikattu fans' woes was the preceding long hospitalisation of AIADMK's charismatic Chief Minister, Jayalalithaa Jayaram, followed by her not-so-unanticipated death on 5 December 2016, all of which had brought the State and State government to a virtual stand-still for nearly three months. When two-time Chief Minister O Panneerselvam was chosen again after his mentor's death for the third time, 'Cyclone *Vardha*' turned Chennai city and suburbs upside down in December 2016, and all the energies of the State government had to be re-directed towards putting its house in order. The government without Jayalalithaa did measure up, maybe better than when Jayalalithaa herself was around and active. In the process, the State government leadership perhaps chose to forget that Jallikattu would be around as a socio-political issue soon. It is also possible that at least some sections of the leadership had concluded that after the Vardha, the people would understand and that they could be hopefully convinced.

However, the efficiency of the administration possibly ensured that Vardha was forgotten earlier than expected, and Jallikattu returned to the centre table in time for the ensuing Pongal season. It, however, became apparent that Jallikattu was not to occur in 2017. Both, the Centre and the higher Judiciary, had clearly sent out a possibly unintended impression that they were not at all serious about the issue or the larger causes involved. The flash-point was reached, without even anyone seriously trying or igniting it, at least at that very point in time.

As if to justify the protests and protestors *post facto*, the State government and the Centre rushed in, for the former to promulgate an ordinance, to conduct the event in the days that followed and the latter to stand by it, in legal and political terms. The Animal Welfare Board of India (AWBI), an arm of the Centre, which was the main petitioner seeking the ban, would suddenly find sense in going slow on its challenge to the post-protests ordinance of the State government, promulgated with the blessings of the Centre. In turn, the Centre too did not have options. That also formed a part of the Tamil angst, so to say.

Once the street-protests in 'distant Tamil Nadu' (had) captured the nation's imagination, the Supreme Court too became more aware than earlier. The court rose to the occasion, and accepted the Centre's submissions to put off the anticipated verdict on a pending case against the earlier lifting of the ban, by a week. Thus, a more immediate, though temporary, resolution to the protestors' cause became possible.

This, in turn, led to the consequent dispersal of the lakhs of protests-participants across the State. As may be recalled, only three days prior to the D-day for the annual Jallikattu fair, the Supreme Court had tersely told counsel for the two governments that the Bench could not be rushed into pronouncing the pending verdict from a 2016 case, as though it had already begun dictating the judgment. It meant that the case in which arguments had been closed months ago could not be decided upon in time (even if it was the proverbial last minute), one way or the other, for the 2017 show.

It also implied that pending the Supreme Court verdict, against what essentially was a notification of the Centre from the previous year, 2016, in turn facilitating Jallikattu all over again, the Union of India could not promulgate a fresh ordinance or notification even if it wished to, pending the Supreme Court's disposal of the case in which all arguments had already closed. It is not as if such a thing was not attempted earlier, but it would mean that the Centre had flouted constitutional norms and healthy precedents in relation to the higher Judiciary, the proverbial 'watch-dog' of the Constitution and Democracy. Why the Centre did not approach the Supreme Court for an early decision, or even a postponement of the verdict, earlier no one knows.

Alienation and Angst

It is here that the Tamils' angst and unhappiness showed up, as it did through the Marina protests and elsewhere across the State, equally peaceful and successful. But the roots lie elsewhere, from the sublime to the trivia. Be it the Cauvery water dispute involving neighbouring Karnataka, or the Mullaperiyar dam storage level where Kerala is the other party, the Tamils have felt cheated by the system. In both cases, there have been a series of governmental initiatives from the Centre and a succession of Supreme Court orders, favouring Tamil Nadu, whose farmers have suffered enormously over the past several decades.

In both cases, the Supreme Court was the adjudicator and the Centre the enforcer under the Constitution. When those orders of the nation's highest judicial body had not been implemented—instead flouted—in the weeks preceding, Jallikattu's Season 2017, that too in yet another bad year for the State's farmers, it snapped something from inside. As if this was not enough, on national TV talk-shows, leading legal luminaries from the North began talking tough against the possibility of a fresh ordinance to facilitate Jallikattu even at that late hour. To the average Tamil, not the ignorance, but the purported, or perceived, partisanship of these 'worthies' showed up. For the first time possibly, the elite of Tamil Nadu concurred with the opinion of the masses, without sharing their angst to the same degree. The proverbial Tamil patience was lost.

Yet, the average Tamil maintained his cool and peace, even as he/she answered the calls for a show-of-strength, again peacefully. The contradictions began showing up then. On the social media, many protestors (not necessary that any or all of them went to any of the venues, or were even residing in the State) made out their case thus. If a new ordinance, whether by the State or the Centre, would tantamount to contempt of court, what was the legal luminaries' 'verdict' against or justification for Karnataka and Kerala when they had 'blatantly flouted' successive orders of the very same Supreme Court? The elite could not claim to be honest and disagree, too. The social media did not leave out the Centre, either. Those that posted the social media messages/calls asked, what kind of Centre was it that would agree to the Apex Court's explicit direction for constituting a Cauvery Management Authority (CMA) one day, would go back to the court, seeking a review of the earlier one, that too, the very next day.

Social media campaigners had a more explicit point. The arguments having been placed long ago, and the court having decided on the setting up of the CMA, how could the Centre, which only had the duty to enforce that order, go back and seek a 'review' of sorts? If anything, Karnataka as the stake-holder State could have sought a review one more time, not the Centre, so to say.

Did not the Modi government at the Centre, too, qualify for 'dismissal' just as the court was hinting at the Tamil Nadu counterpart if it did not ensure that the Jallikattu protests did not become a 'Law and Order' concern under the Constitution? It is another matter that as per the Supreme Court verdict in the 1971 case, *U N R Rao vs Indira Gandhi*, there has to be a government headed by the Prime Minister to carry out the affairs of the Indian State at the Centre, thus denying the President of India autocratic powers of a kind. the Jallikattu protestors and their social media campaigners were seeking to make out only an argument—which had all the valid socio-political elements in it. Though some saw the State government caving in on the 'Jallikattu protests', to ensure that no such gatherings were ever allowed, when it came to the subsequent anti-NEET agitations, firmer *diktat* from the Supreme Court had its effect. In between, the State government's Law and Order response to various minor protests against methane projects and the like were mixed, at best.

The Jallikattu protests were the first of the kind in a long time, where the tempo especially had not built up over time—unlike in the case of those earlier on the Cauvery water dispute and the Sri Lankan ethnic issue, among others.

Multiplied Agony

The agony of the average Tamil had multiplied in 2016-17 because they had lived much of the months preceding the Pongal season of 2017 with a non-functional government in the State. First, it was the Assembly elections in the State and the long run-up of campaign. This was followed by Chief Minister Jayalalithaa's hospitalisation. Before that, the nation was witness to Tamil Nadu's shame of mishandled 'Chennai floods' of December 2015. From one December to the next, it was like a long winter of discontent. Chief Minister Jayalalithaa should have held herself morally responsible, in the eyes of many in the social media, but no one was held even legally accountable.

Through the year, an unprecedented number of farmers had committed suicide across the State. But the State government and political leadership were seemingly concerned only about Jaya's hospitalisation, later death and the post-Jaya politics within her AIADMK. The local media, both print and TV, were equally uni-focused on politics and political personalities.

It left only the social media as a tool for those that it impacted, to share their pains and sorrows, tears and shoulders.

The irony was striking. *If Chennai City suffered owing to unprecedented floods, the rest of the State suffered from unprecedented drought. Common to both was the unprecedented callousness of the political leadership and mismanagement, or non-management by the bureaucracy, relatively efficient though dubbed corrupt, compared to the distant past. The drought highlighted the farmers' plight even more, in the face of denial of Cauvery and Mullaperiyar waters, so to say, and the even more unprecedented callousness of elected governments in the State and at the Centre.* Or, this was what the perception was in the eyes of the commoner.

Through much of Jayalalithaa's previous, fourth and fifth terms in office—the latter during 2011-16—the State government was officially in a 'denial mode', whenever and wherever dengue-deaths had occurred frequently and in large numbers. If media reports were to be believed, the government wanted the State's medical fraternity, too, to go on a denial-mode, even in the face of increasing number of dengue cases and dengue deaths. There were also reports of government doctors who talked to the media on dengue prevalence and death being handed down 'punishment transfers'. Like farmers' suicides, such infection and deaths had occurred across the State, and the victims were mostly children and infants, and for no fault of theirs.

Fastest Urbanisation

In context, even mostly sedate sections of the growing ranks of the State's urban middle class (at 50 per cent or so, Tamil Nadu is the fastest urbanising State in the country) felt helpless and hapless. In their own silent way, they ended up comparing the unfolding scenario in their neighbourhood and native villages (where much of the dengue deaths occurred, for instance) and contrasted it with the unevenness of the system and scheme governing them all. These newspaper readers and television news viewers also took mental note and made mental calculations *vis a vis* the time taken by the Supreme Court to pronounce the verdict in the 'Jayalalithaa wealth case' or the consequent contribution to anticipated instability in the administration.

They were also deeply pained and hurt by the impossible situation that some of the other (*read:* DMK) politicians like Kanimozhi, MP, and former Union Minister Dayanidhi Maran, had got themselves into and tarnished the State and its public honour and fair image, through their own alleged role in mega-corruption and their consequent involvement in court cases. Those cases were not about to end soon either. Unlike the Jaya cases, present and past, those against the DMK leaders would continue to make constant news in the local and national media even more, adding to the embarrassment of the State's population.

The Tamil social media compared the Centre's determination on demonetisation and other political moves of Prime Minister Modi, with their reluctance to promulgate a pro-Jallikattu ordinance on the one hand, and the Centre (too) not coming up with convincing communication on Chief Minister Jaya's health condition and its deterioration, when it was known to have access to the same. 'If successive governments at the Centre could promulgate so many ordinances to set at naught various Supreme Court verdicts at different times, and the Modi administration, too, for its part, could keep issuing Executive Orders by the dozen on demonetisation-related issues and clarifications, why not show the same interest and initiative *vis a vis* issues that are dear to the people of a State that is very much a part of the Indian Union?' was the crux of the social media arguments in this regard.

Unknown to most and unacknowledged by the few in the know, the Jallikattu protest was also an expression of the youthful protestors' anxieties about their own future, near and not-so-near. Many of them, especially boarders, had taken the 'short-span inconveniences' caused by demonetisation an affront on their dignity. Those that stayed away from a college/university hostel were the worst hit. News reports and analyses about the negative fall-out of demonetisation and anticipation of industrial sluggishness meant that campus recruitments might either not happen, or those thus recruited might not actually land the promised jobs. Travelling distant in mind and time, those already holding jobs, especially in the much sought-after and most-employing IT sector, also feared that demonetisation and the Trump presidency's H1B visa rule-changes in the US could mean 'pink-slips' for many of them. None in power cared, not even understood their agony.

For the younger generation of students—and more so, their parents—the Supreme Court order for national-level common entrance test (NEET) for admission to professional colleges in the State, as across the country, was/is a problem. It is more of a concern for their parents, especially those from rural areas, who have inherent limitations to match up to the best in the State and across the country. From a constitutional view-point, Jayalalithaa as Chief Minister had been pressing for a review of the court order, and/or for the Centre to exempt the State and its students from the same. If other States did not take up the issue or were all for NEET, it was their problem—Tamil Nadu could not be made to suffer, was the refrain.

Less said about the reservations in professional colleges the better. Ever since the Supreme Court fixed a 50-per cent upper-limit for all reservations in the 'Mandal case' verdict *(Indira Sawhney vs Union of India, 1992)*, Tamil Nadu has been playing hide-and-seek with its original 69 per cent reservations. This has meant that the State allots seats under 69 per cent quota, but later adjusts it to 50 per cent as and whenever the Supreme Court hears the case—by increasing the number of general category seats for the year, to meet the 50-per cent upper-limit.

Owing to the indecision or unwillingness of the Judiciary to hear and hear out the Tamil Nadu reservations case over the past two decades, the number of engineering and medical college seats in the State has increased every year—impacting on quantity as much as quality. Over the past years, high-end IT jobs at entry-level have become fewer than originally thought of, also because the employers can afford to start at the low end of the pay-gradation and yet hope to mine a wealth of moderate to high talent. Unlike their predecessors from the 'dot-com bust' era at the turn of the millennia, the present-day youth also knows that if you lost a private sector job once, you had lost it for good. It is more so within the highly-paying IT sector, where most of them belong. With Tamil Nadu, among other south Indian States especially, producing over 250,000 engineering graduates each year, employers just limping out of recession would rather go in for fresh hands at low salaries and other hand-outs instead of re-employ those that had been 'benched', and for reasons of economy and not non-performance.

It did not stop there, either. Concerned more about TRP ratings than people's pain and farmer's anguish, the famed Tamil media, both print and TV, had focussed more on the Assembly polls in the first half of 2016 and on Jayalalithaa's hospitalisation, death and AIADMK's 'succession battles' than farmers' suicides and creditor-banks' sending raiding parties to farmers' homes and humiliating them. Where sections of the local media reported issues of people's concerns, the report and the channel had a slant. There were also deliberate attempts to counter the same in and by equally politicised channels on the other side. The less said about the national media, including print and television news, the better.

For a State that has generally been high on the score-card for national (*read:* English) magazines sold, and English talk-show and news-watchers, the coverage of local news and views by the so-called national channels has remained sparse, at the same time exhibiting the ignorance of the anchor more than the knowledge of the participants, if at all.

Reaching Across

For an agitation that was to have been Tamil Nadu centric, how did the Jallikattu row reach across foreign shores for similar protests (though much, much smaller in numbers) to be held wherever Tamil-speaking people were present? If social media postings of the time were to be believed, not only in the US and Canada, Europe and Australia, Gulf countries and South Africa, but even in communist Russia and China, such protests were claimed to have been held (reportedly Tamil Nadu students studying medical schools there). The social media did carry pictures of such protests, of anything between a handful to a couple of dozens gathered in protests out there. The faces were visible though names were not mentioned. Verification, if one wanted to check the authenticity of the claim, was still possible. There are reasons for the same. One, the Tamils from India, working or studying in those countries, have felt the hurt and angst. It was very similar to, or at times more, than the helplessness and consequent anger at the system, felt but rarely exhibited by the 'upper castes' over the reservations system. It was directed against their own State-level politicians, politics, including 'family rule' of the DMK, on the one hand and of the indifference of the AIADMK leadership. More importantly, it was against the Centre.

The overseas Tamil protest-participants empathised not only with the angst felt by their brethren back home for long, and which they had carried with them to the far off lands. Their hurt and anger at the Indian scheme and system flowed from a sense of agony and helplessness that they had felt initially over the Government of India's handling of the Sri Lankan ethnic issue, war and violence, ending with the ultimate exit of LTTE leader Velupillai Prabhakaran and scores of his armed cadres and hundreds of unarmed, innocent men, women and children on the battle-front in 2009.

The agony was widespread and shared, both back home in India, and more so in countries where they lived, with their Sri Lankan Tamil friends and neighbours unravelling more details and stories every day since then. It had turned into a sense of betrayal against the Congress-ruled Centre as a political entity, the Government of India as a constitutional institution, and the ruling DMK of the time in Tamil Nadu.

The political reaction was slow in coming. But constant communication between a relatively enlightened member overseas and his/her family back home, ensured that the message got across, clear and sure. The DMK-Congress combine felt the electoral heat in the Assembly polls of 2011. More importantly, for the non-resident Tamil (NRT), if they could be described as such, the 2-G scam cases involving the then DMK of Tamil Nadu became a matter of shame overseas, as their Sri Lankan Tamil (SLT) colleagues and non-Tamil Indian neighbours were also watching the elections in the south Indian State.

Their sense of shame got transmitted back home, reflecting in the poll results even more. Since 2011, that uni-polar unilateral feeling of hurt and neglect by the Indian state system as a whole, and the Tamil Nadu polity closer home, has only deepened and widened. Today, their belief in themselves and the power of their youthful colleagues back home may have only increased, not decreased. This apart, there is no denying the role and participation of SLT Diaspora in many/most western nations, in guiding political campaign in Tamil Nadu, over the Sri Lankan ethnic issue, war and violence, and targeted against the Government of India on the one hand, and select political parties and leaders in the State. If in war truth was a casualty, in peace, again, in this case, truth still seems to be a casualty—one way or the other, one size or the other.

Yet, the question remains as to why and how India's most peaceful and spontaneous protests in a long time ended in and with violence. Truth be acknowledged, the size of the protesting crowd was totally unanticipated. Even government agencies of the Centre and the State might not have considered the possibility. But it was not entirely unanticipated, that whenever massive crowds gathered anywhere in Tamil Nadu or even elsewhere in the country, on any issue, fringe-elements often seek to capture the imagination of larger, peaceful sections, try and leave them with little option but to stay along, and play along—and direct it in a way where violence against and/or by the State became unavoidable, and for which the State alone would have to take the blame.

In recent times, it had begun with the 'Kudankulam nuclear protests' in southern Tamil Nadu earlier, and had got built into the psyche of low-profile protest organisers of the kind. It is not as if Kudankulam protest-organiser, Dr S P Udayakumar, with an American doctoral degree, and his group were directly involved in organising or even guiding and coaching the 'Jallikattu protestors', but the lessons learnt there, and acquaintances made there would have been of help and assistance.

Once the Jallikattu protest act got together, the Tamil Nadu police began publicly addressing and advising peaceful sections of innocent participants not to get involved with someone who was seen to be pro-active in their midst. In particular, the police advised participants not to share their coordinates like phone numbers, address and political thoughts with a stranger in the protest venue, especially in Chennai's vast Marina venue, lest they became unwilling victims of political indoctrination and worse. It may also be thus that the State police, reacting late to the emergent reality on the ground, might have decided to take a chance, and try and isolate the 'trouble-makers' from the mainline mass of protestors, and act against them, one way or the other.

The police and the protesting mobs in the end-game of the Chennai campaign especially blamed each other for the violence. After holding back for a couple of days, then Tamil Nadu Chief Minister O Panneerselvam ordered a judicial inquiry into the violent act of the protests, especially at Marina. Justice S Rajeswaran, a retired Judge of the Madras High Court, has been appointed under the Commissions of Inquiry Act 1952, and his report is expected to throw some light on why it happened.

With the post-Jallikattu period witnessing more protests, be it on relocation of State-run liquor shops, or against a hydro-carbon project in interior Neduvasal or on farmers' plight, violence has been time and again seeking to rear its ugly head—be it on the police side, or on the protestors' side, or both. After a break, the people of Neduvasal re-commenced their agitation, but then in some other villages across the State, the local population mistakenly stalled drilling by Central Ground Water Board (CGWB), leading to the latter suspending ground-water mapping operations.

Sure enough, the police can also be expected to pursue independent cases of arson and more against some of those arrested for violence at the Marina protests. Among them may be some/many possibly wanted for other/specific offences already committed but had stayed away from the police radar for long. To the extent that the peaceful protests had ended in violence, it could also open up new possibilities on State action against anti-national elements. Whether or not the methods that they pursue are right and legal, the causes that they might have flagged in the Tamil Nadu/Indian context may have sense and meaning to it.

The uninitiated and spontaneous Jallikattu protests have flagged the underlying angst of a people within the Union, decades after the anti-Hindi agitations had set afire the Madras State of the mid-Sixties, but under the authorship and leadership of the then unified DMK Opposition. To the extent that the agitation and its aftermath forced the Congress out of power in the subsequent 1967 Assembly elections, there was a message in it. Now there is another one for the divided State polity and leadership, and yet another for the larger Establishment and the national psyche!

Part-I

Message from Marina

THE MORE recent Tamil Nadu protests over the continued ban on the ritualistic annual bull-taming game of Jallikattu took an unprecedented turn in January 2017. Over the past decade or so especially, the 'bull game' of the south-central Tamil Nadu's martial farming community had faced opposition from animal-lovers, leading to political involvement of every kind. In turn, this led to administrative initiatives, for and against the continuance of the game, year on year, ultimately leading to a complete ban, ordered by the Supreme Court in 2014.

In between, the court had conceded the Tamil Nadu government's request for approving a regulated and regularised game, which however, did not go as planned and promised. This led to the Supreme Court ban all over again, and in turn became a contributing factor for the State-wide protests of January 2017.

The surprising element about the 2017 protest against the ban related to the unanticipated levels it reached, and the short time it had taken to reach up to the zenith. The protests began peacefully, igniting curiosity and interest in prospective participants as in political parties and the State administration. The curiosity soon became infectious, with the Centre, the Supreme Court and the rest of India, not being able to comprehend—or, ignore—it any more. This in turn ensured that the early protestors captured the imagination of the larger population, leading to a mass of people gathering in different venues across the State, and for as long as five days. 'Days' included 'nights' in most cases, when only the elderly, women with children and some office-goers left the venues. Both the venues and the groups of protestors chose themselves, and included both urban and rural centres, and those where local people had seen Jallikattu only on the silver-screen. No, they were not whipped up sentiments by political or other groups, but an expression of a sense of denial that went beyond the issue on hand.

As it turned out, in all these venues, participants who had left the protests the previous evening owing to age or other reasons would return the next day, with food and water for the mostly youthful crowds that had stayed back. Noticeably, young girls and middle-aged women spent the nights in the protest venues through the nights, sharing protest space with strangers belonging to the opposite gender, without fearing—or, having to fear—for their personal safety. Their numbers were relatively higher in urban centres. There were no lights or lanterns and they all had to do with whatever light that their mobile phones provided, if it was charged in some neighbourhood home, a kilometre or so away. So much so like the honking of car horns at a fixed hour in protest of something or the other in western countries, and the 'candle-light vigil' that got imported and became popular especially with the 'Nirbhaya protests' across the country, Marina especially, the lit mobile phones became a sign and symbol of the cause. What the participants ate, where they performed their ablutions, or just re-charged their mobile-phones did not matter, but they were still doing it all, nonetheless, possibly in neighbourhood homes, whose residents welcomed them with open hands.

Leave aside the owners and residents of those homes, reportedly neighbourhood fisher-folk in Chennai, even fellow-protestors were strangers, and the girls did not have to fear for their safety and security. This is contrary to conventional beliefs about Tamil Nadu, including the capital city of Chennai, which was still being considered orthodox and conservative, compared, to say, a city like Delhi, Mumbai or Bengaluru. This triggered a comparative discourse on the safety of women in other cities.

The second aspect of the protest was that it did not have any leader or leaders to pinpoint or project. Those that emerged at the morning of the day were replaced by another the next day, or that very evening. If the idea was to deny the hovering police personnel, in uniform or civvies, access to them, it seemed to have worked. Rather, it was also a choice of 24 x 7 television news channels, for a 'quick byte', accompanied by clarity of thought and in communication, rather than that of the participants, who were anyway not homogeneous in anyway whatsoever.

The only commonality among most was their Tamil identity—though after the first two days, there were reports of youth from neighbouring States, travelling especially to Chennai, to join the protest in solidarity with the local youth and their over-arching angst against the existing governmental system and scheme. It meant that the authorities did not know whom to talk to, or what solution would satisfy whom. Not long after the protests had commenced, especially in the sprawling sands of the Marina beach in Chennai, politically-conscious, self-styled groups of social activists began taking the lead, from within the larger gathering. Yet, there was none to call a leader, no group to claim ownership. This may have also been a cause for the avoidable, end-day violence.

Spontaneity and More

Deliberately, every one of those groups was careful not to claim authorship or ownership lest the rest should feel upset and agitated. By conservative estimates, about 300,000 had gathered at the Chennai venue at the peak of the protests. Other figures put it variously between half a million and one. No preparatory rallies had been held, no organisation set up at different localities and different levels to mobilise people for the purpose. There were no posters and blaring audio-campaigns through the streets in any of the towns and villages, where the protests began to take shape, all within the first 24 hours of commencement of the rally at Chennai, where it all began. Who gave any cue, to whom, when and how remained a mystery even after it all had ended successfully. But there were enough indications to what could be in store under circumstances of the kind, if an occasion and a cause presented itself was known to those who should have known them—but nothing much seemed to have been done to assuage the hurt, or otherwise assess the futuristic situation all through the previous months and years, when sentiments were welling up on such diverse issues such as reintroduction of prohibition or protection of natural resources, to which the Establishment continued to turn a blind eye and a deaf ear.

What was known, however, was that a group of youth—or, so it seems until it is contradicted with evidence—had triggered it all through a series of social media messages to friends and others on their 'Contacts' list. The coincidence of a private sector telecom launch with free messaging service is said to have provided an initial impetus, if any, but there was no motive whatsoever. In hindsight, it can be said that even without such free SMS service, the protest would have happened, and at the same levels. Many among the front-liners were young professionals drawing decent salaries in the IT/IET sector, and they were said to be spending from their pockets to make it happen first, and make it a success, later on. Once the momentum had caught on, it is doubtful if anyone would have cringed on spending a little more, to send out those messages, updates and other campaign material.

Bandhs and Protests

Tamil Nadu has had its last serious series of street-protests spread across the entire State way back in the mid-Sixties. The anti-Hindi agitation of the mid-Sixties was a localised affair, barring the handful of university campuses, where students from across the State mingled. There were not as many professional colleges and deemed universities then, nor were there as many private sector jobs employing educated and highly talented youth. The post-Independence Industrial Revolution of the Fifties and Sixties had generated semi-skilled manufacturing jobs and agriculture labour, not as in IT and related sectors, in the more recent years and decades. Later on too, the State had witnessed mass movements and protests, but they were again mostly localised, or/and had organisers preparing for the event for days and weeks together. Against this, the anti-Hindi agitation of the Sixties had a history of its own, with the Opposition Dravida Munnetra Kazhagam (DMK) giving the call against 'Hindi imposition' and also organising itself and the local students across the State for the success of the protest.

Later, the State's farmers, and also various caste groups would organise protests, on specific demands—at times covering substantial parts or regions. On issues like the Cauvery water dispute with neighbouring Karnataka or on the Sri Lankan ethnic issue, or the Sri Lankan fishing problem, there were State-wide *bandhs*, protests and fasts. Some turned violent, most of them remained peaceful. They all had experienced political parties or other powerful organisers sponsoring them, and at times funding them, too. The organisers of the recent Kudankulam protests against the nuclear power plant in the southern Tamil Nadu village too were not totally inexperienced. It was the third in a series, launched at intervals of about 10 years. In comparison, the Jallikattu protests did not have an author or owner, yet its width and reach in comparison was unprecedented. It was more so in the eyes and experience of GenX Tamils.

Yet, none of these earlier protests was in the same league as the Jallikattu protests. Even the equally peaceful and awe-inspiring fortnight-long '*dharmic* agitation', or *Satyagraha (Ara Porattam)* that the late former Chief Minister, K Kamaraj, in turn reduced to being the high-priest of the Congress Party in Tamil Nadu against being the party's national chieftain earlier, launched against the DMK State government in the early Seventies should pale into insignificance for the same reason. It was as massive as the Jallikattu protests in some places, and was even more peaceful—that there was no end-game violence, either. It was again organised by a political party, and all its resources had been commissioned to make it a success and peaceful, at the same time.

The Congress' protests were planned for a full fortnight. As per instructions, the respective district party leadership obtained police permission for the procession and protest. They also submitted to the police a day in advance, the names and addresses of cadres who would be courting arrest the next day, at the earmarked venue. All other party cadres and members of the public were advised to avoid getting mixed up with the identifiable agitators, who would not resist arrest or involve themselves in any violent act of any kind. The idea was to revive fading memories of Gandhiji's *Satyagraha* method of political protest during the freedom movement, and contrast it to the violence that had topped the anti-Hindi agitation only years ago, a reversal of roles for the main political players.

It was also possible that Tamil Nadu was still recovering from the after-effects of the anti-Hindi agitation for the new-generation students to be motivated to jump into the fray at the time of the Congress' protest. The ruling DMK had by then split. The local focus was on the up and coming breakaway Anna Dravida Munnetra Kazhagam (ADMK), founded by charismatic actor-politician, M G Ramachandran, or MGR as he was/is popularly known. In Tamil Nadu, the Emergency was marked also by the death of Congress stalwart K Kamaraj (to natural causes) and the first of the two dismissals of the Karunanidhi-led DMK government, accompanied by indiscriminate arrest of party second-line leaders under the draconic MISA (Maintenance of Internal Security Act) and the institution of the Justice Sarkaria Commission, to probe the alleged misdeeds of the regime.

Under the Governor's Rule, Tamil Nadu did not have to suffer as much as the North, and in fact there was popular acclaim for trains running on time, officials disposing of commoner's papers without fail, and benefits accruing from Prime Minister Indira Gandhi's 'Twenty-point programme'. The intervening Governor's Rule initiatives such as the 'Janata meal' at Rs 1 in restaurants came up in the estimation of the Emergency in common view against the perceived lawlessness, price rice and rise-shortage under the Karunanidhi rule.

Without reference to Emergency and its benefits or shortcomings, the post-Emergency scenario witnessed the arrival of the '10+2+3' pattern of education. Tamil Nadu was among the first States to adopt the scheme. In the succeeding era of economic reforms, Tamil Nadu was also among the few States to catch up with the market-driven need for professional education. Coupled with the fear psychosis that the Emergency had instilled on the campuses in the State, the education-related changes soon ensured that school, college and university campuses in the State forgot what protests and agitations of the anti-Hindi days looked like. Nor was the new-generation students even inspired to imagine the scales and levels of any past protest.

Keeping Politicians Out

If, however, any street-protest of the kind succeeded in the decades after anti-Hindi agitation and up to the Jallikattu protests, it mostly related to the pro-reservation agitation of the Vanniar Sangam, a caste grouping, predominant in the northern districts. The Sangam was the forerunner to the present-day Pattali Makkal Katchi (PMK), a political party identified still with the Vanniar community. During the Sangam's protest, demanding 'most backward class' status for the Vanniar community, the North-South traffic and transport across much of the State was affected badly in the late Eighties. There was unprecedented violence, mostly unilateral, as protestors would cut down massive trees along the national and State highways, and at times burn them, to stall traffic. Once again, there was an identifiable leadership and organisation, though they were still honing their skills.

Through the Nineties, and even during the succeeding decades, protest calls on the 'Cauvery water dispute' had elicited much support and sympathy, especially in the affected districts. In comparison, the support for Mullaperiyar-centric protests was not as big, but it was slowly gaining greater recognition, nonetheless.

Periodically, fishermen across southern Tamil Nadu coast protested the intervention, arrests and killings by the Sri Lanka Navy (SLN). On occasions, mostly ahead of elections, Opposition parties took it to other parts of the State, too. Political parties from Tamil Nadu continually raked up the issue in Parliament, at times bringing the proceedings to a stand-still for days together. All through, agitations and protests over the 'Sri Lankan fishing issue' were peaceful. All those protests were definitely non-violent, wherever, whenever.

Closer to the Jallikattu agitation, the State had witnessed a series of protests for years together, in support of the Sri Lankan Tamil cause. In most cases, political parties, and at times the State government or the party heading the State government, gave the call for the protest. In the early Nineties, demanding 'Cauvery waters' from Karnataka, then AIADMK Chief Minister Jayalalithaa went on an indefinite fast, until the Union government, under Prime Minister P V Narasimha Rao, intervened. In his time, Jayalalithaa's political mentor, M G Ramachandran as Chief Minister also called for a dawn-to-dusk fast, over the 'Sri Lankan ethnic issue', which was yet to capture the imagination of the State, enough.

On one occasion, after the conclusion of the ethnic war in Sri Lanka and the decimation of the fearsome LTTE in May 2009, young professionals especially cornered a part of Chennai's Marina, to press their cause. For the first time ever, the protest-leaders who had not been known anywhere earlier shooed away political parties and leaders, saying that they had politicised the ethnic cause for their own electoral benefits—and had done nothing meaningful. Soon, some of these leaders became prominent in their own right, both as annual protest organisers for the cause. Some appeared frequently on Tamil TV talk-shows. Going beyond the immediate Sri Lankan Tamil issue, they argue a larger pan-Tamil cause. Some of them, with their relatively dwindling following, were seen at the Jallikattu protest venues, too.

Kudankulam and After

In between the anti-Hindi protests and the PMK agitation on the one hand, and the PMK agitation and the Jallikattu demonstrations in 2017, there had been intermittent issues and protests that impacted on the State. One such was the State-wide farmers' protests when the united DMK was in power in the early Seventies. After 17 farmers had lost their lives in police-firing, as party treasurer, MGR taunted their memory, asking, 'You cannot fire rose petals from police guns. They only fire bullets, and bullets kill'.

Intermittently, there had also been caste and communal clashes in different parts of the State, especially in the North in the Eighties and the South in the Nineties. Again political parties or identifiable interest groups were behind them. The State also witnessed incidents of 'communal violence', including the anti-Muslim riots of November 1997 in the 'Cotton City' of Coimbatore, followed by the 'serial blasts' of 14 February 1998. The 'Rajiv Gandhi assassination' of 21 May 1991 and the 'EPRLF killing' of 16 Sri Lankan Tamil political leaders, both by the LTTE, was a blot on the State's fair image. But all of them belonged to different genre, compared to the later-day Jallikattu protests.

The decades after the anti-Hindi agitation also witnessed the Tamil film industry, a powerful public organ, joining the Cauvery or Sri Lanka-related protests in full bloom, drawing national attention. At times, as in 2016 and in the early Nineties earlier, the Cauvery protests did produce violent street reactions in Karnataka. In more recent times, the mass-protests against the Russian nuclear power-plants in the sleepy coastal village of Kudankulam evoked great interest and scientific discourse in many parts of the State and also elsewhere in the country. Whether the Kudankulam protests triggered later-day protests against the proposed Jaitapur nuclear power-plant in Maharashtra is unclear but then the issues had been debated across the country for other locales of the kind not to have been made aware of the 'issues and concerns' involved.

Two other major protests that were anticipated to become massive but ended up in a whimper related to political issues and political leaders—rather their arrests over allegations of corruption. Former AIADMK Chief Minister Jayalalithaa's arrest by the successor DMK government in 1996 was expected almost since she lost power. So was a retaliatory arrest of DMK's Karunanidhi when Jayalalithaa returned to power in 2001. But television news channels made more noise on, and or against the respective arrests than even the party cadres on the streets. Both arrests were marked by studied silence by the respective party cadres, who had correctly read the message from the election results and the mood of the voter that caused it.

Gender Revolution, too

On the question of participation, there was no comparison between the numbers in the various venues this time and earlier agitations and rallies, including those spurting out from local/localised caste issues and class concerns, of whatever denomination. Heightening the holiday mood, especially on the third day of the annual Tamil harvest festival of Pongal, non-protestors came as families with food and soft-drinks for their own consumption as if they were on a picnic. Anyway, it is ritualistic to picnic on the day of Kaanum Pongal, the third day of the Pongal festivities. The word, *kaanum* in Tamil means seeing, meeting or visiting. Traditionally, on that day, people visit their family elders, relatives and friends, and exchange greetings, wish one another prosperity ahead of the upcoming harvest season and beyond. They also gather as families in public venues such as the village quadrangle (*chaavadi*), temple grounds or river-banks, and spend the whole day together, sharing home-cooked food. In Chennai, traditionally, people visit the Marina beach, or the zoological park or such other places of relaxation, in large numbers. Many of them came from the suburbs, which again was expanding over the previous years and decades, in terms of area and population, making access to the city easier than earlier. Gone were the days when they came by bullock-carts and, later buses. While the latter practice at least continued, in most cases, the suburban youth came into the city venues, including the malls, in their swanky motor-bikes, which had become possible owing to the massive 'installment schemes' unavailable to their earlier generations. What was remarkable in 2017 was that they came every day after that with the same zeal. It was a different kind of zeal than in all these very many years.

Even on the day of Kaanum Pongal, people had come in large numbers despite anticipation of trouble of some kind or the other. That was because as fast as the news of the Marina protest spread, so did the added news that it was being organised by students and youth, keeping the political class and film personalities away. Even more impressive was the news that it was absolutely non-violent, hence safe for entire families, including infants and women, to be around. So much so it was common to see college girls and their siblings in school chatting and dosing alongside their male counterparts. Thus a quiet, gender-revolution was also taking place with full acceptance by parents and other family elders. They had shed their social inhibitions of the past, as everyone's daughter or son that they knew was there too, along with their own. Not only the female participants but also their parents on-site or back home had no anxiety about their physical safety or upright behaviour.

Nothing of this kind had happened before and on such a large scale. Tradition-ridden Tamil Nadu was breaking old social barriers and mindsets. It went mostly unnoticed nearer home and unacknowledged elsewhere. A 'new Tamil Nadu' had arrived and what a way to pronounce it, announce it!

The spontaneity did not stop with teenagers of both genders joining hands without any reservations, or their families not protesting. Nor did it stop with the large numbers that gathered in every district town, and every village where traditionally Jallikattu had been staged through past years and decades, generations and centuries. No other protest prior to this one, originating and focussed on Tamil Nadu and a

'Tamil tradition' had attracted so much attention, sympathy and support as the Jallikattu protests of January 2017. Again, they were equally spontaneous, responding mostly to whatever social media messages that local Tamils had picked up and local Tamil organisations were capable of organising.

Identification Overseas

Outside of Tamil Nadu, wherever Tamils lived in the country, the protest motif caught on like hot-fire, in city after city. Many and at times most of the Tamils elsewhere might not have even seen the State once, after their forefathers had migrated over the previous decades and possibly centuries. Many of them might not have even heard or known of Jallikattu. Now they found their identification with the 'Jallikattu cause', in the land of their forebears, and it was spontaneous, so was their participation in local protests. It had not happened before, whether involving local Tamil communities in other parts of the country, or Tamil-speaking people elsewhere in the world, wherever their origins could be traced to India. After the pan-Tamil protests of the Sri Lankan kind, a cause centred on Tamil Nadu, its people and their sentiments echoed on the streets of London and New York, Dubai and Abu Dhabi, Canberra and Ottawa. True or not, social media even carried pictures of similar protests in some Russian and Chinese cities. Wherever Tamils from India, and more especially Tamil-speaking people lived in some numbers in Europe, they gathered to give vent to their angst.

True, such Tamil-centred and Tamil-organised protests, some even with local whites participating in numbers, had been held across Europe, Canada and Australia, in the none-too-distant past. Included in the list were nations such as Singapore and Malaysia, Mauritius and South Africa, where all Tamil indentured labour had migrated during the British Raj. But almost every one of them was organised by and for the Sri Lankan Tamils, with their Indian counterparts participating, putting their heart and soul into it, all the same. It was more so in the closing months of Sri Lanka's decisive 'Eelam War IV' of 2009, and at times afterward, too, demanding international, independent investigations into 'war-crime charges' against the Sri Lankan armed forces. That the LTTE propaganda machinery had experience, expertise and funding could not be overlooked, either.

However, it was for the first-time ever that Tamils from India, mostly first-generation migrants and at times those with permanent residency or citizenship in the host-nations, were showing an interest in a cause that agitated their brothers and cousins back home. Fair enough, local Sri Lankan Tamils did participate in substantial numbers, at times out-numbering their Indian brethren. There were also reports that in some places at least, Sri Lankan Tamils took the initiative, leading to their Indian counterparts demonstrating their own commitment to the cause before long. The Sri Lankan Tamil Diaspora was among the various motivating factors and initiators of the early social media calls for the Jallikattu protests in Tamil Nadu. Of course, this one can be verified and confirmed only by government agencies with equipment and information. But there is no denying the fact that at the height of the war-related protests in support of their Sri Lankan brethren in Tamil Nadu, the Diaspora pressure was visible. This time, though, the Tamils of India, wherever they were the organisers of Jallikattu protests, were not really known to be adopting such tactics.

On more than one occasion, Sri Lankan Tamil film promoters, producers, distributors and exhibitors, with their base in the West, would arm-twist highly-paid Tamil Nadu film actors and icons into adapting their line on the ethnic issue. After a point in the past, the Tamil Nadu film stars became as demonstrative as their larger Sri Lankan Tamil brethren, some of them feeling strongly about the cause, having educated themselves on the issue, in between, some others not wanting to rub the rest on the wrong side, and yet others, without even having to wait for any cue from elsewhere. They joined industry-organised token fasts and other forms of protests, in the cause of the Sri Lankan Tamils. Those that could not or did not participate had to pay a heavy-price, in terms of their film-releases, overseas collections and early pull-out from cinemas in those countries where Sri Lankan Tamils dominated the Tamil film viewership. There were occasions when a Tamil film-star who had missed an industry-organised protest would end up organising one of his own with full participation from his fans' associations. Whether or not such tactics of forced participation by Tamil film stars in relatively unrelated protests have continued afterward, the Sri Lankan Tamils' behind-the-scene presence in Kodambakkam, or 'Kollywood', the Tamil equivalent of Hollywood, continues and is obvious, too.

Violence Unexplained

Yet neither the size nor the spontaneity attaching to the Jallikattu protests could explain the 'Marina violence' accompanying its successful conclusion. Questions remain as to why a section, or more than one section of the protestors—sections still, they were—did not want to disperse after then Chief Minister Panneerselvam had initiated convincing measures to have the martial sport back soon enough, remains unexplained. The Chief Minister had followed up his promises and initiatives with immediate legislative measures, which had the unqualified support of the political Opposition, too, in the 234-member State Assembly. For its part, the Centre implored upon the Supreme Court of India, to go slow on the enforcement of the ban that it had imposed earlier, for all practical purposes. The court too had been alive to the ground realities, and the final disposal of the case, where the new facilitating Tamil Nadu law, too, would be added as among those that needed to be heard and decided upon.

Pongal and Aadi Perukku

AS PER the Tamil-Hindu astrological calendar, or *panchang*, and coinciding with the nation-wide Makar Sankaranti observances, falls the Tamil harvest festival of Pongal. In astronomical terms, it signifies a phase of the movement of the sun, worshipped as god across ancient civilisations, as among the most visible and continuing symbols of Nature. Either out of fear for calamities and destruction that they can wrought, or out of sheer awe and respect for giving him all the bounty, Man has always worshipped sun and other aspects of Nature.

In Tamil Nadu, and wherever Tamil-speaking people live, Pongal announces the arrival of the Tamil harvest month of *'Thai'*, which is by itself a sign of prosperity. *'Thai piranthal vazhi pirakkum'* is an old Tamil adage, a belief. It means, 'Come the month of *Thai*, and new vistas will open up' (ending problems and miseries). The term 'Pongal' too signifies 'overflow' of the harvested crop, hence prosperity, again. On every Pongal day, inevitable prosperity is denoted by letting milk and rice overflow from the cooking pot,offered to sun god and then shared as divine *prasad* or *prasadam*.

Here possibly comes the first signs of the Tamils treating the cultivable land and the animals that help to plough his fields, or the female of the species, as equals to future prosperity—as he cooks the rice in milk and adds jaggery or sugar to it, again representing sugar-cane, now a commercial crop.

In most parts of Tamil Nadu, the Pongal prasadam is cooked in the courtyard of the house, open to the sky and to sun god. In some places, it is a community affair. Even in places that are near inter-State borders, the old habit of celebrating Pongal only as a family affair with regular kitchen cooking is changing. However, it remains the same as far as the timing of the 'cooking' and ritualistic offering to sun god and other gods of Nature, both as a thanksgiving and prayers for the future, go.

Like Makar Sankaranti observances elsewhere across the country, the Pongal cooking in Tamil Nadu is done at the exact time of birth of *Uttarayana*, the aspect of sun's phase signifying the birth of the Indian calendar month of *Makar*, coinciding also with the Tamil month, *Thai*. In some communities, it remains regular morning cooking but with added prasadam, piety and festivities. In most others, the Pongal cooking is done at the exact hour of the birth of the new month. That again is changing. Yet, none of these differences and changes has made Pongal any less of a tradition and custom.

In much of rural Tamil Nadu, there is also the custom of ritualistically preparing and offering pongal (which also becomes the name of the milk-rice-and-jaggery cooked offering) to family deities and village deities, periodically. Entire families and communities gather on such occasions. To distinguish the annual harvest festival of Thai Pongal from the rest, some village communities also refer to the former as '*perum* Pongal', or the 'big Pongal' festival.

Of equal significance is the use of only wet-land crops like rice, sugarcane and banana leaves on the occasion, so also tender/matured saplings of turmeric, which is considered auspicious in southern India, especially Tamil Nadu. For Tamil women, the use and application of turmeric on their foreheads at morning bath is a sign of their marital status and strength. Turmeric also protects the feminine face from the sun and heat, and has other medicinal qualities too—especially considering that she too is going to slog it out, dividing her time between home and farm, and needed protection from sun and heat, all the same. This is either the main cause for the use of turmeric, or is an added cause—but once again, the practice continues.

More importantly, Tamil women have their *mangalsutra,* or *thaali* in Tamil, tied only in a thread soaked in/with turmeric powder at the time of their wedding. Some may later on tie it in a gold chain, worn around their necks, others continue to wear both. In literature and films, real-life and fiction, turmeric tied in a yellow thread is a ready substitute for mangalsutra. On the reverse, crude as it may be, one of the early acts of widowhood in Tamil Nadu is the removal of the woman's mangalsutra and abstinence from the use of turmeric, or yellow thread, along with the red *tilak* on her forehead. If the use of turmeric signifies prosperity and fertility in a woman, its removal means the exact opposite. Rather, turmeric saplings to which again *puja* and offerings are made on the Pongal day, and which is then offered to sun god, is a sign of prosperity.

The same can be said of the use of fully grown sugarcane, banana leaves and fruits used on the occasion. Sugarcane is seasonal and does not grow in all parts of the State. Yet, for Pongal, it is a must item. Seasonal shops sell matured sugarcane stalks and turmeric saplings in push-carts on the eve of the Pongal festival. It is more so in urban centres, where the local population mostly comprises migrants from rural and semi-urban centres, even if for decades and generations.

Until successive Dravidian party governments began making rice available regularly in ration shops and at cheap rates in the dry peripheries of the land, rice was a rare commodity for the rural population in many parts of the State. Living on millets through most of the year, they used to have rice-based meal only on two or three occasions. Being the harvest festival, Pongal used to top it all, along with Tamil New Year in mid-April, and possibly Deepavali. Today, millets cost more than rice, which is available for free for the poor through the State government's public distribution system. For those that could not afford rice even that one day in the year, it used to be a sign of continuing poverty and penury. Tamil fiction and films have narratives of children from poor families protesting to their mothers, howling at the top of their voices, if they did not have their annual taste of rice, even if not rice pudding or *payasam*, on Pongal day at least.

Hence, everything associated with Pongal has a great social and economic, emotional and psychological significance for Tamils, living in or away from the regions where Jallikattu too is a tradition—and for generations, centuries and millennia together. So, has Jallikattu been a part of it all, in communities and localities where the sport was a part of the annual fair for local martial communities. Even granting that Jallikattu was/is a seasonal past-time, and was/is only a crude and cruel entertainment, it is historically obvious that only a prosperous community can afford it. Nearer home and elsewhere, only rich kings and landlords have been the patrons of arts and architecture, over the centuries, and only they could act as preservers and sustainers of cultural heritages too. The poor had little time or energy for what remained a rich man's past-time. Over time, Jallikattu had become an add-on sign of such prosperity, relative as it may have been.

What is not available readily becomes an idea for hope and dream. It is thus that in Indian mythology,' a 'sea of milk', or *'paal-kadal',* became a sign of prosperity, where Lord Vishnu rests with his consort, Lakshmi, the Hindu goddess of wealth. In Tamil literature, there are constant references to a river of milk, or *paal-aaru*. Tamil literature also mentions rains thrice a month, indicating it as a sign of eternal prosperity. Some early Tamil historical films, either seriously or out of jest, had the line, *'maadham mum-maari'*, meaning the same, the idea itself borrowed from ancient literature all the same.

In context, it signified either a kingdom's prosperity or absence of it. In the works of Omar Khayyam and other poets and writers, an oasis with some shade and water in the midst of desert conditions, was/is a sign of hope, if not outright prosperity, for a weary caravan. Call it superstitious or ardent belief, it is here that Tamil practices too become tradition, and tradition, custom. It is like anywhere else in the country and the rest of the world, too.

Fresh Flooding

Apart from Pongal, there is yet another farming-related festival that the people across Tamil Nadu celebrate every year. Owing to the inevitability of over-imposing religious connotation, it is confined mostly to Hindus, but other communities join in, in some places and on occasions. It is the *Aadi Perukku*, or 'fresh flooding' (of the river Cauvery) in the Tamil month of *Aadi*. Essentially, the celebrations should have commenced in the Cauvery delta region, but sure enough it has spread to other parts of the State too. They have continued to date despite the known and acknowledged fact that the Cauvery does not flow much in the State, over the past decades. On most occasions in recent decades, the State government has also discontinued the practice of releasing limited quantities of Cauvery waters from the Mettur reservoir for the festivities, owing to shortage of rainfall and also non-release of water by the upper riparian State of Karnataka.

The river Cauvery has its origins in Thalacauvery in the Kodagu/Coorg hills, now in Karnataka. For decades and centuries now, the south-west monsoon commences its Indian sojourns in the Andamans around 25 May each year, and reaches the Kerala coast on 1 June. From there, it spreads out across the country's west coast before turning in-land and travelling up to the North, East and the North-East. In the normal course, it should not leave out the dry West, either. The Aadi Perukku festival is timed for the eighteenth day of the Tamil month by the name Aadi, when the first floods of the year's rains in Thalacauvery will flow down to the Thanjavur delta, still considered the granary of Tamil Nadu.

Early Tamil literature has references to the Aadi Perukku festival on the banks of the Cauvery. The *Manimekalai*, written between the eighth and ninth centuries, is one of the five long epic-poems (*Aiyum-perum Kappiangal*) in Tamil. The epic has a scene wherein the male protagonist Kovalan (of the *Silappadikaram* fame) parts company from his lady-love Madhavi, to return home to wife Kannagi, at the annual *Poom-punal* festival—which is, celebrating the year's fresh flow of Cauvery waters in native Poompuhar. It is another matter that the Cauvery waters and irrigation have strong evidence in the Grand *Anicut* or *Kallanai*, a stone-dam across the river built by the Chola King Karikalan, as far back as the second century after Christianity was born. Whether or not there is enough Cauvery waters to fill it each passing year, the Kallannai itself stands tall, in all its pristine glory, over 1,800 years after it was built—thus becoming one of the oldest man-made structures that has still survived in these parts—and continue serve the purpose for which it was conceived and constructed.

There is a link and relation between Aadi Perukku and Thai Pongal in the contemporary context of the 'Jallikattu dispute'. As religious festivities, Deepavali (as pronounced in Tamil, and Diwali elsewhere) and Dussera have an all-India presence and prominence in the annual Hindu calendar. But

Thai Pongal is an out and out Tamil custom and celebration, though there again Makar Sankaranti is a national equivalent, so to say. Like Pongal festivities are confined to Tamil Nadu, Aadi Perukku should have been limited to the Cauvery delta. In practice, it is not the case. It may owe to the greater identification of the Tamils with agriculture and agrarian economy over generations and centuries. It may not be without rationale that Aadi Perukku and Thai Pongal (both named after the respective Tamil calendar months) fall six months from each other. The former is for thanking the gods for good rains, to help in irrigating the farms and fields. The latter is thanks-giving for a bountiful harvest. Tamils celebrate both wherever they are, in even this 'IT *yugam*', or era. They may be in distant Mumbai or Delhi or Kolkata, or Boston or Belgrade. Like Aadi Perukku, Jallikattu too is an extension of the average Tamil's identification with his roots, whether or not they might have participated in the sport, or organised one in their villages, be it in the past or even at present.

Unlike the Aadi Perukku festivities, not all the migrant Tamils from India, took Jallikattu with them to far-off hands. It was/is not without reason. Those that went in the first lot to the West were from the upper crust of the Tamil society, and were not from the traditional 'Jallikattu communities'. It is only in recent times that the latter too have ventured out. But where Tamils went out in earlier times, and are settled in their host-countries for long, they are hosting the sport there again, as part of the Pongal festivities. The Upcountry Tamils of recent Indian origin in neighbouring Sri Lanka are an example. Elsewhere across the British Raj where Tamils from India were taken as indentured labour, they did not have the freedom or wherewithal to practice their religion or celebrate their religious festivities. Not only Jallikattu, but even their other religious and community practices and customs were lost, some retained in some form, and others revived in more recent, post-colonial times, out of the fading memories of the generations that succeeded the forerunners.

Regional, Sub-regional?

At the height of the Jallikattu protests in 2017, there arose the question if the sport had a State-wide reach across Tamil Nadu. The campaign too was done mostly through the social media, and the authorship of the protest could not be ascertained. But the argument that the sport was limited to a minority section was gaining ground at least until crowds began swelling and drowned it.

In a way, the gathering of massive crowds at different venues in the State for the Jallikattu protests was a demonstration of the sport's wider reach. The local television media also showed this time, how young boys and girls from other parts of the State and even other parts of the country, had travelled to traditional Jallikattu centres like Palamedu, Alanganallur and Avaniyapuram, all in the southern region. Many of them did not even know the name of those villages/localities. To some, it also became a pilgrimage of sorts. In the mouths of some other youngsters, it sounded like a penance for not doing what they should have been doing through their growing-up years. They had overlooked it, either owing to ignorance or peer-pressure or parental neglect. Now that they had been made aware of it, and they were also on their own, earning and living their own lives, they were atoning for the past. Whether they will do so in future remains to be seen, but they at least have stories of the same to tell their children and grandchildren that they had not heard from their parents, mostly based now in urban centres.

Like Pongal, and more like Aadi Perukku, suddenly, Jallikattu too started spreading wings, beyond the traditional geographical sphere of influence within Tamil Nadu. Maybe, the sport may never be staged in Boston and Berlin, especially with the traditional fervour native to the customary Tamil Nadu villages. But there is already an announcement about the State government hosting it in Chennai's famed Marina, the venue of the historic January 2017 protests.

Over the past several years and decades, the sport has already spread to some peripheral areas, outside the traditional confines. If the State government is serious about it and also has its way, on the Marina sands, the State Tourism Department can make it an extension of the annual 'Pongal Industrial Trade Fair', at the other end of the world-famed beach, in the Island Grounds, and draw huge crowds even without the 2017 controversy.

It can well be like neighbouring Kerala making the annual boat-race, again coinciding with local harvest season, a larger tourist attraction than already. Karnataka has its annual Dussera procession in Mysuru. Nearer home, many addicts of the annual 'December *kutcheri* season' of Carnatic music in Chennai believe that the fortnight-long celebrations, now going up to a month, may have preceded the birth of the city. It was transported from the rich Thanjavur delta, where fine arts had its patrons in the local land-lords. The *brahminical* organisers of the 1927 Madras session of the Indian National Congress, all lovers of traditional music-forms, added the kutcheris by Thanjavur-based *vidwans* in the evenings, for relaxation and entertainment. Today, it has been institutionalised as never before, either in India or outside.

It is not only about Carnatic music but even various forms of folk music, instrumental or otherwise, which had originally belonged to traditionally prosperous regions of the State—particularly in the kingdom cities of Thanjavur, the erstwhile Chola capital, and Madurai (Pandyas). When kingdoms fell and went beyond repair and recognition, new patrons emerged—in the form of local landlords and *zamindars*. When they also became weak, politically and financially, newer sponsors appeared on the scene, in some cases—though not in all.

Some of these patrons/sponsors did not belong to the regions where the art forms had thrived and prospered. Some artistes migrated, some others still stayed back in their original homes, and travelled to different places in different seasons for different purposes, based on what the new-generation patrons wanted. It is not unlikely that Jallikattu, otherwise a dying tradition and art-form in its own way, can take such a turn, and a turn for the better, over time.

Who knows, half a century down the line, a casual visitor to Chennai may claim that it was an ancient sport native to the city, though even the city itself would have only been 400-plus years young. Better still, with the current impetus and new interest, Jallikattu can also be staged in other non-traditional areas of the State other than Chennai—or, even outside Tamil Nadu. No one can then say that Jallikattu was only a sub-regional sport, as some tend to say now. If *kabadi* can become a national sport, and vying to become an Olympic event, who knows, with Spaniards in Europe and across the Americas taking the lead, bull-taming of the Jallikattu kind, if not of the blood-letting bull-fight kind, could become an accepted international event over the medium term.

Taming or 'Fighting' the Bull?

IT IS ironic but true. Jallikattu has now gained new popularity and desirability, owing to the protests—rather, the spontaneity of the protests. In turn, the protests and spontaneity owed to the ban on Jallikattu. All of it thus made it more popular than earlier. The question is, would Jallikattu have died a slow but possible sure-death, if only overtime, like many of the other forms of traditional art forms, but for the ban? Or, can it still happen in the near or distant future?

The prime problem in the understanding of Jallikattu as a martial game for those outside of Tamil Nadu springs from their pre-conceived notions. They start off on a negative note, given their vast knowledge and varied views against the Spanish bull-fight. The Google era has not helped matters, for a better and clearer understanding of Jallikattu and in distinguishing it from the Spanish game, if it can be termed so. Nor has it helped clear clouded ideas.

Spanish Bull-fight

The Spanish bull-fight is bloody and gruesome, often shown and watched on television worldwide for decades now. Until the 2017 street-protests, Jallikattu had not made it to national news channels. Where it was shown in the past, it was a brief news item, about the Supreme Court stay of the year's event or an outright ban. The viewers from outside the State did not have even a second-hand idea of the sport. Barring select animal activists, genuine as they otherwise may be, most people evaluate Jallikattu from their relatively 'better knowledge' of the blood and gory attending on the Spanish bull-fight.

Considered in this light, naturally, Jallikattu would have to go.

The Spanish bull-fight is all about well-armed, well-trained men, at times on protective horse-back, taunting and spearing the fighter-bull to a slow and painful death through an instalment of deep cuts and wounds on the hapless animal, otherwise well-fed. They also have lesser men on their feet showing the proverbial red-rag before the bull, to provoke it even more, so that the 'gladiator' can charge with practised ease and cunning than already, to enthral an audience of a hundred thousand or so, that they will want more of the 'action'. This also ensures that the 'game' does not end as a tame, one-sided affair. And the spectators have their money's worth of fun and entertainment.

Having done the deed, and letting the animal die in pain, inch by inch, the 'victorious' bull-fighter drags the majestic animal's massive carcass around the stadium, like our victorious cricketers taking their trophy around in celebration. The crowds cheer the bull-fighter even more loudly. It happens even today despite all noble claims to civilisation and Christian beliefs and catholic behaviour. Simply put, it takes you back to the era of gladiators and their ruthless audiences in over-crowded coliseums. A child who reads a little more than school text-books these days might be reminded of the valorous stories of *'Androcles and the Lion'* and/or *'David and Goliath'*, but they too would not have read about anything as bloody as the Spanish bull-fight.

The animal rights activists do protest, but neither the governments, nor the courts in those countries have stopped, or stalled, the game—or, is it game-hunting in public and in urban/urbane settings. In India, the courts, governments and the legislature have been protective of the animal and animal's rights much more than is acknowledged. Instead, there is demand for greater intervention by the very same INGOs that have not succeeded as much elsewhere. To be fair to them, there is no harm in trying, here or elsewhere.

In Contrast, Jallikattu

In comparison, the sport of Jallikattu in Tamil Nadu is one of valour, and not blood-letting, of the animal in particular.

The bull-fighters do not generally train themselves for the task though overall they might have been into martial arts, in earlier generations especially. It is not even bull-fight in the Spanish sense of the term, but bull-taming, at best.

If someone's blood falls to the ground, if someone is irretrievably injured, it is the man fighting the animal, not the animal. As Tamil writer Ti Su Chellappa (1912-98) says in the brief introduction to the first edition of his novelette, *Vaadi Vaasal* (1949), '*Human blood can spill at the vaadi vaasal, but not a drop of animal blood should (even) be seen.*'

Like Jallikattu, the term *Vaadi Vaasal* too suddenly became familiar to TV news viewers with the Marina protests, starting with those in native Tamil Nadu. But then, every petition before the courts against Jallikattu, every judgment that has banned the sport have cited instances after instances, where cruelty to the animal seemed to have been the norm, not an exception. Independent of political parties and leaders in power, successive

State governments have not been able to convincingly explain to the Apex Court especially, why they did not, or could not, enforce the regulations for relatively humane handling of the animals, and also for the orderly conduct of the sport, as outlined in the provisions of the 2009 enabling law, and repeated commitments made to the Judiciary, whenever the matter came up. This includes the post-protests Season-2017, if PETA's (People for Ethical Treatment of Animals) latest petition, against the new Tamil Nadu law, and also media reports during the period, are to be believed.

Chellappa's *Vaadi Vaasal*, originally written as a short story, is all about Jallikattu. It is about a brave young man, Pichchai, taming a notoriously ferocious and equally well-trained bull, Kaari, or the 'black one', at a local Jallikattu event. In a way, he fights the bull to avenge the death of his father at the sharpened horns of Kaari. In doing so, Pichchai is restoring the family honour, which is what martial communities have lived for and died for in the distant past. This tradition is still being handed down from generation to generation, in increasingly dwindling numbers, as originally known. Today, it is just about keeping up the family's tradition more than its name and fame of generations and centuries. At the end of Chellappa's story, the animal is killed, but not by tamer Pichchai, who does not even hurt or injure the bull even remotely. Instead, Kaari's owner, the zamindar, or landlord, from a neighbouring village, shoots the defeated bull, as if this alone would restore his own honour and that of his village and zamindari. The zamindar also honours the talented youth, Pichchai, throughout the day's events involving other bulls, and grudgingly so when his animal too is tamed.

Indus Bull Seal

The game of bull-taming may have had its origins in southern Tamil Nadu. But it is in western Tamil Nadu, that we have an animal with a striking resemblance to the depiction of the one in the famous 'Bull Seal' from the Indus Valley Civilisation, dating back to 2,000 years BCE.

Although in modern times, speakers of the various Dravidian languages have mainly occupied the southern portion of India, Dravidian populace must have been widespread throughout, especially before the Indo-Aryan migration into the sub-continent, or as is believed by some. The Brahui-speaking population in Balochistan (Pakistan) and their language have been taken by some as the linguistic equivalent of the present-day southern Tamil Nadu population, perhaps indicating that Dravidian languages were formerly much more widespread across the country, and may have been supplanted by the incoming Indo-Aryan languages. The Indus Valley Civilisation (2,600-1,900 BCE) may have been the pre-Aryan manifestation of the Dravidian peoples and languages in south Asia. From there, they spread to south India, according to some anthropologists. The 'Bull Seal' (and also the animal) is one important indicator of the close links between the present-day cultures of South India and the Indus Valley civilisation of the past.

The Kangeyam Bull

The 'Kangeyam bull' is a local breed found in and around the town known by that name, not far away from the district headquarters of Tiruppur, the 'knit-wear capital of India', in western Tamil Nadu. The animal has superior draught strength. It can also adapt to lesser availability of nutrients. These are all qualities that the normal eye or the common man cannot know or detect. What catches the eye of anyone with even a faint acquaintance or memory of his primary school history lessons is something else. It is the visible link to the animal on the 'Bull Seal' from the archaeological excavations in the ancient sites of the Indus Valley Civilisation. Apart from those in western India, an extension of the Indus Valley, it is doubtful if any other bull stock from across the country bears such a close resemblance to the 'Indus Bull' as the Kangeyam animal does.

Apart from the Kangeyam bull, there are at least 70-80 varieties of bulls in Tamil Nadu, fit for taking on a Jallikattu tamer. Only half of them have survived the ravages of time and neglect. There are many more varieties spread across the country, big and small. At the height of the Jallikattu protests, some social media campaigns wanted their readers to believe that the ban in the name of ending animal-cruelty was a ploy to make draught-resistant local breeds extinct so that western dairy industry could grow manifold in the country.

The symbolism of the 'Indus Bull' seal needs to be contextualised and properly understood. Apart from the fact that the 'Indus Bull' might be among the seals and symbols from the past that may have survived the ravages of time, there is also a close linkage between fertility and hence prosperity, and the male of the species. This has been true of almost every ancient community and civilisation. Archaeologists and anthropologists believe it to be so. Their claims have not been disproved.

At the height of the Jallikattu protests, one campaign theme also centred on western animal entrepreneurs wanting to market their bull varieties in India and said that soon, the locally-adaptable native breeds would become extinct if Jallikattu was banned. All of it was again to promote western dairy industry in this country in more direct ways. Some even claimed, without proof again, that like broiler chicken and BT brinjal, the aim was to control the reproductive pattern of local breeds of cows, if only over time. Convoluted as the argument may sound, the Jallikattu ban was only a first step in that direction. According to this line of thought, at times posted in the social media and/or posed in TV talk-shows, a ban on Jallikattu would make strong breeds of local bulls unwanted and extinct. The campaigners argued that the specially-fed Jallikattu bulls served a greater purpose in the reproductive cycle of the animal, and maintaining them was also a costly affair, if they did not serve the reproductive purpose.

Expanding on the argument, it was said that with the ban, India, with its current stock of the largest number of cattle-head, would become the net importer of milk and milk products—and in large quantities, in this era of market capitalism and wanton globalisation. In short, a ban on Jallikattu would lead to an ultimate extinction of high-breed bulls for re-production. It would ring the death-knell to Verghese Kurien's successful 'White Revolution', which has changed the face of rural India as much as the 'Green Revolution' before it. The argument, however, appears as much contrived as many others that were thrown up on the social media at the height of the Jallikattu protests. Yet, all those that campaigned for Jallikattu ban, and quoted chapter and verse from various literature did not even seem to have attempted to challenge these claims of their critics.

How Old is Old?

Questions have been raised, and at times answered, at least partially on how old is old, for Jallikattu to be described as forming a part of the Tamil culture.

How long should a practice be in continuous or even continual usage for it to be accepted as a 'living culture'? For instance, if living practice is to be a yardstick for acknowledging the long cultural history of a people, barring a lone village in Karnataka, and may be such isolated places elsewhere in the country, Sanskrit cannot be said to be a 'living language'. Even in Mattur, the village in Karnataka's Shimoga district, the tradition of all-Sanskrit usage in daily life and living, was revived only in near decades. Yet, the Government of India in its wisdom has continued to honour the ancient language identified exclusively with the nation, in terms of its origin, antiquity, richness of literature, and identification as the 'divine language' in some parts of the country, and also one-time growth and the present stage of near-extinction.

In the post-demonetisation currency, Sanskrit numerals find a place, triggering yet another avoidable controversy. Sanskrit was in the news, and did not lose its place in the new currency notes because of the controversy. Instead, the controversy only drew attention to the new and contemporary status that the language has acquired. It is another matter that none can question the antiquity or flexibility or relevance of Sanskrit as a mother-language in the Indo-European linguistic context. Nor can the antiquity of Sanskrit and its application in ancient mathematics, astronomy and other aspects of science and medicine, be ignored. But *if continuing usage is the yard-stick, all arguments fall flat.* As for Jallikattu, the January 2017 protests have helped revive awareness about the sport, both inside and outside Tamil Nadu. There is already a talk of taking Jallikattu to places outside of the traditional centres.

The question of age and period of Jallikattu still remains. Possibly, the earliest of authenticated Tamil literary references to the sport is found in *Mullai Kali*, a set of poems dating back to the later part of the *Sangam* literature, 2000 years ago. In a unique exercise, ancient Tamil grammar, *Thol-kappiam*, has addressed lifestyle and livelihood of people under the third of the three sections, *Porul Adhikaram*. The phrase *Thol-kappiam* translates as 'ancient epic', but then it is a book of grammar. The first two parts of the book are titled, *Ezhuthu Adhikaram* and *Sol Adhikaram*, respectively relating to language and linguistics, and the grammar thereof. In turn, the third, *Porul Adhikaram*, deals with land and its people.

It is not only poets and poetry that wrote about land and people in the context of ancient Tamil. Even grammar books did it. They, in fact, defined and delineated land and people, their lifestyles and livelihood in great detail. The *Thol-kappiam* divides the land that people lived under five different categories, based on topography, fertility and plant population. The term *Mullai* in *Mullai Kali* refers to forests and forest lands. The *Mullai Kali* is about people who live there, living on and off the forest wealth. It forms a part of the larger, five-part *Kali Thogai*, a compilation of rich poetry on the land and people living in the five different geographical regions in the Tamil country. As writer-chronicler, Perumal Murugan, author of the Tamil novel, *Madhorubhagan*, points out in his introduction to the sixth edition of Ti Su Chellappa's *Vaadi Vaasal,* there are poems in the *Mullai Kali* that refer to Jallikattu.

Surely, neither the *Mullai Kali*, nor the larger *Kali Thogai*, is science-fiction type of work, where the poet can imagine the martial art-form of Jallikattu centuries and millennia before they had come into practice. The otherwise accepted argument that poets and writers often exaggerate the qualities of men, good or bad, cannot be applied in this case as there was/is nothing of discovery or invention in a game of Jallikattu.

References to Jallikattu kind of martial art-form in ancient poetry is not an 'R2D2' of the filmi *Star Wars* genre. It is much less than missiles like the *'Brahma-astra'* and flying saucers like the *Puspak-viman* that finds occasional mention in our mythologies, and even the millennium-old Tamil epic *Silappadikaram*. Conventional wisdom still has it that poetry and grammar are only an expression and codification of an existing practice. Poetry uses flowery language. Grammar, the codified form, is shorn of such niceties and exaggeration. Jallikattu has both poetry and grammar going for it. The ancient grammar book, dated back to the third century, places the martial sport in the context of land and people. The *Mullai Kali* speaks of the sport in some detail, thus establishing its antiquity, and hence cultural relevance. If the *Mullai Kali* is acknowledged as a part of *Kali Thogai* and the latter forms a part of the famed

Sangam literature, then Jallikattu too has been around for 2,000 or more years.

History and Etymology

BJP leader Subramanian Swamy, too, comprehensively brought out the historicity of Jallikattu in his petition before the Supreme Court. At the height of the Jallikattu protests, some social media activists did find fault only with his criticism of certain developments, but he is possibly the only one who has presented arguments favouring the martial art as a part of the Tamil cultural practices. Swamy claimed, 'Jallikattu was known as *Eru Thazhuvuthal* (hugging the bulls) in Tamil Nadu during ancient times.' That is to say, Jallikattu was about hugging on to the bull's hump, and not hitting or hurting it otherwise. This is also what it has become after the pre-ban Supreme Court-approved Tamil Nadu government regulations said, as against head-on, face-to-face taming, where the tamer literally takes the bull by the horn.

It is Eru Thazhuvuthal that is now being witnessed on television channels, whenever Jallikattu is in the news. But the more courageous part of the sport did involve the man, standing alone in the instant or improvised arena, with on-lookers standing in a flexible circle, taking on the fierce bull by the horn, and literally so, to try and bring it to its knees, again literally so. It is a contest between competing strengths, will-power, powers of concentration, all required in a battle-field later on. The physical strength is visibly weighted in favour of the animal. Will-power and powers of concentration are common to both. Valour and bravery, the man at the centre understands. If the bull too understands it, there is no way for the common spectators to know it. But the animal's care-giver and owner have their own ways of knowing and understanding it, just as they instinctively appreciate it when their bull is at times irritated and is off-colour. It is just like how the owner, trainer and jockey of a race horse know all about the animal's mood and methods with just one look.

Subramanian Swamy's affidavit and/or written arguments, filed as late as October 2016, pertained to the 'Jallikattu case' already pending before the Supreme Court. The case became necessary after the government of Prime Minister Narendra Modi sought to nullify the earlier court-ordered ban, through a Government Order (GO), issued by the Executive wing. As Swamy points out, Jallikattu as a 'practice has been clearly recorded in the *Sangam* literature of Tamils. *Sangam* literature flourished between 400 BCE and 300 CE. *Sangam* poet Cholan Naluruthiranar has sung seven poems describing *Eru Thazhuvathal* events'.

At a time when *swayamwaram,* or *swayamvar* in most non-Tamil Indian languages, included martial contests and competitions for winning over the hands of a woman across ancient India, Jallikattu was a common practice for the purpose. It has been acknowledged as such. Just as breaking of Lord Shiva's bow, *Shiva Dhanush,* was the game-setter for the swyamvaram, or groom-hunting, in the Hindu epic *Ramayanam,* and all those skill-games with the bow-and-arrow, culminating in the 'Machcha Entram', in the *Mahabharatham*, Jallikattu was one in its own way, in its own environs. In our times, Tamil films, from Sivaji Ganesan's *Veerapandia Kattabomman* (1959) to super-star Rajnikanth's *Murattu Kaalai* (1980) and later-day films, too, all have had episodes on bull-taming, where again, no blood was/is shed.

To quote from Swamy's affidavit, and in turn citing ancient literature, Jallikattu 'would be held in villages abutting forest lands....Their livelihood depended on these cattle and from the produce of the cattle *viz.*, milk, curd and ghee. They raised bulls of great valour and strength in their houses. The event of *Eru Thazhuvathl* would be held after beating the drums in the village and announcing the festival. The parents of girls who are to be married would then announce that the one who tames their bull alone can win the hands of their daughter in marriage. After the event of *Eru Thazhuvathal* is over, the bride to be and the groom would sing the praise of Lord Vishnu along with friends of the bride (*Source: Mullai Kali* poetry by *Sangam* poet Cholan Naluruthiranar).' Thankfully, no father or girl offers her/herself as a prize for the winner any more—not in living memory or even the immediate past. Instead, it is in cash or as gold coins, originally tied in a piece of cloth around either one of the horns or the neck of the animal. In more recent times, the prize for the winner has become more contemporary. Possibly there are sponsors, but the prizes these days come in the form of motor bikes and bicycles (the latter in larger numbers), TV sets and refrigerators, and of course, cash in varying figures—thankfully, not all of them tied to the animal's horns or around its neck for the fighter-bull to drag it/them along while facing the free-hand tamer at the other end.

Krishna Connection

The *Mullai Kali* refers to the people of the land as *Aayars*, or Yadavs, to use a more contemporary caste identity, made popular and acceptable in recent decades—people who are associated with cattle-rearing from time immemorial. Hindu mythology says Lord Krishna comes from the same community, and he is also pictorially and poetically presented in the company of cows and cattle-head. A story in the *Srimad Bhagavatham*, one of the eighteen *purana*s (scriptures) of the Hindus in Sanskrit, narrating Lord Krishna's life, has an episode in which he tames not one bull but seven, as ordained by a local ruler, who had been rearing them with great care only for the swayamvaram of his daughter. Needless to point out, Krishna did precisely that and took the hands of the princess.

Swamy's Supreme Court affidavit too speaks about the *Bhagavatham* narrative, to date the sport of bull-taming and its mythological/historical roots. As the affidavit submits, Jallikattu or *Eru Thazhuvathal* 'probably had its origins in the life of Lord Sri Krishna narrated in detail in the *Bhagavatham* and in the earlier works about Sri Krishna'.

The *Bhagavatham,* like all the other *Puranas,* is dated back to that of its author, saint-poet Veda Vyasa. He also authored the *Mahabharatham*, the other Hindi/Sanskrit epic after the *Ramayanam.* Forming an important and integral part of the *Mahabharatham* is the *Bhagvad Gita*, Lord Krishna's percept on life and death, good and evil. It is the last word on Hindu *dharma*. The *Bhagavatham*, in the *Vishnu Purana,* (the Puranas are said to be post-Christ compositions by some but there are others who believe in its greater antiquity, and believe strongly so) in turn, encapsulates Krishna's life-story, the ninth of the ten *avatar*s of Lord Vishnu, the second in the divine Hindu Trinity. Hindus believe that Lord Krishna returned to His heavenly abode at the end of the *Dwapara Yuga*, the third of the four ages, or life-span of the universe, as per Hindu mythology and beliefs. Using astrological and scientific calculations, some have put the date of Krishna's death as 21 July 3227 BC. Krishna had lived up to 125 years. All of it would mean that Krishna's taming of the seven bulls could be dated back to 5000 years before our time. Of course, there are other versions, which puts the date back by millions of years, but the 5000-year mark is the closest that we cannot ignore, if the argument is one of beliefs and beliefs-based customs.

Whatever the truth or otherwise of such beliefs, even internal linguistic evidence have been marshalled to fix the age of Adi Sankara's interpretation of *Srimad Bhagavatham* to at least in the eighth century after Christ, that is at a minimum of 1200 years. As recalled in Swamy's affidavit as well, the *Bhagavatham* describes how Lord Krishna had tamed seven bulls to win the hand of Naknajeeti, daughter of Naknajeet, the king of Kosala. Tamil literature readers know Naknajeeti as

Nappinnai, a Tamilised version of her name. Krishna is believed to have come from the western coastal town of Dwaraka, and Kosala was in central India. In the *Ramayanam*, the story of the seventh avatar of Lord Vishnu, Kausalya, the mother of the divine, came from the kingdom by that name. Both towns were far away from the action ground of Jallikattu, deep down south. True, there may not be one too many references to Jallikattu or another form of the sport in subsequent times and the history of the rest of India.

Apart from the *Bhagavatham* in Sanskrit and the *Mullai Kali* in Tamil, religious literature of the Vaishnaviite sect has recorded, rather re-recorded, Lord Krishna's bull-taming prowess. The *Azhwars*, as the title goes, were Tamil-speaking Vaishnaviite saint-poets in the era of Hindu revivalism, post-Jainism, in the Tamil country. The compilation of their poetic rendering on Krishna and other avatars of Lord Vishnu, are collated as the *Naalayira Dhivya-Prabhantham*, meaning a collection of 4,000 sacred compositions on the name and fame of the Lord. To this day, Vaishnaviite Hindus in Tamil Nadu recite *paasuram* after *paasuram*, or composition after composition, set to music, from the *Prabhantham,* at all important family, social and temple functions. They also recite it at home every morning. At least two of the twelve Azhwars, namely, Nammazhwar (or, *Nam Azhwar* 'our *Azhwar*'), and Tirumangai Azhwar, sang about Lord Krishna taming bulls. Some claim that Nammazhwar dates back to around 3500 BCE, or some 5,500 years ago (possibly around the time Krishna tamed the seven bulls) but the more acceptable date is around 800 CE. Likewise, the traditional and acceptable dating for Tirumangai Azhwar are from around 2,700 years before Christ to around 775 CE, respectively.

It was the era of Hindu revivalism, and of Adi Sankara, and also Tamil Saiviite saint-poets like Thirunavukkarasar, Thirugnana Sambandar, Sundarar and Manika-vasagar. While Sankara and the rest helped revive the Saiviite traditions of

Hinduism, the Aazhwars did so in the case of Vaishnavism, in Tamil Nadu.

The closest that one can date the Azhwar paasurams on Lord Krishna's bull-taming is around 1,200 years ago. Even arguing that the sport was not prevalent in Tamil Nadu, and the two Azhwars were only singing what had appeared in the *Bhagavatham* in Sanskrit, there is a lot of explaining to do. If Jallikattu was prevalent in the Tamil country, it dates back to the Sangam era, the age of the *Mullai Kali*, 2,000 years, if not more. If these paasurams had their origins in the *Bhagavatham*, the sport has to be dated back at 5,000 years ago, and also acknowledged to have been played out elsewhere in ancient India, beyond and beside the Tamil country. It would then be conclusive that Jallikattu was not confined to a sub-region in present-day Tamil Nadu, or belonged exclusively to only one community, as was/is being made out by some, when the January 2017 protests came out of nowhere.

Incidentally, Krishna was a Yadav, and so were the residents of the Mullai landscape in the Sangam era, but today, the sport is prevalent and more popular among the martial Mukkulathore community, clearly indicating that there was possibly no community bias to the sport. If one looked at the fact that Krishna, the Yadav, was not just a cow-herd but was also a ruler at birth, and there were other kings too from the Yadav and other communities across the country, it would justify how bull-taming as a swayamwar sport was important to test the valour of royal men, born and sworn to protect their land and people from enemies. In Tamil Nadu, the Mukkulathore community is identified as an erstwhile ruling class, who had fallen into modest times with the exit of blue-blooded royalty, very many centuries ago.

Whose Jallikattu?

THERE IS no denying that Jallikattu being a sport of valour and bravery, it has an element of community/caste-centric approach attached to it. In a socially-structured society like India's, whether such divisions were/are repugnant otherwise, it was/is a reality. It is also a fact that some of the past stigma refuses to go away, despite legal and constitutional measures that have gone a long way to change the situation. There are reports that Dalits, at the lower end of the societal order in every part of India, are said to have been kept out of the sport.

At the other end, one does not expect the upper-most Brahmin caste and most of the other upper-caste youth to participate as bull-fighters, tamers or whatever. Some of them might have prided themselves as owners of the best Jallikattu bulls in the neighbourhood, some may have also learnt martial arts of some form or all. There have also been hereditary Brahmin kings and those from non-martial, non-Kshatirya castes, elsewhere in the country, but they were exceptions. This also owes to tradition and culture of another kind. Barring local temple priests and a few other Brahmins and other upper caste members of the rural society, the upper castes do not take part in most of the village-level events of the kind. It is mainly because their numbers are few. The Brahmins, for instance, do not constitute more than 2.5-3 per cent of Tamil Nadu's population. Nor have they accounted for a higher percentage at any time in the comprehensible past. That cannot be said of the Dalits, who comprise 20 per cent of the State's population.

Pastoral Background

Going back to the origins, Lord Krishna came from the Yadav community of cow-herds. The Tamil literary work, *Mullai Kali*, in which Jallikattu gets detailed mention, is also about the land and life of the community. It may thus be of interest to study as to how far did the sport stay on in the rest of India, especially in the North, and how did it disappear, or does the tradition still continue in the same form or such other forms in any of the cowherd communities elsewhere in the country?

One possibility is that the constant battles that the northern princely states had fought, both among themselves, and with those coming constantly from Central Asia, could have ended patronage and also the practice of sports and arts of various kinds. The present-day Tamil Nadu too witnessed such internecine battles and wars between its rulers. It is likely that such wars and victories might have contributed to communities that were/are identified as more martial than others and might have adapted the latter's sport, especially because it was an expression of a warrior's valour, courage and bravery.

If Jallikattu survived in the south and south-central parts of Tamil Nadu especially, there was also no major and sustained foreign politico-military intervention in the Jallikattu country. The closest in this regard was the advent of Malik Kafur, born Manik, a Hindu, the fourteenth century army commander of

Delhi Sultan, Allaudin Khilji. In his third military campaign to the South in as many years, Malik Kafur intended capturing the Tamil kingdoms, laid siege on the Pandya capital of Madurai for weeks, but lost out, ultimately. Though he had taken the Pandya king prisoner, Malik Kafur ended up negotiating an honourable way out, and went back home.

After Malik Kafur, the only outsider-rulers of these parts were the Nayakkar kings of the Krishnadevaraya clan from what is now the Andhra-Karnataka country. The Nayakkar dynasty ruled from Madurai, in which kingdom the Jallikattu country too fell, for nearly 200 years (1529-1736). The Nayakkar kings were also born Hindus, they too worshipped bulls as the vehicle of Lord Shiva, the third in the Hindu Trinity, after Brahma the Creator and Vishnu the Protector. They did not have any reason, cultural, religious or any other, to interfere with local customs.

In the post-Nayakkar era, the British entered the scene. They were interested more in revenue-collection and civil and police administration that facilitated and ensured it. They did not interfere with local customs beyond a point, unless they feared it as a means to overthrow them. Across the country, they were thus happy to rule the people through local zamindars and *jagirdar*s. South of Madurai, it was the *poligars*, many of whom were descendants of the Telugu-speaking Nayakkars. In parts of the Madurai and the adjoining Tiruchinapoly (now, Tiruchinapalli, or Tiruchi) revenue districts that the British created for their administrative convenience, Jallikattu has flourished to this day. This was so despite the fact that it was in these parts, 'rebels' like Veerapandia Kattabomman, the Maruthu brothers and Rani Velu Nachiyar, had challenged the British, and ended up paying for it. Though the anti-thuggery laws and their crude and cruel measures did extend up to these parts, yet there is nothing to suggest that the British rulers discouraged the annual Jallikattu festivities in anyway. All of it was also in an era long before the likes of Gopalakrishna Ghokale in western India had begun using religious and community congregations like the annual Ganesh festival, to light up the fire of freedom in the local population. The constant reorganisation and division of inherited revenue districts after Independence might have given a wrong impression about the politico-geographical location of the traditional Jallikattu villages and communities.

There is also an explanation, how a martial sport of what essentially was a pastoral people of Yadavs, or *Aayar*s, came to be identified even more with an essentially martial community of the Mukkulathores. Warrior communities were concentrated mostly around the capital towns or in barrack-towns as might have been the case those days while pastoral people lived elsewhere across the country, where their life-support systems were available in abundance. In context, it needs to be remembered that ancient Tamil kingdoms, like others across the country, were essentially city-States in the Roman mould. They were anything but how a present-day Indian State is visualised. Battles were fought, won or lost over the control of the capital of a kingdom, with the enemy laying siege on the city.

The Tamil grammar *Thol-kappiam* also sets down the rules of warfare, just as it has detailed the lands and people. In listing out early preparations and provocations for a full-fledged war on a rival king, enemy rulers start with *Aanirai Kavarthal*, or capturing the cattle-head from within the enemy territory. They would have been attempted along the border villages, where anyway, a military cantonment would have been established. Naturally, there would have been defences to protect the animals even in peace times, but their numbers increased when war is in the air. Either the people protecting the cattle would have come from traditionally martial communities, or the best among the local communities of cattle-herds and others would have been trained and equipped to do the job, at least until the regular army arrived.

It was thus not unlikely that the ruler retained a small group of families from warring communities along the border villages, to protect the border and also the people and their cattle there, from the enemy. It was the natural thing to do, just as it was commonplace for kings to post their intelligence men in the border villages, to report back on suspicious men and movements of every kind. The interaction, especially in times of peace, could have led to martial communities taking to the valour-sport of the pastoral people and adapt it as their own. In due course, the ruling class and communities would have taken to the sport, as a way of proving and testing the valour of their soldiers without blood-letting of any kind. Ancient rulers across India, other than born-villains like Kamsa, or Kansa, adhered to dharmic principles as much in war as in peace time. The *Mahabharatham* clearly states that war was fought only during day-light hours. There is even an episode when Lord Krishna 'cheats' on the rival Kaurava clan of his favourite Pandava brothers by creating an illusory dusk.

In Tamil, *Thol-kappiam* insists that a warrior should not attack his enemy in the battle-field when the latter is re-setting his hair, or tuft to be precise, or has lost his weapon, or thrown it down, indicating surrender. In the same vein, it could be expected of rulers and communities from those days to have full respect for the life and health of the Jallikattu bull. It was thus laid down that if ever there was a casualty in Jallikattu, it had to be the man, not the animal. Written close to 70 years back, in the late Forties, Ti Su Chellappa's *Vaadi Vaasal* describes it all in some detail, after the writer had spent time in the Jallikattu country, researching for his work. It was a different time, different people, who still practised the precepts and beliefs of the forefathers, immediate and distant—long before electricity and protected drinking water came to Tamil Nadu villages, and even more before the 'IT era' arrived.

Though politically the 'Dravidian movement' as loosely understood in caste/casteist terms, had anti-Brahmin moorings, the real issues in rural Tamil Nadu, then or now, is between the Dalits and the 'intermediary castes' of different hues in different parts of the State. In modern times, casteist approach and consequent untouchability are acknowledged as a curse on Tamil society, as with many others across the country. It is not an argument or defence, but only a statement of facts as they exist. Jallikattu is a sport from the past, and did not possibly escape the conventional caste overtones of the times. That such a casteist approach to societal and social interactions remains to date cannot be denied. Yet, as the Marina protestors showed, at least in the urban milieu of the kind (and spreading across most urban centres in the State on the occasion), no one asked the next man or woman in the crowd as to his or her caste or religion. Nor did anyone complain that he or she had been excluded.

The traditional base of Jallikattu comprised most of the erstwhile Chola kingdom from the distant past and also the contemporary Pandya kingdom of those times. The undivided Tiruchi-Thanjavur districts from the more recent past relate to the Chola kingdom. The adjoining old Madurai district down south was the centre-piece of the Pandyas. The ruling class of the two kingdoms are believed to have come from the warrior Mukkulathore community, with its own three sub-divisions. Their soldiers also came from these three communities in particular. However, there is nothing to show that other communities, especially Dalits, were excluded. It is not unlikely that through war and victory, one kingdom influenced the practices of the other, and in a 'positive' way as was acceptable to the martial classes of the times.

Hero's Death

The caste hierarchy in the distant past and continuing caste-divide in our times derive from the conventional *Varnashrama*

Dharma of ancient India/Hindus. In this case, the Mukkulathore community constituted a warrior class, equivalent to the Kshatriya clan in ancient India. Like elsewhere in the country, the martial class took different names even in different parts of Tamil Nadu. They are still identified as such though the traditions of soldier-recruitment near-exclusively from those communities died very long ago. Jallikattu became a sport for the young Mukkulathore men to display their prowess in public and prove their valour. The alternative for them to taming the bull would have been for two or more youth to fight it out among themselves–and there was no knowing what would come of it—death, family and village-level enmity, and possible break-up of the kingdom, as well.

There is another factor, also historic. Until the Muslim 'marauders' came with their armies from across the Hindukush mountain ranges, Indian rulers were not known to have maintained a large standing army. They had a minimal army for all times. For fighting a war and other emergencies, they would send out messages and messengers to villages comprising the kingdom. The villagers would contribute men of valour and some martial training/experience, if at all, to what would essentially become a 'volunteer army', or army of volunteers.

Thus, '*Naattaikakka, veetirkku oru magan purapaduka*' was the line typical of Tamil historic novels and films, announcing the arrival of war. Translated, the call, often sent out through the village drummer-messenger, means that at least one able-bodied man from each family should come forward and join the army and the war, to protect and secure the nation and its honour (from the enemy). The second line of the war-call is often, '*Maanam kakka, veetirkku oru magan purappaduka*', or '*Nattin maanam kakka, veetirkku oru magan purappaduka*', both of them asking the youth to join the war, to protect the nation's honour. This is one scene in which the written language of novels have invariably outsmarted the visual effect on the silver-screen, with every aspect of it detailed in paragraph after paragraph, at times chapter after chapter. The scene would be followed invariably by one in which the youth from across the country would be shown running, again haphazardly (to where?), but with long spears in their raised right hands (invariably, the sword is reserved for the film's hero-king, even as he mounts his war-horse), and shouting in unison, *Vetri-vel, Veera vel*—meaning, 'victorious spear, fearless spear', implying that they are going to win the war.

Film scenes and scenarios apart, all that these volunteer-soldiers knew was to fight, die or win. Of course, many of them would have been trained to fight, but not all of them, though. Some of them might have had inherent skills at leadership, but often untested and unproven. Anyway, they had not been honed into a fighting force, linking various aspects of war strategy and tactics before each battle. Other than what the *Shastras*, the *Ramayanam* and the *Mahabharatham* have told us, there was no trained, drilled and disciplined force that could be expected to follow a pattern and deliver. They fought as they came, either to win or to die. But that being the status and standard with all native armies, superior training and skills as a fighting force did not matter. It was a story of individual valour and the individual's valour.

Military historians say that Indian kings did not have a standing army until about a thousand years ago. In the absence of a standing army, it would thus become difficult to identify field commanders at different levels without some way out to identify and nurture them. This is despite the fact that the *Mahabharatham* details how commanders of the Pandava and Kaurava armies named those down the line, and in naming them, how Bhisma insulted Karna, if only to ensure that someone remained after his time, to protect Duryodhana and the latter's interests. Despite the otherwise arbitrary nature of selection of individuals for various posts in villages, kings needed field commanders at different levels who could lead by example, rather than experience, especially of the command experience kind. Between two wars, even victorious rulers would have to have countenanced the inevitability of 'hero's death' embracing many if not most of their field commanders, at times right up to the top. Replenishing them between any two military missions would also require them to recruit new commanders. It would have been no different for the other party, but there is no clear explanation, where from these new recruits came and how were they discovered, as otherwise, the best of soldier material had already been to fight the previous war.

While Indian religious texts and historic poems are full of stories about *guru-kulams*, or *guru-kuls*, meaning residential training centres, where the ruling class learnt the art of war, too, there are not many references to one for training the foot-soldier. By convention, organised military training along with other aspects of education, religious learning and statecraft were all reserved for the ruling class and the nobility. The charioteers, it would seem, had inherited it as a family profession from their fathers and grandfathers, handing it over to their sons and grandsons, in turn. The foot soldier, then or since, does not get the same type of training or treatment. In turn, these differences and distinctions are based on the acceptable norm, as applicable to any other trade, then or now—like between doctors and their para-medic staff, for instance. Yet, there is no gainsaying the story of Karnan, an anti-hero in the *Mahabharatham* acknowledged as the 'son of a charioteer', implying his low-caste 'birth' (which it anyway was not, as the latter was only his foster father).

At the height of the Jallikattu protests in January 2017, suddenly the social media was abuzz with allegations of high prevalence of casteism in the sport. Before the Jallikattu mood caught on with much of the State, prominent political leaders from the Dalit community had expressed reservations bordering on outright criticism against the need to revive it. Thol Thirumavalavan, the founder of the Vidudhalai Chiruthaigal Katchi (VCK), with cadre-concentration in the northern districts, and K Krishnaswamy, leader of the Puthiya Tamizhagam (PT), another Dalit party from southern districts, were in the forefront at one stage. However, they quietened soon. Yet, for a while afterwards, the social media campaign, inserting a Dalit element to the Jallikattu discourse, continued. The references were in contemporary terms, but the roots were in history, both social and political. Yet, nothing much was clear, nor could they be clarified.

There is nothing to suggest that the Jallikattu protests of 2017 have helped bridge the caste-divide between the Dalits and the rest. It may have been more so in relation to the Dalits and the Mukkulathores, who are seen as mutually-antagonist on a wide socio-political firmament. Yet, motivated attempts through the social media, to introduce or re-introduce the caste elements into the Jallikattu protests did not succeed. Without much trace, such efforts at branding Jallikattu as an 'anti-Dalit' Mukkulathore community sport did not succeed. If it has not happened already, there is no gainsaying the possibility of the two communities rubbing shoulders with each other in future Jallikattu events. It might start possibly with urban centres, but its spread cannot be stopped after a point. In turn, this could open a new chapter in the bloodied caste and casteist history of the State, more especially in areas where these two communities have a substantial presence. This could be especially so if the State government were to organise Jallikattu events in Chennai, and possibly the Marina sands where the 2017 protest took place, as promised by an incumbent Minister, as a part of the decades-old annual Pongal Tourist Trade Fare.

It is not that the Mukkulathore community from the southern districts had the exclusive right to valour and thus the sport of Jallikattu in ancient Tamil Nadu. In the western districts, comprising what is now the business cities of Coimbatore, Erode and Tiruppur, among others, the local 'Kongu Vellalar' community, or Gounder community, have conducted bullock-cart races for decades and centuries. The *Rekhla* race might not be as valour-centric as Jallikattu was/is, but it is again a competitive sport involving the cattle-head. In some other parts of the State, or even in some parts of the Jallikattu country, it still goes by the name, Eru Thazhuvuthal. The one difference is that in Jallikattu, the tamer faces the animal straight and brings it down, holding on to its sharp horns, which could hurt and even kill. In Eru Thazhuvuthal, he holds on tightly to the bull's hump and tries to stall its run. Here, the tamer does not face the animal head-on. Instead, he comes from the side, to be able to hold on to the animal's hump at the first available opportunity. Still, if he has to match the bull's run and speed, he cannot jump out of nowhere from the sides, and surprise the animal, and obtain a psychological gain at the start. He has to be at an arm's length to hold on to the hump lest the animal should leave him behind by a legion.

Both sports require different kinds of skills and training, and in a way, even different scales of valour and mental strength. In the case of Jallikattu as used to be known, death at the animal's horns was/is always a possibility that the tamer cannot overlook. Nor can he ignore the real possibility of a slip and fall under the heavy-weight bull's front hooves or even those of the animal's rear feet. In the process, the tamer could be trampled upon or gored or both. In both Jallikattu and EruThazhuvuthal, it is stopping the animal on its track, unlike in horse-racing, where the animal too knows where to go and how to go. Anyway, the race-horse is trained much more than a Jallikattu bull. There is also a jockey sitting on the animal, whipping it all the time to top its speed and other animals it is running with. But both in Jallikattu and Eru Thazhuvuthal, the man's strength of the heart, mind and limbs have to be of unparalleled quality and quantity. One slip, he loses, possibly including his life.

The 2014 Supreme Court ban on Jallikattu covered Eru Thazhuvuthal and Rekhla race as well. References in the court order do not make much of the Rekhla race also because a similar sport in Maharashtra was a part of the petitions before the Bench that banned them all. Pending the Supreme Court hearing in the case, the Maharashtra government had complied with a ban ordered by the Bombay High Court, and also reported compliance. Hence, the Supreme Court Bench did not have to deal with the racing part of the sport in detail.

In the case of Jallikattu, which included Eru Thazhuvuthal, the ban imposed by the Centre was contested. They were grouped together, argued and orders passed. Though post-Jallikattu protests, a Rekhla race in western Coimbatore, marked the legal departure of the court ban with a protective State government ordinance, approved by the Centre, neither had the ban on the Tamil Nadu races been challenged in the courts, nor did the new ordinance, or the one earlier, cover the same. Incidentally, in Tamil Nadu, which encourages Jallikattu, the State government banned horse-racing decades ago. This was primarily to control betting as poor people were losing heavily every week-end, dreaming dreams that would remain a dream in most cases, leaving their families poorer and hungrier.

Swelling Numbers

Apart from the Dalit angle, feeble attempts were made through the social media to argue that women had been kept out of Jallikattu all along. No women thankfully seemed to have fallen for such a campaign. If anything, their numbers at protest venues only swelled from one day to the next. It is again an inheritance (not exactly commendable) from the past. The tradition had evolved at a time when women needed protection from enemies. Families too needed them the most as their guardian-angel. Already, there are women drivers, pilots and astronauts, corporate executives and independent entrepreneurs. There are women soldiers, boxers and wrestlers, who keep bringing Olympian glory to the nation. Traditions apart, not far away from now we may have women bull-tamers too. But like everything else, this can also take its time and may have to await greater secularisation of the sport. Who knows, it could well start with the entry of women bull-tamers, and spread to other segments of the society, cutting across, class, caste and religious barriers, real and imaginary.

Noah's Ark and More

ON THE one hand, Jallikattu, or Eru Thazhuvuthal, was about testing/proving man's valour and courage. On the other, it was also about testing the animal's prowess. It needs to be remembered, and at every turn, that *bullocks formed the core of agriculture activities across the country*, until mechanised methods like tractors and other farming machinery began replacing them, in a big or small way, that too half way through after Independence. Independent of the present-day political discourse and controversies, cow was a life-giver of sorts. 'Cow worship' flows from 'cow economy', even now for homes, especially in rural areas, where they are reared. Agriculture, including animal husbandry, is not only the food and nutrient-provider for the community and the country as a whole. It also employs or engages close to 75 per cent of the nation's population, even at present.

Bullocks used to be the main tool for ploughing paddy fields, pull large water-bails from deep-wells for irrigation and also carts, to and from the farmland to the home and to the market place. The introduction of horses to pull carriages was a later-day addition, and was affordable only to the ruling class, nobility and the village elite. Horses were required for the cavalry. Yet, history and literature also have many references to old-day armies using huge bullock carts to carry weapons and stores through long distances, undertaking arduous and at times hazardous journey. Possibly, after the war, the victorious army used the same carts to take back the booty and the loot to their kingdom, towns and villages.

It is thus a point to ponder if the ancient war-time practice of *Aanirai Kavarthal*, mentioned in the *Thol-kappiam*, had something to do with denying the enemy the animals that would be available for war-time use even while denying his population the use of the animal in the farm and home fronts, simultaneously. Though the story is not about the use of bullock carts for military purposes, there is also this episode about Sanjeevaka the bullock and Pingalaka the lion-king in the *Panchatantra*, which is a compendium of just and moral stories for children, dating back to 2,000 years.

Whether for agricultural use or for battle-time deployment, only castrated bullocks, as different from fertile bulls, were/are in demand. Reproduction-challenged bullocks were maintained far greater in number than fertile bulls—and naturally so—in all communities, cutting across classes. Castrating the bull was almost the rule and retaining the fertile bull as such was an exception, but a very necessary exception at that. It was equivalent to the farmer retaining a few measures of food grains, millets or vegetable seeds for planting the next crop even while consuming much of the rest of the harvested crop. The consumer may not know or even understand, but to the farmer, collecting and preserving the seeds are as important as piling up the harvested crop, marketing it and/or consuming it for family use. This meant that fertile bulls too needed to be protected and preserved, as with paddy seeds, in an era when mechanised farming was light-years away and artificial insemination had not been thought of even as a mythological or fictional possibility as many other sci-fi like characteristics.

Temple and Temple Towers

For understanding the relevance of Jallikattu in the context of customs and traditions from time immemorial, there is an equal need to comprehend the attendant socio-political practices. South Indian rulers of the distant yore, especially in the Tamil country, had the practice of building massive temples in granite, mainly on a higher plane than the river banks. Many of the massive, surviving temples of Tamil Nadu date back to 800-1,200 years, the same as the time-line when Nammazhvar and Thirumangai Aazhwar were singing the praise of Lord Krishna's bull-taming prowess, and their Saiviite equivalents in the Nayanmars, creating the *Thevaram* and *Thiru-vasagam*, in praise of Lord Siva. There are other granite structures that date back to 2000 years, if not more, in Tamil Nadu. The more famous among them is the Grand Anicut, known in Tamil as Kallanai, or the stone-dam, across the Cauvery. It served the cause of irrigation and agriculture. Built by Chola King, Karikalan, the reservoir has been in the news almost every other year over the past four decades, because of the 'Cauvery water dispute' with neighbouring Karnataka.

The need for large granite temples with two, three or four courtyards, and tall temple towers has to be contextualised to the times and the purposes that they had possibly served. The temples do mark the war-victories and glory of a particular king or kingdom to the present-day, yes. They were also funded by the war-loot in many cases. In an era when people had to traverse across the country by whatever mode possible, the tall temple towers served as the beacon for the weary traveller looking for a safe resting place to spend the night. The tall temple flag-masts too served the same purpose. Bronze or brass bells, big and small, at the top of the mast would chime in the breeze, hailing the traveller and indicating the direction of the village concerned, even if heavy winds were to blow out the lamps, lit up in the multiple galleries of the towers and serving as a light-house, at night hours. All these need to be imagined in an era without noise pollution and other towering buildings, to make some sense and to understand the practical wisdom behind those constructions.

In times of natural calamities like heavy rains, floods and droughts, or even possible pestilence, the temple courtyards would have served as refugee camps for the local communities. The temples thus had substantial stores and massive kitchens, feeding the poor, the needy and the weary traveller in normal times and the distraught communities in times of natural calamities. The size of the community possibly decided the size of the temple, more especially the size and number of the courtyards. In the Tamil country, only such massive temples built of granite have survived the ravages of Time, more than even the palaces of their kings. This meant that the palaces too were possibly built of mud, wood and mortar, like any other commoner's home, but maybe of better quality and larger size, while the best was reserved for the gods, and through them, the people themselves.

However, even in normal times, temples reared cattle-head, both cows and bulls. If bullocks were also there, they were used for all the common purposes that the people used them otherwise. It is common for temples in Tamil Nadu to maintain cow-sheds even at present, as may be the case elsewhere in the country. As is known, invariably in all Indian temples, the idol is given a ritualistic bath, or *abhishekam*, every morning, noon and at times night. The existence of a cow-shed ensures that the milk for the abhishekams and other offerings to the gods is guaranteed. These offerings invariably include(d) sweets made of milk and milk-products like ghee, apart from rice, or wheat as the case may be, and sweeteners like sugar or *gur*, based on what is available locally. Suffice is to point out that these are daily nourishments and nutrients for the local population too.

Tsunamis of the Past

In Biblical terms, the Tamil country's granite-temple is reminiscent of Noah's Ark, the ship on to which the Biblical character Noah collected a sample of every living species and set sail through the storms and stayed afloat, for letting them off on land, when Nature's fury subsided, for the world to recommence its reproductive cycle.

The temples in the Tamil country provided food, space and security for the local population in times of natural calamities. They also protected the cows and bulls, to ensure that the local village economy was not totally destroyed by the heavy rains and high floods. Protecting these animals would ensure that people could hope to pick up their lives, even if in bits and pieces, and hope to recommence various activities associated with agriculture, including animal husbandry. Thus, it may not be an accident of history that the Tamil kings thought of building granite temples, with storage spaces for food, and shelter for men and beast.

The Sangam literature refers to two tsunami-like experiences that had submerged many a city and town, country and kingdom. Accordingly, the ancient Pandya kingdom, for instance, was originally located in a place called '*Then* Madurai' (not the present-one), or 'Southern Madurai', which was submerged in the seas. The city-State was re-located and recreated slightly up north, in a place called Kapadapuram. When that city was also gobbled up by the hungry seas, then alone was the present-day temple-town of Madurai founded, as the third recorded capital of the Pandya kingdom. This new city of Madurai itself dates back to the Sangam era, 2,000 years ago.

There are literary references to the third of the three 'Tamil *Sangams*', or assemblies of scholars, being situated in the present-day Madurai. The common references to the term 'Sangam era' relates only to this period. It is possible that other Tamil kingdoms of yore also suffered similarly, if not to the same extent. If there are no literary references to any of them, it may be because only the Pandyas were/are seen as the keepers and guardians of the Tamil language, and thought themselves to be so. Still, with the available material, one can imagine the antiquity of Tamil history and culture, though not recorded as history but only as literary references.

Successive tsunami-like experiences, or *kaal-kol*s as mentioned in Tamil literature, had destroyed what was then the geo-political landmass of 'Kumari Kandam'. The present day Kanyakumari, at the land's end, is believed to have derived its name from the submerged Kumari Kandam, further and farther south. (The Lankan Tamils believe, the island is part of this Kumari Kandam.) In Malayalam, the language that continues to be spoken in Kanyakumari district even after the Linguistic Reorganisation of States in 1956, the term *kandam* means a piece or plot of land. It is also a literary word in ancient Tamil, the likes of which Malayalam has freely adopted when the new language was born. But after Kumari Kandam was washed away, the rulers who built their new city-State seemed to have thought well and proper.

According to literary and other evidence, this is the present-day temple town of Madurai. It was built in the sixth century BC. The present-day Madurai may not be as old as the Syrian capital of Damascus, considered the oldest continuously inhabited city on the planet, dating back to seventh century before Christ, but it could still be among the oldest. The tsunami-like death and destruction also educated the later-day kings to build superior structures with superior material that could withstand sea-surge of every kind that they could have imagined by that the time. It was also the reason why those temples came to double up as emergency granary and refugee camp for the villagers and a temporary cow-shed for their cattle-head, too.

Though limited only to the protection of the cattle-heads, there is still the western Indian practice, in States like Gujarat and Rajasthan, for the community to erect emergency cattle-sheds, or *pinjara-pols*, in times of severe droughts. Further up North, Punjab has the unique tradition of *langar*s, or community kitchens, in Sikh *gurudwara*s. Like Tamils' Aadi Perukku festival, the Sikhs have taken their langars to wherever they migrated, inside the country or outside. In both cases, namely, pinjara-pols and langars, their economic reasons and social relevance are the same as with those of the ancient Tamil Nadu temples. The reverse is also true.

Bulls as Offering

To date, in the temples of Tamil Nadu, and in some neighbouring States, too, the traditional practice has been for the people to make the first offering of their paddy and every other farm produce to the local temple and deity. Even vegetables and fruits from the family's kitchen garden are first offered to the local temple. The first temple-entry of a new born in the family is a ritualistic, community affair. It is so across the country, cutting across religions and regions. Some also offer the first born of their cattle-head, sheep and lamb, and even eggs from the hen in their homes. In temples in neighbouring Kerala, to date, people also make an offering of elephant calves. As per custom, the temple idol is carried atop the pachyderm on festive occasions and other rituals. As it happens, in the wooded country, elephants are otherwise used to pull/carry logs, and thus the donated pachyderm serve that purpose, even more, especially in forests and farms belonging to the temple and the community. While the famed Sri Krishna Temple in

Guruvayur has many elephants thus donated by devotees, in the Sri Vadakkanathan Temple, Trissur, the annual '*Pooram* festival' is famous for the parading of temple elephants, in all glitter and glory.

In the temples of Lord Siva in Tamil Nadu, it is customary for families to offer a bull-calf at the conclusion of 13 or 16-day long funeral rites/ceremonies for a departed elder. People also make money offerings along with the animal, to ensure that the temple is not burdened with providing for the upkeep of the animal as it grows up. During these days of funeral rites, the village priest, generally a Brahmin/vegetarian, is also offered a matured milch-cow. The community custom thus ensures that the priest and his family have a source of (additional) income, through the sale of milk. More importantly, the animal did not get slaughtered for food, in times of the worst droughts. The animal's prospective bull-mate was preserved in the temple, with their future generations in mind. No doubt that old, draught animals were killed for meat and skin, the latter used for all purposes to which it is being used now.

Mythology has given a religious touch to it all. Bull is the vehicle of Lord Siva, the third in the Hindu Trinity. In some schools of Hindu thought, Siva is also the God of Death. Offering a bull-calf to the Siva temple is thus pleasing and placating Him, for and on behalf of the departed ancestor. The offering of a bull-calf to the temple is a penance, or *prayachittam*, for wrongs and sins that the dead man might have committed on earth. This, in turn, is expected to ensure that the dead ancestor went to heaven, and not hell. In rural Tamil Nadu, shooing away the village/temple bull even if it had jumped the fences of a farm or grazed on standing crop could lead to the village ostracising the entire family. This practice is in vogue even today. So much so, every Jallikattu event in every village in Tamil Nadu commences with the temple bull being let off through the Vaadi Vasal.

By custom and convention, it is not expected to be checked or stopped on its way. The question of seeking to tame the temple bull just does not arise. It is both a sin and dishonour. Stopping the temple bull in a Jallikattu can lead to the barring of the tamer from all events in every village in the entire neighbourhood and elsewhere, for all time to come. Even if it had happened in another village, his native village also ostracises the tamer and his family.

At another level, the *Garuda Puranam*, one of the eighteen *puranams* like the *Bhagavatham*, talks in detail about the soul after death. The *Garuda Puranam* talks about life after death very extensively—rather, about the 'life' of the soul, or the travels and travails of the human soul after death. Lord *Garuda*, the divine bird kite, the vehicle of Lord Vishnu, recites the knowledge given by Lord Vishnu, to Sage Kashyapa. According to the *Garuda Puranam*, while traversing from this world to the other, the soul crosses the river of blood and gore, representing the sins committed in human form. Lest he should sink in it, the dead man, rather his soul, holds on to the tail of the cow, which reaches him to the other shore. Or, that is the religious belief. Hence, the ritualistic gift of a cow to the Brahmin.

It is not as if all these legends linking gods and rituals had a denominational issue about them. From the Vaishnaviite perspective, or that of the other major sub-sects of Hinduism apart from Saiviism, so to say, Lord Krishna was/is always depicted with cows. He came from the Yadav community of cow-herds, and his affection for the animal went beyond his birth. Invariably, only in the midst of a large herd of cows is a young Krishna shown as wielding a flute. Stories about his playing on the flute and the cows getting 'intoxicated' by the music are legendary. Though located in Gokulam (or Gokul) and Brindavan (near present-day Mathura, his birth place in Uttar Pradesh), these stories about Krishna, his community background and the charm he wielded over cows have always had equal currency in distant Tamil Nadu, the whole of India, and wherever Indians lived. It is from Mathura to Gokul to Brindavan and back to Mathura and onward that Krishna goes to Dwaraka, never to return to his old homes and foster parents, Nandagopan and Yasoda.

Thus, between them, Shiva was the Lord of the bulls and Krishna, that of the cows. Considering that farming and related activities formed the mainstay of ancient societies, and cows and bulls in turn were the backbone of agriculture activities in an era when land and irrigation water were not issues, such godly identification with sound socio-economic initiative for preserving cattle-head has been given a religious touch so that people follow that code, and not violate it. It is the case with most Indian customs and traditions, which otherwise may have an equally scientific or practical reason behind them. But the comparison should end there. Extending the issue to the contemporary era, citing the Krishna-and-Shiva identification to the opposite genders of the animal, should be more politics than economics or religion.

Community's Vow

Training the bulls for the purpose of taming in public and feeding them well for the purpose as a public sport event were aimed at ensuring that they grew and matured into stud bulls, better than the rest. Cows and bulls do not fight each other in such events. The bull-tamer grew up with the family belief and community commitment that it was a dishonour for all if the animal was injured or its blood let off.

The question of a bull dying in the undefined and traditionally un-blockaded arena was just unthinkable. But fighting the man without knowing that it was the safer between the two, and being trained for it, was supposed to enhance the virility of the bull, too. If any or all of it was entirely scientific or not is a different question. But in village communities the world over, customs, traditions and religious beliefs matter more than science and systems, including the governmental laws of whatever kind. Civilisation and the 'Rule of Law' are all about changing those beliefs and practices, if only over time—from years to decades to centuries, even after which many of those customs refuse to either go away or get replaced—a sad thing, after all.

One common refrain of the womenfolk of the villages during the Jallikattu protests in January 2017 was that owing to successive years of ban on the sport, and the consequent sacrilege—or, so they believed—the rain gods had failed them for as many years. But no explanation or justification could be sought or obtained if one were to refer to them, previous occasions, over decades and centuries, when there were droughts but with no question of any ban on Jallikattu. It should be conceded that Jallikattu too thrived as a major annual event of the Tamil villages only in years when they all had a bountiful crop and the rain gods too did not fail them. That is also what traditions and customs are all about—not linked to scientific verification, but based on blind beliefs bordering on superstition at times, nothing else and nothing more.

In the land of Ahimsa

IF JALLIKATTU has such a long history and a tradition of valour attaching to it, why was there so much of criticism and marches, seeking a ban on an innocent sport of such a great importance? At the end of it, it is the man, if at all, and not the animal, that gets hurt and even gored and killed.

Post-protests, the delayed Jallikattu events were held in traditional venues in many places. The State government sanctioned it, the Centre stood by it, and the Supreme Court seemingly looked the other way. Yet, weeks and even months later, many Jallikattu events witnessed tamers and spectators dying from injuries by the animals. The governments that had long ago promised the Apex Court to ensure the safety of the animals and the humans did not seem to have done enough in this regard. Their callousness at different levels continued as in the previous years, ban or no ban.

Yet, even the most committed of animal activists with their eyes and ears glued to the ground did not take their usual social media route to complain about specific cases and/or issues of inhuman handling of the animals this time. It is likely that there was no cruelty to the animals. PETA however has since documented such instances of cruelty to the animals even in the post-protests Season-2017, when the governments in the State, and also the Centre, were expected to be more cautious and were thus expected to enforce greater supervision over officials who were tasked with ensuring that all provisions pertaining to the safety of the animals, tamers and participants, under the 2009 Tamil Nadu law. As was expected, PETA has attached video footage, observers' concerns and comments, and media reports to support its argument against bringing back Jallikattu bulls under the list of 'performing animals' under the 2017 Tamil Nadu law, to help restore the martial sport. In doing so, the new legislation proclaimed Jalliakattu as part of the local 'culture', after the earlier Supreme Court judgment of 2014 had declared it was not. The pending case assumes great interest and greater urgency, given the fact that the Jallikattu Season of 2018 is upon us, and the State government and other stake-holders, all needed to know where they stood—in terms of anticipating preparations, including one for a possible ban, if it came to that.

For all the animal-sacrifices and at times human sacrifices that had found a place in early Hinduism, or whatever sect to which such practices belonged, overall the religion is seen as passive and peace-loving. It may not be to the same levels that Buddhism preaches peace and Jainism practices '*Ahimsa*', meaning non-cruelty of any kind to any living being. Hinduism may not be in the same league, and for the average practitioner, even bloody wars as in the *Ramayanam* and the *Mahabharatham* were necessary evils. These were wars that the gods themselves either participated in or fought directly, for good to overcome and eradicate evil. If it has to be given a religious-tag, Jallikattu belongs in Hinduism, or whatever sect of the religion that was being practised in that part of Tamil Nadu of the yore.

Going by mythological and literary evidence on the antiquity of the bull-taming sport, Christianity and Islam, the world's two largest religions of our times, had not reached the Indian shores when Jallikattu began to evolve as a community sport. Catholicism especially was all about loving fellow living-beings, but it did not extend to cover non-killing of animals and birds for eating or for fun. Those thoughts would enter the human consciousness much afterwards in the West, and elsewhere, too. But even from and in their midst, bloody wars did not go away. Even decades after the two crippling World Wars of the twentieth century, the 'Christian West' bombs hundreds of thousands of humans in the Asian neighbourhood (*read:* closer to India) in the name of fighting 'global terrorism'. Their authors and analysts predict and perceive them as an emerging 'clash of civilisations', which has had its roots in the Crusades a millennium ago. All these even when their social activists are crying foul in the name of war orphans in their thousands and raise their voice in protest against the rape of Nature and cruelty to all life-forms, including animals. It is another matter, none of those sentiments or strong catholic beliefs has helped end a bloody game like the Spanish bull-fight.

Older a civilisation, as the Indian civilisation as a whole is, it however began to adopt western thoughts of governance, politics, military strategy and even civic and civil priorities only about two hundred years ago when these began to influence local customs and traditions, laws and law-making. Even earlier, Buddhism was the fountainhead of Ahimsa in thought, deed and action, and was born in these parts of the world, close to 500 years before the time of Jesus Christ, who again preached similar values and paid for them with His life, and left behind a message that has since caught on. But it was the British common law influences that have codified modern Indian law and jurisprudence and have mostly been improved and/or built upon the same through the post-Independence era, and for good reasons. The question was/is simple, but the answer is complex, or almost non-existent. The why and how of the commencement of opposition to animal-centric sports like Jallikattu are not clearly identifiable or definable. So is the rationale for a ban, in the eyes of those that are opposed to the ban.

All in the Nature

Both opponents to cruelty to animals and meat-eaters, which is a form of such cruelty, have co-existed in India for thousands of years and continue to do so. Jainism and to a greater or lesser extent, Buddhism, are acknowledged exceptions. In Hinduism, upper-caste Brahmins are sworn vegetarians, that too mainly in western, central and southern India, so are some the 'Saiva Vellalar community' in parts of southern Tamil Nadu and the 'Lingayat Veera Shaiva' brethren in Karnataka, both exclusively worshipping Lord Shiva, and his pantheon.

In neighbouring Sri Lanka, both the majority Buddhists and the dominant Saiviite Vellalar Tamils of Jaffna, the self-appointed guardians of minority Tamil rights in the island-nation, are staunch non-vegetarians. Across central India, substantial sections of the local population are non-vegetarians, but most are tribal, non-Brahmin, non-upper caste communities, especially in States and regions such as Jharkhand, Chattisgarh, southern Madhya Pradesh and northern Andhra Pradesh. In East, North-East and northern-most Jammu and Kashmir, Brahmins too are fish/meat-eaters. The long and short of it is that wind, weather and consequent availability, or non-availability, decide the food habits of people. Where there was/is abundance of rain and/ or ice-melts down the slopes of the Himalayas and down to the plains, people can afford to be vegetarians. If nothing else, those that chose to be vegetarians by choice and community inheritance can afford to do so. In regions where visitations of dry-spells and drought were common, people, including upper caste Brahmins, make their choice of fish and meat.

If the argument against Jallikattu was/is against causing harm and cruelty to animals, killing and eating them is the crude and cruellest of all forms. It does not stop with one breed or genre of animal, to be conferred any special status, whichever be the religion or social customs, or whatever the animal.

The common argument that the animal does not know it is being subjected to cruelty in the form of Jallikattu, and also did not have a choice applies even more to killing and eating it. It is here the western vegan submissions from a relatively recent past, that all life-forms are created to live on their own, not off each other, triggers some favour. Such an argument is equally wrong, as no living organism can live without living off another—other than air and water that are common to them all. And no living being can live only on air and water alone. Even trees and plants require minerals, but they can be obtained—and are obtained—from non-living sources. But even among the least protesting plant-forms, there is the story of parasites living off a healthy, stronger and bigger plant. The list expands when it comes to other life-forms, beyond plants, fruits and flowers. It is all in the Nature just as they are all a creation and part of the very same Nature. It is so even in terms of religious, political and social morals–and laws flowing from the same.

Trade, not Sword

Both Christianity and Islam had reached southern India, especially south coastal Tamil Nadu and Kerala, before they were known to the rest of the country. These coastal regions had a tradition of trade with the Arab world in that distant past. It is here that all three Abrahamic faiths, namely, Judaism, Christianity and Islam, came. Tamil literature dating back to that period graphically describes how the local rulers in southern coastal Tamil Nadu had let those traders erect settlements near where their ships berthed, for them to live and store their wares during their long stays here. When some of them took to a new religion back home, they also brought it to these parts. As coincidence would have it, both Christianity and Islam came to the present-day Kerala coast, first. It is, therefore, reasonable to believe that they had reached the Tamil coast not very long after or alongside. In both cases, the Abrahamic faiths arrived on the back of trade and tradesmen, through peaceful means. Definitely, they were not through the tip of the sword and/or through forced or even enticed conversions. Such a course seemed to have been reserved for northern India, a few centuries later.

But before Christianity and Islam, and also the mother of all Abrahamic religions, namely, Judaism, India did have two other religions, deriving from ideology propounded by individuals. Both Buddhism and Jainism have had their origins in ancient India. The former has spread out of the country of its origins, and there are more Buddhists of different sects and sub-sects in Sri Lanka, Japan and countries of South-East Asia. Jainism however is confined to India, still. The number of Buddhists in India are still not big, despite B R Ambedkar, the 'Father of the Indian Constitution', embracing the religion along with his followers, especially from the native State of Maharashtra.

Fewer still are the number of Jains in this country. Unlike Buddhists, most Jains in the world still live in India, the land of their origin and of their religion. Jain religious persons influenced rulers in yesteryear Tamil Nadu at a particular point in time. Buddhists too had populated and preached in southern India. There is a version that Buddhists migrated to Sri Lanka and elsewhere when hounded down at the turn of 'Hindu revivalism' from the seventh and eighth century on. However, there is no such story about Jains, though the ruins of Jain temples are there across Tamil Nadu even today—some having been converted to Hindu places of worship.

The Jains are known to Tamil literature and works of history as *Samanar*s, and the religion prospered through a certain period in Tamil history after their practitioners and preachers influenced local kings, mostly Saiviites, to embrace the faith. That period, spread over two or three centuries in the middle of the first millennia after Christ is known as the 'Dark Ages' of ancient Tamil Nadu. It is believed that all written history and literature, if any, and stone edicts, again if any, from that period, were either destroyed by 'Hindu revivalists' or by the ravages of time.

The Ahimsa Contradiction

Buddhism in India too remains mostly a religion of peace and non-violence. As a part of Ahimsa as an abiding trait and marker, both Buddhism and Jainism preach and practice vegetarianism. Ironically, Buddhists outside of India are mostly non-vegetarians. It may owe to the food and other social/community habits of those that had embraced the religion in those nations.

If Jains had controlled or influenced public policy and governmental programmes in ancient Tamil kingdoms, even their exit in the normal course should not have altered the food habits of larger sections of the population. It implies that either Hindu revivalists re-introduced non-vegetarianism, or the habit did not die even when the Samanars had control over native Tamil kings and their administrations in the preceding centuries. The question thus arises, whether Jains could influence policies involving animal sacrifices during their time, or even could have attempted the same, unless they had been able to convert the whole lot of local populations to their faith and beliefs. If they did succeed, did those policies and practices go away with them, or were they even forced out with their exit?

Literary evidence records that a cow (of course, a coincidence in this context) sought justice from the King, Manu Needhi Kanda Cholan, for his son running over its calf, killing the latter. The king was Justice Personified and his name too reflects it.

When the cow would settle for nothing else, he orders his son, the crown prince, to be similarly run over. It turns out later that the gods were testing the height of his justice, and the prince is spared. Yet, there is no mention in the story, before or after, that the king did not kill animals or did not eat non-vegetarian food. These are different levels of animal-protection.

The Prevention of Cruelty to Animals (PCA) Act, 1960, acknowledges as much in express terms. The ban on Jallikattu flows from this piece of legislation though enforced in this case, decades later.

Before or alongside the Chola king who ordered his son run over by chariot, there is the story of Emperor Sibi, who sliced out a piece of his own flesh, to compensate an eagle for its lost meaty food. Chased by the eagle, a bird flew into the hands of the 'King of Justice', as Sibi was known. Sibi took the bird under his care and protection. But when the hungry eagle complained that the king had denied him his day's meal, the ruler could not deny justice in that argument either. Of course, god appeared before them all when the king was slicing off a piece of flesh from his meaty thigh portion (as chosen by the eagle?) and blessed them all! The Chola and Sibi stories, true or not, were aimed at underscoring and underlining as much the rule of a king's dharma, or value-system based on justice, or a justice system based on the morals and values of ancient dharma.

It is often argued that there is no equivalent word or adequate phrase in European languages to describe or explain the word dharma, and what all its meaning(s) stand for. Either way, Ahimsa, or non-cruelty to all living beings, is a part of the Indian dharma, to whichever local religion or form of practice its origins are attributed to. Yet, non-vegetarianism has co-existed with such principles of dharma since the *vedic* age(s). Whether or not Sibi and Manu Needhi Chola were vegetarians, non-vegetarianism remained. Gandhiji adopted Ahimsa as his political creed at the height of the freedom movement. Yet, he would condone/advice mercy-killing of an ailing lamb rather than letting it agonise in pain.

In contrast to Sibi and Chola is the story from the West, Shakespeare's *Merchant of Venice*. In the play, Portia argues for her lover, Bassanio, saving him from losing a pound of flesh from near his heart in repayment for the moneys that he owed to Shylock, the Jewish money-lender. Shylock gives up after Portia argues that he was entitled to his pound of flesh, and from near Bassanio's heart, but not an ounce more, not an ounce less—and not to a drop of blood, either. The story is about greater cunning of Portia against that of Shylock, and also the latter's greed. It is not about Justice of the Sibi and Manu Needhi Chola kind.

No god appeared at the end of *Merchant of Venice*, to certify Portia's smartness or even Shylock's avarice and lack of basic humaneness. There are communities even in present-day India and rest of the world, where loan-sharks put their heart into their moneys and do not mind putting other people's heart too, if that's what's going to get them their money back. Is it the creditor's dharma, in the Indian way of thinking or what? Extended, this could well explain and justify one living by over-lording the other or killing for food or fun, whatever the circumstances. Or, isn't it as simplistic as that?

In early Tamil literature and ancient Tamil Nadu, the authors of *Thol-kappiam* and *Tirukkural*, the latter called the 'Tamil *Veda*', were believed to be Jains. The other popular Tamil grammar book after *Thol-kappiam*, namely, *Nannool*, and many, if not most books in the pantheon of Sangam literature, too were believed to have been written by Jains. They are different from the Jains now living across Tamil Nadu, some families as long as five centuries and more, who are relatively recent migrants from Rajasthan and speak mostly Marwari or Hindi at home, but are equally at ease in Tamil, too.

The early Jains in Tamil Nadu, especially the authors of *Tirukkural*, *Thol-kappiam* and *Nannool* were all Tamil-speaking Jains, or 'Tamil Jains'. It possibly also implies that either they or their forefathers had embraced the religion. According to Census-2011, there are 83,000 Tamil Jains in the State, who are much less visible than their more recent cousins coming from western India. There are Jain archaeological finds across the State, mostly dating back to the eighth and ninth century. Even at present, to whichever station in life they belong, or in whichever part of the world they stay, Jains' adherence to Ahimsa and their persisting with the inherited food habits of centuries are worthy examples.

Whether Hindus or Jains or whosoever, the kings of the yore, Tamils or others, here or elsewhere in the country, did train and maim animals, to fight battles or get killed. Indian epics, including the *Mahabharatham*, mythology and literature in every language is also replete with incidents of kings resorting to animal sacrifice at the commencement of wars and also as thanks-giving after victory. Both warring parties in the *Mahabharatham*, we are told, performed sacrificial rites before the commencement of the war. Both the *Ramayanam* and the *Mahabharatham* also talk of the *Ashwamedha Yagna*. The details in this case are about the valour and victories of emperors and their armies. The yagna is successfully concluded only when the horse is sacrificed to propitiate the gods that had made all those victories possible. That was the dharma of the ruler.

Training a horse or elephant to be battle-ready required all kinds of preparations and training, worse off than for Jallikattu. Unlike the Jallikattu bulls, those animals were sent to their death, knowing well that they would get hurt, maimed or killed, or even allowed to die a slow, bloody, painful death. The only saving grace in their case was like the animal sacrifices in some of the temples across the country even today, anything more than a single chop to dismember the yagna horse was considered inauspicious—or at least, less auspicious than otherwise.

Yet, protecting animals and their rights to survival and more, and putting them to death in war and for food, are two sides of the same coin. Wars and battles on horse-back and on atop the elephants are gone. Hence, they do not have to get killed in battle. But the cultural remains of getting other animals like the bull trained alongside have survived to date.

Animal Rights

Stories and philosophies from across religions and regions of the world and languages can be marshalled to argue both for and against continuing with a Jallikattu-like sport and more.

Yet, arguments against cruelty to animals, including sports like Jallikattu, have a relatively recent origin compared to the ethos of this nation and its multiple cultures. All those diverse cultures had known vegetarianism as a creed at least for a section of their people. Yet, from the priestly Brahmin community of the Vedic age, they had/have also encouraged ritualistic killing of animals for propitiating the gods. Killing for eating animals never stopped. Even law-makers and enforcers that favoured animal-sacrifices in public places like temples, were/are not known to have given up eating meat, or are known to be considering the same.

Letting animals participate in war alone has stopped, not because of man's sudden love for animals. Instead, science and technology have invented very destructive tools of war, with which our poor animals and humans put together cannot stand even light years away leave alone, against them. It is recorded that the clever use of the cavalry by the marauding groups/armies from across the Khyber Pass a thousand or so years ago, and also the use of gun-powder, both of which were unfamiliar to the local rulers at the time, alone changed the tools of war, even locally. If local folklore and tales from a more recent past were to be believed, even the European rulers, down to the time of the British, fought or otherwise frightened the local rulers only by the use of gun powder, which alone gave way to the end of the cavalry in local wars. Across Europe, the cavalry ended its long history only after the First World War, just a century back again, not because of the sudden love for the animal or animal rights, but because more destructive forms of warfare was found with the deployment of air-power, after the centuries-old use of gun powder. Has the sudden love and care for animals erupted after they have become dispensable commodities as tools of war, is a distant question.

True, between the two Great Wars of the twentieth century, in a matter of less than two decades, the role of animals as tools and vehicles of war have diminished but have not vanished altogether yet. Today, horses and elephants, camels and mules at best have a ceremonial role in select armed forces of the world. India is no exception, and here one of the less than handful of Cavalry Regiments in the world has survived to date. Fair enough, the cavalry forming a part of the President's Bodyguards enthrals the audiene in every Republic Day, so does the Camel Regiment of the Border Security Force (BSF), the latter more especially against the setting sun on the ramparts of Delhi's historic Red Fort in the closing hour of the 'Beating the Retreat' event, on 29 January each year. But they also need to be trained, they also need to be made to stand tall, as the pride of India. But cruelty of the kind outlined by animal rights activists in every court case against Jallikattu, they do not face. With the need for letting animals get killed in very large numbers in wars gone, man can now afford to turn human and humane towards and about them. In turn, they have actually done it, too. Just as human rights as a concept and conditioning was born out of the deaths and destructions of the two World Wars especially, the idea of animal rights too has grown alongside without many noticing it at birth. *Step by limited step, we have reached a stage where sports like Jallikattu can be de-legalised and certified as causing cruelty to the animal.*

Blame it on democracy, or praise it for the same, the advent of human rights, both as a concept and practice, was thus the first step towards the current talk, awareness and pro-active initiatives in the name and for the animal world. The Prevention of Cruelty to Animals Act, 1960, is such a piece of legislation. Subsequent notifications of the Centre, including those banning the use of animals in circuses and Jallikattu, were a part of the process. Whether we would have reached this stage of caring for animal welfare and rights, if these animals were still fighting the wars of humans is debatable.

Today, even primary school books or picture stories for young minds do not carry Greek short stories like *'Androcles and the Lion'*, about a prisoner being let loose to fight a hungry lion, before a large gathering of onlookers. If the animal did not kill him, it owed to an old debt, of the prisoner having removed a thorn from the lion's foot when it was in pain some years earlier, and the animal recognised him, as they are said to. Thus the story of Androcles and the lion is more than about the inequal man-animal fight of a kind different from that of the Jallikattu, and more so the Spanish bull-fight. Public execution and flogging may remain in parts of the world, but they have been eliminated elsewhere. Many countries and also many States/Provinces with penal provisions separate from the federal government, as in the US, have abolished death sentence as a part of their own human rights initiatives. Where death sentence is still on the statute book, authorities are discussing and discoursing upon the most humane way of executing death-sentence, even for the most heinous of cold-blooded killers who had premeditated those killings.

In our country, Section 302 continues to remain as a part of the Indian Penal Code (IPC), dating back to 1860. However, in 1980, the Supreme Court ruled that death sentence could be awarded only in the 'rarest of rare cases' (*'Bachan Singh vs State of Punjab', 1980*). There is a common misconception about this phrase/provision. As the relevant portion of the Supreme Court judgment read, 'Death penalty should be imposed when collective conscience of the society is so shocked that it will expect the holders of the judicial power centre to inflict death penalty irrespective of their personal opinion as regards desirability or otherwise of retaining death penalty.' That is to say, the Judiciary should award death-sentence judiciously, and not otherwise. Courts across the country, going all the way up to the Supreme Court, have not shied away from applying this rule, and continue to send the 'most deserving' to the gallows.

Rape of Nature

The human spirit and endeavour of seeking to live down the past mistakes of our forefathers, and create a new and just, equal and equitable world, is also behind the commencement of thinking, talking and working about animal rights and welfare. Such initiatives have come to cover other creations of Nature, including Nature as a whole. It is more visible and continuous in Tamil Nadu than in many other parts of the country. In this State, over the past decade and more, it has become a grassroots-level movement, to fight for the cause of Nature, and fight against the 'Rape of the Nature' even more.

Almost every one of the Tamil Nadu village and town already has at least one contemporary tale about the local people's struggle to protect the environment and ecology, Nature's gifts like rain-water and rain forests, and natural resources like minerals, plants and paddies. The battle for the protection of one of them in a particular instance may help in the protection of others alongside. The irony is that those that are opposed to cruelty to animals in the context of Jallikattu do not approve of mass protests in defence of Nature and natural resources. The pro-Jallikattu protestors too do not seem to acknowledge the contradiction in their positions, where they want natural resources saved but do not extend it to animals and bull-taming.

Such battles for Nature's rights have become infectious across the State. By default or design, Man is at the top of this pyramid of Nature's gifts. He is also at the bottom of it at the same time. Man needs to protect himself from himself, and for this he is looking at options to protect other life-forms. Maybe it is for selfish reasons, maybe not, but protection of Nature and natural resources have triggered a great interest and gained greater support all across the southern State, never as before and never as elsewhere in the country. Written into all such scripts, even if as an unintended after-thought, is the larger cause about animal rights for survival and survival with the same dignity that Man has been fighting for himself.

Every such argument or submission or protest points to animals, especially cattle-heads as among the victims of the 'Rape of the Nature'. Chemical contamination of drinking water, river-sand scams, blasting of hillocks for granite, deforestation and faster urbanisation all have a bearing on the life, health, and food-and-water availability of animals, both domestic and wild. In cows and bulls in context, it has meant loss of milk-yield and other ailments, caused by consuming food and water, chemically contaminated. Hence contradictions in the professions of the pro-Jallikattu groups also remain.

Falling for 'Drunken' Bulls

On specifics, there was said to be some truth in the early complaints of the activists that the Jallikattu animals used to be made to drink liquor regularly and more so on the days of the event. There have also been reports of chilli-powder being sprinkled on their eyes before letting them off the Vaadi Vaasal, to irritate and provoke them. Activists have produced video-recordings of such unhealthy and at times cruel practices before officials and later before the courts hearing the case for a temporary or permanent ban on Jallikattu. The fact was that on most occasions, neither the authorities, nor the pro-Jallikattu lobby, including local organisers, could deny such charges as convincingly. Some Jallikattu oganisers in particular and their social media supporters did claim at the height of the 2017 protests that all such practices have ceased after successive court interventions. Experienced tamers say that they are not the ones to fall for 'drunken' bulls or bulls with chilli-powder in their eyes. Drunken bulls can be dangerous and kill them instantly. No one wants to get killed in the brave Jallikattu arena in such a mean fashion, unless he is also drunk. In recent years, especially after Supreme Court directives, medical doctors and veterinarians test and certify both bull-tamers and the animals as free from liquor, as has become the standard practice in all other sport forms across the world. The argument against the use of chilli powder to provoke the animal is also contested. Some of this chilli, some bull-tamers point out, would rub off on their own hands and then onto their eyes and mouth, rendering them immobile before an animal that is angrier than already. They would instantly know the truth, and from then on, no bull-tamer, and hence organiser, would encourage owners of such animals to field their bulls in Jallikattu events anywhere in the neighbourhood. In this, the tamers maybe concerned only about their own safety, but the fact still remains that it helps save the animals, too, from cruelty. But the PETA petition on the post-protests Season-2017, as mentioned, too repeats similar charges, authenticated in a way by local media reports, which were otherwise pro-Jallikattu, mostly.

Contradictions of the kind galore, both in theory and practice. Arguments that Jallikattu does not involve cruelty to animals any more turn tame if one were to compare the tamers holding to the animal's long tail and hurting it, to even a bullock-cart driver doing so, to make the animal pick up speed. There is some meaning in activists dubbing 'castration' as the most extreme form of cruelty to the animal but this is a regular animal husbandry practice all over the world—and no animal-lover is protesting. There are fewer instances of castration now than earlier, but it does not owe to a new-found love for the animal and animal rights. It owes entirely to the fact that proportionately, fewer bullocks are required in this age and time, as science has found substitutes for bullocks in motor cars and buses, tractors and mechanised oil mills—as with modern-day war-machines when it comes to elephants and horses in particular.

Cutting Both Ways

FOR ALL of India and all Indians, dharma, by whatever name called, is an 'Article of Faith', or '*The* Article of Faith', or even going as far as '*The* Article of *The* Faith'. It is independent of religions and castes to which they may belong now, or may have belonged in a distant and near past. There is no equivalent, or even an all-embracing word or phrase in any world language to explain or describe the Indian word, dharma. Wherever Buddhism has spread, as in Sri Lanka equivalent phrases like '*dhamma*' (in majority Sinhala language), for instance, do exist. Sri Lanka cannot be said to have embraced Ahimsa as a creed as in the days of Lord Buddha, the founder of the religion. Nor have such other nations given up war and war-mongering, violence and cruelty, as Emperor Ashoka.

Maybe, the origin of the word and the concept it stands for are better explained through Sanskrit or any other Sanskrit-linked language like Pali or Prakrit. But it is also one of the many remnant Sanskrit words prevalent and in free use in every

Indian language—and with the same meaning, understanding and force—as with the phrase 'dharma'. Yet, in application to daily-life situations, conflicts and contradictions galore! But it is to 'dharma' that every Indian instinctively looks at, and looks into, even while discussing global geo-strategic situations and worse. If one takes a closer, intuitive look at what the *Bhagwad Gita* preaches as one's '*karma*', it is also an intricate yet intrinsic justification, inter alia, that every *karma* comes with its own form of dharma, suited to its circumstances, and should not be confused with others. So, the job of the butcher and the soldier is to 'kill', not to preach 'Ahimsa'. The peace-negotiator's role is to preach peace, equity and equality—which is what Krishna attempted before the *Mahabharata* war commenced, but not afterwards. Then, he became one of the Pandava war-team, though sticking to his avowed commitment not to use any weapon in the war. Krishna, the god in human form, was also the greatest of strategists and also executor in Team Pandava, deploying crucial non-weaponry tactics at critical hours in the war. Krishna even used his weapon, the Chakra, or disc-like weapon, in non-attack mode to hide the sun, to help the Pandavas, in one instance.

Justification for and against Jallikkattu too is thus only one of the very many instances that ancient civilisations such as India's constantly confront. For age-old situations, there are only age-old explanations, not necessarily immediate solutions. It is tempting to compare the Jallikattu ban with the *Sati* ban of burning widows with their dead husbands in the pyre. Raja Rammohun Roy is credited with making the ban-demand a social movement. The British rulers passed a law and enforced it. In a democracy, the voice has to become still deeper and come from a wider body—from the masses—for it to become successful at implementation. Even centuries later, instances of Sati are being reported from parts of India but it is no more a question of culture or community habit.

'Civilisational' societies, such as India's, having evolved over a time and with Time, have been both accommodative and assertive at the same time.

'Fate' and 'fatalism' are words that could explain, or explain away, the accommodation or in-built escapism(?) of such 'civilisational' societies as India's. This is also one major concept that has distinguished Indian philosophies—and religions—from the rest. If bent too much and too far, it could yield, or give away. Twenty-first century India cannot afford it. Nor can twenty-first century world afford India moving away, or being forced to move away from the 'inclusive' platform of yore, as different from the 'exclusivist' scheme imported, or sought to be imported from outside.

The abhorrent and obnoxious practice of Sati has mostly gone away from India. Though still news reports keep coming up every now and again, re-introducing Sati, for instance, in the name of re-discovering India and Indian culture, for instance, is not on. Likewise, Jallikattu may become extinct in its time, not necessarily before it. Maybe without the more recent reiterations over the ban, and the subsequent—not necessarily consequent—protest for restoration, which in turn derived from a larger 'denial' perspective, even the revival call might not have come up in such a form and size when it did. Retaining the law in the statute book and offering justifications is one thing. Enforcing it without concern for the consequences is another. The former can facilitate the acceptance of the ban as time goes by. The latter can render the law irrelevant as communities contest it, not just in courts but more so, on the streets. Tamil Nadu's continuing opposition to the 'imposition' of Hindi even decades after the acceptance of the language as one more in the Indian societal and constitutional milieu is a case in point. Discretion is the better part of valour. For authorities in high places, discretion is the best part of democracy too.

Contradictions and More

At the height of the Jallikattu protests, a new line of argument came to be put across through the faceless 'social media', again. It pertained to the 'constitutional commitment' to 'cow protection', and extending the argument to cover 'Jallikatatu bulls'. Nowhere else in modern India and Indian-ness does the discretion-centric self-contradiction stand out more than in the nation's Constitution, which is less than 70 years old—or, young, as one wants to look at it.

At Independence, and later on while writing a Republican Constitution, India was looking at modernisation of its industry and industrial production, as a way to ensuring equality and equity of humans. Prime Minister Jawaharlal Nehru described industry as 'Temples of Modern India'. Yet, his leadership also walked backward—in the eyes of his critics—to let 'cow protection' into the Statute.

It was still not 'animal protection', covering all non-humans that do not belong to the plant species. It covered only 'cows'. Yet, the 'protection' did fall within the four walls of the larger concept of animal protection and animal rights. In India it happened long before the contemporary West had thought about it. It was thus that India at Independence went in for universal adult suffrage. Western democracies took their time in reaching there. It has proved to be the great arch-way to an India of equality and/or equity, under a modern State structure—or, whatever has been achieved thus far, and continues to be attempted continually, if not continuously.

The Indian Constitution is the only one of the kind in the world that promises cow-protection, or possibly the protection of any animal, as a national creed and deed. The 'Directive Principles of State Policy', under Chapter IV of the Constitution, clearly enjoins upon the Indian State a duty to frame laws to ensure that cows especially are protected in the country. Cows here explicitly include 'draught' animals, but otherwise should also cover bulls and bullocks, trained for Jallikattu or hard labour.

Under the title, 'Organisation of agriculture and animal husbandry', Article 48 of the Constitution reads thus: 'The State shall endeavour to organise agriculture and animal husbandry on modern and scientific lines and shall, in particular, take steps for preserving and improving the breeds, and prohibiting the slaughter of cows and calves and other milch and draught cattle.' There have been occasional protests demanding cow-slaughter ban from time to time since the inception of the Constitution, but nothing much has happened beyond a point. Just now, it seems to be taking a bloody and unwelcome turn. Laws are for the State to enforce, not for street-corner vigilantes to force down upon.

There may also be a need to remember and recall that while conferring constitutional protection for 'cow', India has not adopted the same as the 'National Animal'. That honour is reserved for the 'Royal Bengal Tiger', not even for the 'Elephant', which is acknowledged as India's 'Heritage Animal', instead. Different yard-sticks for different purposes and circumstances is what statecraft is all about, as long as it serves the larger purpose. In the case of cow-protection, too, keeping India and keeping India united at post-Partition era through gestures of the kind was upper-most in the constructive Indian mind, despite the impracticality of enforcing such a ban, then or later.

The very Constitution that seeks to protect the cow under the 'desire' chapter on 'Directive Principles', includes a mandatory and very enforceable chapter on 'Fundamental Rights', committing the Indian state to the Citizen's right of choice in all matters, including food and profession—like beef-eating and beef-selling. It is a settled principle of Indian law that Fundamental Rights are enforceable by and through the higher judiciary whereas 'Directive Principles' are an expression of the state's legislative intent to move in that direction. Thus, it is not only 'cow protection' that finds a place in the chapter on 'Directive Principles'. Even 'universal education' is a desired and very much desirable position of the Indian state with a constitutional commitment to reaching there at the birth of the Republic. It was only when half the well was crossed could India think in terms of making 'universal education' a part of the chapter on 'Fundamental Rights'. The question still remains if that enforceable mandate has been achieved or is even achievable, at least through the medium term.

True, the Constitution proposes 'cow protection', there is a 1960 law on preventing cruelty to animals, but there is also an unending habit and practice of beef-eating, cutting across religions and regions. Now also is added the argument in favour of its export value. It is another matter that the 1960 law did not flow out of the Constitution, which should have then meant a ban on 'cow slaughter', sale and eating of beef. Though the 1960 law still reflects the spirit of the constitutional provisions, it refers to all animals, not just 'cow', which alone gets a constitutional protection. The 1960 law, as may be conceded, flowed from a modern western idea, true to their new-world view in an era after the cruel and gruesome two Great Wars of the last century, and more in the centuries before that. Here again, enforcement of an existing law or lack of it cannot mean that the law does not exist, nor should it mean that the other person does not have the 'Fundamental Right' to eat beef.

Whether enforced or not, the law always provides for penalties and punishments for violations that are proved by appropriate authorities before appropriate legal/judicial forums. Fair enough, a majority of population in central Indian States, traditionally known as the 'cow belt' in politico-electoral parlance, are reported to have (or, even surveyed to have) been non-beef-eaters. But substantial to absolute majorities in the rest of the country have no issues with their selves eating beef or others eating beef, even when some of them do not touch any meat, leave alone beef.

Whether it also has to do with the post-Emergency political belief that you can win national elections with the support of the 'cow belt' States is beside the point but the fact also remains that the much-cited Prevention of Cruelty to Animals (PCA) Act, 1960, has a proviso that clearly states that *killing/slaughtering animals for human consumption is exempt from the application of the law.* Hence, possibly the twist and turn involved in the 2017 Central government notification even on 'cow slaughter ban', if it could be dubbed so, seemingly distinguishing 'slaughtering' from 'selling and marketing' that relates only to cattle-markets, or wherever the cattle is sold. It could well include the house or backyard or farmland of the animal's owner, even if it were a draught animal that he could not afford to feed any more, nor lose the little extra income that comes with the sale, even if to a slaughterer.

In a nation that is acknowledged to worship cow as god, or goddess, to be precise, if a custom-bound cow-owner has been selling his draught animal to the slaughterer too for centuries and millennia together, the 'all-accommodative Indian contradiction' is even more striking. Then there is Sarat Chandra Chattopadhyay's *Mahesh*, written in the late 19th century, about a man Gafoor's love and dilemma over his ox Mahesh at a time of severe drought that still brings tears to the reader's eye. This story, written more than a hundred years ago, depicts the reality of an India which is in complete contradiction of what we are being told is the narrative, dictated at times and in places by today's politics.

'Branding' thus does not stop with animals, but with humans, in terms of their food habits and trade practices, at times obliquely sanctioned by perforce vaguely worded government regulations, like the more recent Central notification on sale and sale-places of cows, draught animals included. In a nation where social practices, availability of free grazing land and even irrigation and drinking water are always different in different States and regions, an uneducated and unexposed one-size-fits-all solution does not work.

For instance, in the case of draught cows, and also bulls and aged bullocks, letting them off in the public land for grazing until death may be practised and is practical in the Gangetic plains, maybe. As coincidence would have it, in 'distant' Tamil Nadu, there are now no *poromboke* lands at the disposal of the government to convert them all into a free grazing ground for draught cows, bulls and bullocks even if the Constitution were to mandate it, and laws and courts might seek to enforce it, too (in the near or distant future). The fast-paced enactment and enforcement of land reforms laws and consequent distribution of the freehold in the hands of the government to the poor and needy has ensured as much. A stage has now come when there is no land available for housing and new industries unless agriculture lands are converted for non-agriculture purposes, through law or surreptitiously. Less said about the availability of water for irrigation and also the drinking and other kitchen uses of humans, starting with infants, infirm and the old, in the State, the better. Anyway, do those that want the draught cows and ageing bulls and bullocks too not to be slaughtered want them to be let loose in the open, without either the one-time owner or the State providing for their upkeep and feed until Death embraces them in the natural course?

If they want to still talk about their own proposals for digital-enrolment of the animals to identify the owners and transferees, or for the Indian State to open up *gousalas*, or cow-sheds, in every street-corner, it will surely remain unenforceable/unenforced law like a million others, with which political and official corruption too can tag on, instead. It is also in this context that the protests against the 'beef-ban' law (though it is only a marketing ban/regulation, so to say) too needs to be contextualised. It is unclear if all these protestors now were/are for-or-against Jallikattu ban.

But as much as the 'beef ban', or even more so the series of un-investigated (!) attacks on 'animal-slaughterers' and beef-eaters (only) across the 'cow belt' States, the anti-ban protestors are proclaiming that governments cannot continue to do so, 'In my name'. Here, they are not as original as they would want other Indians to believe, but the parallel, for and against in this case, too, is striking. The slogan immediately calls to mind the nation-wide protests and rallies across the US, with placards, 'Not my President' after Republican Donald Trump was elected to the high office. The 'Trump protestors' in India were fewer in number than most other protests of any political/social kind before it in recent years in this country.

Yet, the message was clear.

In the immediate context of Jallikattu, it only raised the question, whether the life of a human (bull-tamer or not) is less valuable than that of the animal? And if slaughtering of a cow should not be permitted, and legal restrictions needed to be imposed on not only on such slaughtering but even the marketing of those animals, what about humans that are similarly placed?

First and foremost, can humans be killed by other humans outside the purview of law, which has very clear-cut and centuries-old provisions for the purpose. Two, these laws do not provide for 'execution' of a cow-killer or a beef-eater. Three, even more gruesome, those that seek 'licensed slaughtering' of animals in clean and painless environment, go about slaughtering fellow humans in even more gruesome manner, and still are not held readily accountable. Put on the reverse, some perverted thinking could come up with defence even of pain and harm to Jallikattu animals, arguing that when men could be put to such cruelty and worse, why talk only of animals.

It is not as if self-styled '*gau-rakshaks*' and their protests are new to the country. In the Sixties, such protests included Hindu *sadhus* taking out a rally through the streets of the national capital of Delhi, stoning and setting fire to the residence of Kamaraj, the then president of the ruling Congress Party at the Centre and in most States. Incidentally, the attack on Kamaraj's residence was accompanied by the police opening fire on the protestors, killing many of them.

Then Union Home Minister, Gulzari Lal Nanda, had to quit office, as policing the national capital fell (and it is so even today) under the exclusive jurisdiction of the Centre, and the ministry under his care. Questions were asked by his own Congress leaders as to his efficacy as Home Minister when his police force could not protect the house of a veteran leader (who thankfully was not inside when it was set ablaze). Incidentally, there was a lull in the activities of the 'cow protection' squads after this Delhi episode of 1966, as even the political leaders and parties identifying with the demand could not bring themselves to accepting and acknowledging the violent street-behaviour, that too before their own eyes, in the national capital, of all places, bringing instant dis-repute in the eyes of the national and international media, permanently located in the city.

All of it seems to be changing. In the months following the 'Jallikattu ban' centred on the bull and southern Tamil Nadu, elsewhere in the country erupted independently, self-styled 'cow-protection' squads, bent on enforcing a non-existent beef-ban, and thus even legally-licensed 'cow-slaughter' for beef-making/manufacture. The *Hindutva* driven approach to 'animal protection' is not helping matters. It also remains to be seen if such a mood and trend as exhibited by the cow-protection squads might end up being used to argue the case for continuing/reviving 'Jallikattu ban', too.

If anything, 'cow protection' got as much attention and commitment from the present-day rulers whenever they were in the Opposition, as did the demand for 'uniform civil code' and the abolition of Article 370 of the Constitution, conferring special status on the troubled border State of Jammu and Kashmir. All of them have been on the Hindutva political agenda, and have continued to remain there. No one is talking about the other two anymore. Rather, they were being talked about—and dropped like a hot brick, as the most pragmatic thing to do.

Politicians everywhere are pragmatic. 'Cow protection' is fine, as cows do not protest one way or the other, even if left out in the cold after they had served a limited political purpose. In context, what is going to be the Centre's position on the 'Jallikattu case', when taken up by the Supreme Court again, remains an unmentioned concern of the silent Tamil population. Will it stand by its earlier, post-protest commitment to have the Jallikattu sport back for good? Or, will it remain wishy-washy as any strong support for what some see as 'cruelty to animals' could also go against the spirit behind the 'beef ban order' and the underlying Hindutva tenet in the matter? Though reports do not exactly speak about the Supreme Court serving notice on the Centre, on the latest PETA petition against the 2017 Tamil Nadu law, its involvement/intervention could become a necessity, also given the fact that at the core of the argument of the animal rights activists is the 1960 Central law, and subsequent notifications and legal positions taken before the courts on this and related issues.

'Wishy-washy' is the term often mentioned in this context, as in the post-Jallikattu protest days, the Centre said different things to the Supreme Court on the Cauvery water dispute, within a matter of days, if not hours. After having conceded the long-held Union of India position under different governments and Prime Ministers on the Supreme Court's jurisdiction and the supremacy of the court order, then Attorney-General Mukul Rohtagi turned the tables by submitting one fine morning that the Apex Court did not have the powers to hear the case from day one, under the Inter-Water River Disputes Act. Tamil Nadu critics of the Centre would later draw a parallel between 'cow protection and central Indian State politics' on the one hand, and the 'Cauvery water dispute and the upcoming Assembly polls in Karnataka' where the BJP has a strong base and hopes to return to power in Elections-2018.

Multiple Benefits

The present discourse is not about cow-protection *per se* in a religious and/or constitutional sense, or the lesser or larger Hindutva agenda, if any. Instead, it is about the realities of our times compared to the demands from the past. The fact is that the Hindu majority in the country do continue to revere the cow as an incarnation of *Maa* Lakshmi, the Goddess of Wealth and Prosperity. In many Indian households, especially in South India, Lakshmi is a common name for a cow. The daughter of the family is also named Lakshmi. Religious literature thus refers to cow as *Gou-Maatha*, or, 'Mother Cow', but in effect meaning 'goddess cow'.

Going beyond religious beliefs surrounding the place of a cow in an average Indian family, such other practices have their origins in science or pragmatism, or both. It is not only the cow that is honoured in and by Indian families. Most festivities, whether in local places of worship or in families or communities, also have a place of honour for the plantain/banana tree, the coconut and even the fruit of the *palmyrah*/palm tree wherever they grow.

Indians have had a way of honouring or educating people about the usefulness of things available around them without tom-toming the scientific reasons and justification. Turmeric powder keeps away ants and other insects from homes. In rural Tamil Nadu homes, every Tuesday and Friday, turmeric powder used to be ritualistically and decoratively laid out across all doors and windows, to keep insects out. It did not stop there. God has a design in creating them, they too need to eat and live. Man found an additional use for rice powder. When religiously and decoratively converted as *kolam*s and *rangoli*s in the open courtyards of homes, rice powder provides food for those ants and insects. If they are coming into homes for food and if they get it unasked for even before entering someone's home uninvited and unwanted, why bother to enter that house?

In the same context, cow dung continues to be acknowledged as the best natural disinfectant and manure at the same time. Thus, courtyards of rural homes are sprinkled with cow dung dissolved in water. In some places, or at least occasionally, the floors of the courtyards are plastered with a thin layer of cow dung. In more traditional homes, cow dung is used to wipe out the dining place where the banana leaf is laid out, with the food served on it for eating. In both cases, cow dung acts as a disinfectant. When sprinkled with water every morning and evening, the moist cow dung spreads across the courtyard and absorbs outside dust in the tropical, summer climes.

Cow's Call-sign

The scientific reasons were never explained, whatever the reason. What instead became a habit was a religious (!) adherence to whatever practice was handed down from generations. Thus, an unintended Hindu or larger Indian religiosity also came to be conferred on scientific practices and pragmatic considerations. Independent of religious and/or caste identities, many of those practices are in vogue, across the board, and across many, if not most or all parts of the country. Some of them may have a cross-border identity and identification in the larger sub-continental landmass, post-Independence, post-Partition. Yet, when it came to be condemned as superstition, the argument was equally forceful. In comparison, those that spoke in defence of the scientific and practical reasons behind such practices were meek and weak, or did not at all open their mouths, where and when they should have done so.

The third way was to accept it as a casual 'right to passage' without having to accept or question the rationale or superstition one way or the other. A stand-out example is what is popularly known as the 'Turmeric biopiracy case'. In 1995, two expatriate Indians at the University of Mississippi Medical Centre were granted US Patent: 5,401,504 on the 'Use of Turmeric in Wound Healing'. In 1996, the Government of India's Council of Scientific & Industrial Research (CSIR), requested the US Patent and Trademarks Office (USPTO) to revoke the patent on the grounds of existing of prior art. The CSIR did not succeed in proving to the satisfaction of the US authority concerned that many Indians already use turmeric for wound healing although turmeric was known to every Indian household for ages. Fortunately, it could provide documentary evidence of traditional knowledge, including ancient Sanskrit texts and a paper published in 1953 in the Journal of the Indian Medical Association. The patent was revoked in 1997, after ascertaining that there was no novelty.

It is not as if we Indians are stand-alone types in such matters of age-old scientific practices without acknowledging the practical reasons and justifications behind most, if not all, of them. Across the world, communities have feared, hence respected Nature in its varying forms—the sun, the moon, the stars, the trees and animals. Either these creations of Nature supported humans or threatened them. The result was the same. People worshipped them, unknown to one another in civilisational terms, or otherwise, too, distanced as they were by space and time. It is only in relatively recent times that communities have learnt of similarities in their age-old traditions and custom-bound practices. It should have surprised the world that almost all societies had followed similar paths in the worship of Nature without even knowing that the other(s) existed.

The Tamils in particular take pride, at times half-jokingly, on how the cow calls and cries out only as *'Amma'* (*humbaa*) in their language, no matter whichever part of the world the animal is or comes from. Alternatively, it can be argued that early Tamils adopted the natural cow call-sign as their own way of addressing and referring to their own mother. It is certainly true of every other Indian language, where '*Maa*', the cow's call-sign, refers to one's own mother. Across the country, '*Maa* Lakshmi', '*Maa* Kali', *et al,* are honoured references to female. In English, too, '*ma*' refers to one's mother. Conversely thus it can be argued that early man started talking and developed his language and linguistic skills only by aping the cow, and thus the animal in particular had, and should continue to have a greater place in human life than at present. The reverse would be even truer if one were to counter-argue that despite learning language(s) from cow, early man and generations of his successors over the millennia had continued to kill and eat the animal, across the world and to date. It is only in India that cow is worshipped as god and is also given a constitutional commitment to protection. Every argument in all such matters has two sides if not more, and this one is no exception.

Every religion, more especially Hinduism, reveres woman and womanhood as much as it worships cow, as the giver, keeper and symbol of prosperity in homes and communities. 'Cow' includes 'bull'. Lord Siva is thus depicted as having the bull as his ritualistic vehicle, and has given away half of his physical self to his consort, Shakthi or Parvathi, taking with it the name *Ardha-nareeswara*. Both cows and *gopis*, or women, had an equal place in child Krishna's pranks in his growing-up years. Such acceptance and reverence do not extend to daily lives, where both are equally abused. Here, too, cow includes bulls.

Does the alleged misuse and abuse of bulls thus extend to include Jallikattu, too? The question itself thus offers justification for protection of the animal, and thus the justification for the ban, too. Worse than the Jallikattu bull, it is the others, especially the bullocks and the cows in rural areas that suffer the most and the worst, religious beliefs and constitutional guarantees notwithstanding. If cows are to be protected and worshipped, why is it that its owners let them loose in the streets, allowing them to live off the available refuse, including newspapers and worse?

If grazing was/is the reason, then where are those grazing grounds, instead?

There is also no explaining why flowing from a distant and justifiable tradition, cow alone was seen as a living-being worthy and demanding protection, both of man and law, and not other beings, plants and trees, which also expended everything that they possessed for the welfare of the same Man. By extension, it can be argued, why the cow, and not the goat and sheep, which also do near-similar service to man in their own little ways, have not been considered worthy of such protection? True, goats and sheep cannot plough fields, pull carts and so on, but then, their milk is as enriching as that of the cow's—so much so, Gandhiji, ever an experimentalist, preferred the former to the latter, they are also killed to be eaten, and their skin and even hair are used for human protection in wintery climates in this own country of ours.

On another front, to the average Hindu/Indian, especially in the South, full-grown banana plant is a sign of prosperity, to be displayed at temple festivals, wedding ceremonies and other auspicious occasions. Like the cow, goat and sheep, the banana plant also offers all its parts, starting with the fruit, for man's use. Until recently, even the dried up fond used to be threaded in rural Tamil Nadu for vendors for stringing flowers (though the contemporary generation may not even know it). And banana plant grows below a parent plant, one group after another, one 'generation' after another, with the result there is the Tamil phrase to bless newly-weds to grow and propser, '*vaazhayadi vaazhayaha*'.

The coconut palm also gives everything that it has got to the man, but only the fruit gets a pride of place on auspicious occasions. While the dried up coconut fond was/is roofing material, the green fond was/is considered inauspicious as some south Indian communities use it only in funerals. Worse is the plight of the palmyrah palm. Unlike the banana and coconut, the palmyrah does not expect man to water it, and unlike coconut its strong bark was/is used as cross-bars to support either its own dried up fond or those of the coconut palm as roofing material. Of course, the palmyrah palm is available only in dry belts, including parts of the Jallikattu country in Tamil Nadu, but no honour is conferred on the tree or its produce and products on any auspicious occasion, anywhere.

Worse than Jallikattu?

Contradictions thus galore if one were to compare and contrast customs and conventions, but then that is also what traditions are all about. In this case, if cow is considered goddess and not goat or sheep, that is custom and tradition. If banana plant is conferred all the honours, the coconut palm some, and the palmyrah none, again it is custom. In the modern and our 'post-modern' times, governance and governance schemes of all kinds, especially on issues based on such tradition-centred issues can succeed only when an intelligent delineation can be and is made for appropriate situations. The universality of law and its application can fail without those in authorities taking decisions based on a judicious mix of convention and contemporary practices as often reflected by the existing and ever-improving legal tenets. There is also no permanency to such laws as may have been considered modern until the other day. The evolution of the 'reservation laws' even from the days the new Republic's Constitution mandated some for the underdog communities identified as 'Scheduled Castes and Tribes' to the 'Mandal case verdict' less than half a century later in 1992, is only a pointer. Other instances and examples of the kind galore.

Barring the killing for eating, if cruelty to the animal is the bench-mark, there are worse practices than Jallikattu, which in turn is also only a once-in-a-year affair. In practice, though not wholly justifiable terms, Jallikaattu should become the least, though still unacceptable form of harming the animal. Forced labour extracted out of already castrated animals under the yoke of a plough or a cart, or both is worse than Jallikattu. In context, castrating the bull and fixing metalic horse-shoes with metal nails down the animal's hooves should be considered worse than any other form of cruelty to the breed.

The question also arises if milking the cows to feed our infants and our own selves, and converting that milk into various dairy products—and marketing them at high prices for hefty profits—does not amount to cruelty to the animal, especially their own young ones. While defending demands for banning cow-slaughter and worshipping the cow, we pronounce that after mother's milk, only cow's milk contains all the minerals and nutrients required for a human baby, and in the near-consistency as the former, thus as easily digestible, too. The cow produces that milk for the calf, which clearly possesses a near-similar digestive system as human babies. They also need the same nutrients and minerals at birth and to grow up, even more. The baby has its mother's milk as the first and preferred choice. To the calf, the cow is its mother, and cow's milk is equivalent to mother's milk. There is also no substitute to cow's milk for the infant-calf.

Logically, the same cow protectors should not then drink cow milk or feed it to their infants, infirm and the old. Vegans in the West do it, not we the vegetarians among Indians, who otherwise confer an unparalleled divinity on the animal and worship it as we worship every other god in the Hindu/Indian pantheon. Ironically, is it also precisely to celebrate the humans stealing the infant calf's due all through our own growing-up years that we end up worshipping '*Maa Gau*'? Or, is it a *penance* that has been conferred the status of thanks-giving, instead—and offer the very same 'stolen cow milk' to the very same cow (possibly the same animal, too in one's home) or to other numerous gods in the pantheon? If such arguments are to be extended to cover Jallikattu ban, it could end up nowhere.

For Jallikattu ban, it is argued that the bull is not given a choice, and it is incapable of making the choice. But humans across the world, from time immemorial, have not given the cow and the calf any choice in the use of the cow's milk, either. Besides the millennia-old worship of Nature by civilisations distanced by space and time, the exploitation of the cow and the calf for milk seems to have been another human activity that is universal. Less said about the commercialisation of milk products the better. Worse still is the concept of castration of the bull, and the life-long inhuman treatment of the bullocks, after hurting them physically and psychologically in every which way. Spaying of pet dogs and cats is equally cruel in the same context.

Big Business

The question is not about banning all human uses and commercialisation of cow's milk, but about contextualising the Jallikattu ban in the larger canvas of human activity. If animal rights become the touch-stone, which it should anyway be, there will be no end to ban-demands of such kind. If it is Jallikattu now, such bans on other use, misuse and abuse of cows and by extension bulls, can come up any time in the future, if not in years but most definitely in decades. These are issues that have to be considered logically and not made uni-directional, and more so, unilateral.

But there is commercialisation and exploitation of another kind that a section of the social media was talking about at the height of the pro-Jallikattu protests. The 'commercialisation' related to a so-called western scientific-industrial conspiracy to 'kill' the virility and resistance of the local breeds of bulls in the reproductive age, to facilitate large-scale import of dairy products. The exploitation, the campaigners said, related to India, politically, and Indian markets, commercially. According them, the Jallikattu ban was aimed at ensuring the early extinction of strong native breeds of cows and bulls, capable of producing volumes of milk in India's era of a second 'White Revolution'.

The campaign claimed that overseas business interests were thinking way ahead of their Indian counterparts, and were afraid that later, if not sooner, India could become a net exporter of milk products, hitting their businesses hard. Post-Jallikattu, they were also referring to the coincidence of unexplained and untested media hype against particular brands of food products, including the sudden reference to 'plastic rice' in our food, and the massive publicity for replacement-products from a '*sadhvic*' group with known links to powers-that-be. In the past, they recall, the 'anti-BVO' campaign, on 'brominated vegetable oils', killed the Indian soft-drink industry, only for their American counterparts to hit Indian shop-shelves in a massive way, with their ad campaign boldly declaring, 'Xxxxx does not contain BVO'.

The same can be said about the massive campaign against coconut oil, especially in a coconut-rich State like Kerala of the Seventies and Eighties, where the people were told that their centuries-old food-additive was dangerous to the human heart and general health, and that instantly imported palmolein was the safer substitute. The fact that no one in Kerala had died of heart-related diseases assuming the levels of a pestilence, as were being said did not seem to have occurred to anyone in 'god's very own country', the only one in 'India that is Bharat' believed to have been created by an aspect of god, Lord Vishnu in His *avtar* as Parasurama—and which is also celebrated for its highest levels of literacy, health care and other social indicators, then as since. The government, both officials and politicians, were happy with the import, as subsequent corruption cases on this score too showed.

It is another matter that decades down the line, the very same western scientists and doctors are telling us that coconut oil and coconut products are good for humans, and better for infants. The next in the line seem to be the sugar-levels in humans, where international organisations are busy, reportedly studying the global trends to possibly bring down the accepted levels, originally fixed at 140, to 120 now, and to 100, soon. Which means more people would have to take anti-diabetic medicines and early on, and may also be prescribed special, canned stuff, either as a substitute to their regular food or as add-on nutrients.

Such clinical tests and scientific pronouncements apart, chemical intervention in Indian animals, for them to produce more, be it of milk or of fat/beef, are few and far between. Hence the quality of their milk is also closer to the naturally-produced milk, and is also better in every other way in terms of nutrients-content and possible side-effects on regular consumption. In comparison, excessive use of chemicals to make the cows yield more and faster have created health-safety issues for humans too, after consuming the same—or, so goes the argument. Maybe, as a part of its '*gau-rakshak*' efforts, governments in the country, or the vigilante groups, should initiate research in the matter, even as they talk mighty about the traditional Indian ways of doing things, be it in science or marketing, economy and savings.

Bulls like those being used in Jallikattu are specially fed, cared for and develop in-built resistance to diseases. The calves that they sire grow up into healthy animals, providing healthy milk and other products that humans end up consuming. By attacking the existence of these animals through the 'wholesale scientific method' of the ban, overseas business interests, it is claimed, are ensuring that at some point in the future, our animals have to give place to theirs, or we have to import more of their dairy products for our daily consumption.

The more imaginative campaigners even drew a parallel to the 'British exploitation' of India, and claimed that this alone led to India losing its prime place in the global agriculture and manufacturing sectors. They forget the contribution of the Industrial Revolution in Great Britain to the prosperity of that nation, but then, the argument that the raw materials that fed the British economy of the times went from colonised nations, starting with India is correct. Until the British looms had imported cotton to work on, the nation, for instance, was importing finished cloth-material from countries such as India.

As coincidence would have it, around and immediately after the Jallikattu protests, came the news from across the country, in Haryana to be precise. News reports spoke of an individual bull-buffalo being priced at an unimaginably high Rs 9 crore (appx $ 1.4 m). The owner would not sell it, however. According to the news reports, the animal's semen, when used in a large number of dosages for artificial insemination, could fetch the owner ten times as much money as the price offered for the animal, and each year. Extrapolating such news stories, the pro-Jallikattu lobby sees behind the ban-move, similar efforts at causing the extinction of local breeds, to which the Jallikattu bulls too belong.

It is this pride, of owning the best animal(s) in the neighbourhood, that motivate the owner(s) to spend more money and time for giving that extra and extraordinary care to the Jallikattu bull. It is like the owner of race horses, about which alone the urban elite know more. The race horse owner is elated when his horse wins. He is even more exited if an animal born to one of his horses beat the rest. Like the race horse, in the case of Jallikattu bull too, ancestry is a matter of pride and reference. Of course, the sport has denigrated in pride and purpose in the current milieu. But in the ancient days, kings and local chieftains were the ones who used to maintain high-end breeds at great cost. They used to take equal pride in fielding those animals in the annual Jallikattu events. We need only to imagine how the Kosala king in Lord Krishna's time would have taken special care of his seven bulls, for them to help choose the most valorous of men, to take the hand of his dear princess-daughter. Even stories such as keeping the sport an annual occasion for the display of valour by only members of the warrior communities from earlier times are not entirely untrue.

True, like with all other social practices like un-touchability and cruelty to our women, Jallikattu too seems to have degenerated from a cause for protecting the animal and its species into one of hurting them and at times injuring them, in the name of having some fun. But in a country where denial of equality for the 'untouchables' dates back to the *Mahabharatham* and to the story of Ekalavya and Karna therein, equity for animals will take its time. This was so despite the story of Lord Rama, long before the times of the *Mahabharatham*, when He embraced tribal chieftain Guhan as the fifth among the siblings, after the his three biological brothers, and followed it up with accepting half-monkey Sugriva as the sixth one in the clan.

Culture and Cause

Fair enough, the Jallikattu protest demonstrations did not receive favourable response from political parties in Tamil Nadu identifying with the untouchable communities. But it is still to be found out if those belonging to such communities had stayed away, especially those among the cosmopolitan crowds that had gathered in metro/urban venues like Chennai and Madurai, Coimbatore and Tiruchi just because of caste concerns. If reverse was the case, and which it could well have been, then it flows that Jallikattu protests, though not necessarily Jallikattu proper, did become a great leveller like any other invented in more modern times, whose main aims and goals were far away from ensuring equality of humans and equal opportunities for all humans. In the heat of the moment and at the height of the post-protest Jallikattu events across the country, no one seemed to be keeping record of participation by local untouchables, be it as bull-tamers or as spectators. However, upcoming years could prove the point one way or the other.

Which then is the case for which the jury should vote?

Will it be for Jallikattu, or for the ban?

The question boils down to one between tradition and modernity, culture and 'cause', so to say. As with other aspects of human development, in terms of rights, including those of animals, some progress has been made only in recent times. Like with other aspects of development, including economic development and growth, civilisation-linked cultural aspects, outlook and mindset have remained a drag, a pull-down factor than a push-up factor. To equate modern thinking with growth and development in human and animal rights is one thing, but to condemn the other that is unwilling to or incapable of pulling themselves out of the baggage of their civilisation is another.

The old has its advantage of experience and expertise of a particular kind ingrained into the DNA of those people and their environment—ready to be pulled out the shelves for immediate use. The new has its advantage of thinking and acting differently, at times successful, at time losing out. All the time, both sides are trying to balance each other, and at times balance out each other. The median is somewhere in between, and it evolves with time. If it fails to do so, again disaster waits those that are caught in between, be they nations or humans, or nations and their humans.

History is replete with instances and examples of the kind. The US is what it is today, with all its pluses and minuses, and with a capacity to convert, or at least package its failures as a first step on a success-trip, only because it is relatively young as a nation than many of its civilisation-centred counterparts across the world and cousins across the Ocean. Nearer home in India, there are examples of relatively modern cities like Chennai, Kolkata and Mumbai out-witting ancient cities that now remain a complete hollow of their past self and esteem. If the present-day Delhi is what it is today, including being the nation's capital, it owes not to its history as Indraprastha from the days of the *Mahabharatham*. Instead, it became what it is today, thanks to the more recent British rulers, who developed it as 'Lutyens' Delhi'. They completely re-built a new city, which had been made relatively modern by a succession of Moghul rulers in their times. Yet, the difference and 'distance' between Old Delhi and New Delhi remain.

In the Tamil Nadu context, too, leaving aside Chennai, which again is 378 years young, one other city that has progressed and prospered is Coimbatore. With sobriquet such as the 'Manchester of the South' and the 'SME Capital', this 'Cotton City' was nearly non-existent when Chola capitals of Thanjavur and Tiruchi (then Tiruchirapalli), the Pandya capital of Madurai and the Pallava city of Kancheepuram all flourished, either simultaneously or alternatively. Today, these cities have their glorified past intact but younger cities like Coimbatore and neighbouring 'Hosiery Capital' of Tiruppur have beaten them to it. The fact is that the old cities are trying to balance their past and a promising future through the medium of the present. Cities like Chennai and Coimbatore, and even Tiruppur, do not have to make any adjustments with a glorious past, though they too have had a relatively longer history in parts than is readily acknowledged.

It is this dichotomy that gets translated between old and new thoughts and thought-processes. 'Adjustments' is the catch-phrase here, and it would not have happened in the case of Jallikattu or Jallikattu protests until the emergence of a cross-culture generation as has happened now.

The element of the individual Tamil's psychological need to balance his hoary past and modern thought, as such balance too became a part of such modernity too cannot be over-looked, or over-stated, either. Jallikattu has remained an annual sport of bravery and valour for generations and centuries. This was followed by a relatively brief period of opposition to the sport, and the subsequent ban. The protests against the ban were small and sporadic in the early years. But owing to modern management approaches, the protests became more organised and focussed than the sport itself by 2017. Where then were the options, occasion and opportunity for those that loved the sport and respected the sentiments, religious and otherwise, to get across their views to be able to find a solution of their choice? Earlier, the opposition to the ban was political at best, and politically competitive for most parts. The 'human' and 'social' elements were missing, until both surfaced—rather erupted—in January 2017.

It needs to be acknowledged but not as yet, that the socio-economic churning process across rural Tamil Nadu over the previous decades, almost since Independence and at times even prior to that, culminated in the Jallikattu protests. It has been so with regard to the emergence and acceptance of a series and succession of political leaderships and electoral formations/results. But a total social outpouring emerging out of a politico-administrative process that is rooted in the land and its masses all along came about only with the recent Jallikattu protests. The social and societal message was thus clear. Over and above what was right in the eyes of some, including the nation's highest judicial forum, the social evolution had actually taken the processes back to where some of them still belonged. The protests, rather than lending voice to the voice-less, derived from it, instead.

Fighting and Taming

The balance of arguments would seem to back the common call and cause for continuing with Jallikattu, but with minimal hurt and injury to the animal. Here again, unlike race horses and other animals used likewise, be it in competitive sport or as hunting-dogs (leave aside the prey of the game-hunter), Jallikattu animals are put out in the sport arena only for a few minutes at best in its pre-ban, court-approved form.

The scheme bars the 'fight' between the animal and the man in the conventional sense of the sport. It also prohibits the tamer from holding on to the tail of a fast-running bull. What is thus permitted is only for 'licensed men' to run alongside or behind the bulls that are registered with the authorities in advance, and released from the entry-gate, or Vaadi Vaasal, one by one. The tamers can at best hold onto the hump of the animal, and run only up to a 20-metre distance, marked by the authorities. Government officials, including Revenue, police and medical personnel, are on hand to supervise the proceedings, and at times report back to the authorities concerned. The courts had approved this scheme, but then the authorities were lax in enforcing the same, with the result that the ban could not wait.

Considering that such a limited edition of the event should still attract so many animal-owners, tamers and lovers of the sport from across the region or sub-region should make one thing plain and clear. Either the entire community of Jallikattu bull-owners are all morons and sadists, or they attach great honour and prestige to the event.

Given that costly items like high-end motor-bikes and other prizes are awarded to the successful bull-tamers, the sport seems to be imagined still as one of valour and prestige, not of sadism and cruelty. Are you reminded of the story of race horses and pet dogs of the contemporary rich and mighty? It cannot be overlooked that despite the Supreme Court ban and legal restrictions and judicial directions, the State authorities were callous even when Jallikattu was revived, what with overcrowding and inadequate safety arrangements too leading to the death of at least two persons, including a bull-tamer, and the consequent cancellation of the rest of the day's programme at least in one venue—and the sport being conducted, without the required permission, long after the official deadline for ending the year's season was over.

Part-II

The Ban

IN SUCH a historic and cultural milieu, with vast support and citations from religious and social literature not only in Tamil but also in Sanskrit, all dating back to millennia, where did the question of a ban on Jallikattu arise? And what caused the ban and provided justification, as very clearly underlined by none other than the Supreme Court of India, the watch-dog of the other two pillars of the nation's constitutional democracy—namely, the Legislature and the Executive?

In directing the ban, the Apex Court, especially, quoted extensively from the legislation on animal protection in the country, passed by Parliament as far back as 1960. The court also implied the spirit of the Constitution as a fall-back, if at all one was needed, to curtail the unbridled act of the Executive, namely, the governments at the Centre and in the State of Tamil Nadu. To this end, the Supreme Court ordered the restoration of a 2014 ban, in December 2016. It reserved the verdict in the pending case on

7 December 2016, without setting a date for the judgment—which of course is a very, very normal and even more acceptable and justifiable practice. This particular case flowed from the Centre's notification that aimed at setting the court's 2014 verdict at naught.

Expectations in Tamil Nadu in December 2016 were mixed. People were unsure which way the verdict would go, whenever pronounced. They were even more unclear if the verdict would at all be pronounced ahead of the Jallikattu season of 2017. It was only five weeks away, and staging the sport required preparations, physically at the venue, and psychologically for the tamers, and maybe the bulls, too.

The restoration of the ban became necessary after the Centre had de-notified 'bulls' as 'performing animals', banned from public display under the Prevention of Cruelty to Animals (PCA) Act 1960. Ahead of the Pongal-Jallikattu season of 2016, the Apex Court had stayed an Executive notification of the Centre, issued in April 2014, which added bulls (for Jallikattu) to the list of 'performing animals' banned for such display/use as in circus. In 2011, the Centre had added the animal to the list, notified under an earlier order of 1991—and three years later, the Centre 'de-notified' it, following protests in and pressures from Tamil Nadu, comprising the people, polity and the government.

There was thus an avoidable confusion, flagged by the Centre in the first place.

Likewise, the Supreme Court, which had reiterated the ban in December 2016, did not do so when the Tamil Nadu Assembly passed a facilitating legislation to conduct Jallikattu events after the protests, in January 2017. Instead, on 31 January 2017, the court was content with directing the parties to the pending case, to file their responses in the matter. The PETA filed a fresh petition challenging the new law, and later alleged (continued) 'cruelty' to the animals (and also humans) even in the post-protest Jallikattu season, this time facilitated by the intervening State legislation. The case came up for hearing again on 6 November 2017, when the First Bench, headed by Chief Justice Dipak Misra, directed the State government to file its response to the PETA petition in four weeks. The case is thus expected to be taken up any time afterward.

Ahead of the protests and the later-day State law and consequent restoration of the sport, on Friday, 13 January 2017, when the annual Pongal-Jallikattu season was already upon Tamil Nadu with the day's Bhogi festivities, the Supreme Court observed that it found no reason to rush through its judgment in the pending case from the past, in which it had restored the ban in December 2016.

At the height of the protests, only days later, the court, however, granted the Centre's plea, to delay its verdict in the very same case by a week. This facilitated the proposed Tamil Nadu legislation not being set at naught, *ab initio*. More importantly, the legal draughtsmen in the State who drafted the new legislation, and law officers of the Centre who cleared it for the all-important Cabinet approval and presidential assent, did not possibly have to guesswork the anticipated Supreme Court order, at least in the interim, and until the Bench concerned took up the new legislation for judicial review—which all stake-holders had however taken for real but in the future.

The unanimous passage of the new Tamil Nadu legislation in the State Assembly, its double-quick approval from the Centre and the assent from President, all unprecedented in a way to the complex and otherwise slow and over-burdened Indian legislative system, all came through during the one-week of 'delay' that the Supreme Court gave itself for pronouncing the verdict in the pending case from the Centre's enabling notification of 2014—stayed in December 2016. When the court later heard the case post-protests, the Centre promptly withdrew the 2014 notification, through a tacit understanding with the Tamil Nadu government, leaving only the new State legislation to be agitated upon in the Supreme Court, as was expected then—and as challenged, later on. This in turn meant that the Tamil Nadu law facilitating Jallikattu remained on the statute book, thus legalising the sport, even if for a period, when post-protests Jallikattu came to be staged in 2017. It was a complex and ingenuous way to address a complicated situation, but nothing much more, over the medium and long terms. There, the Judiciary held the last word, still. Yet in the immediate, the year's Jallikattu season was duly restored, and the protests were mostly withdrawn, barring in Chennai, where it ended in avoidable violence, involving the police too.

Innocuous Beginning

If not to the same degree and time as Jallikattu, the ban itself has had a chequered history before the pro-sport protestors took to the streets in January 2017. For around three decades, outfits like the Blue Cross, a non-profit organisation (NGO) fighting for animal rights in the country, had been petitioning the authorities in the State and at the Centre, regarding the 'cruelty' being meted out to Jallikattu bulls. They had periodically submitted memoranda/petitions to the Tamil Nadu Legislature, too, appealing for a ban—but to no avail.

The issue took a new turn when the Animal Welfare Board of India (AWBI), the statutory body set up by the Centre, under the Prevention of Cruelty to Animals (PCA) Act, 1960, went to court over Jallikattu. The Board got noticed in the Nineties when it moved the Supreme Court and obtained an order banning the use of 'performing animals' in circuses across the country. That the industry was already dying a natural or not-so-natural death is beside the point. But the ban meant that the high-cost circus industry could not fight the tide of the new-generation moving away from traditional entertainment and even professions of the kind.

Egged on by the Board, the Delhi High Court later directed the appointment of a committee, which listed out the names of animals that were in common use as 'performing animals', and banned their display for the purpose. 'Dog' was originally included in the list issued by the Ministry of Environment and Forests (MoEF) at the Centre in 1991, as required under the 1960 law. Better counsel prevailed, and the animal, a common pet otherwise, was removed from the list of 'performing animals', later on.

'Animal Welfare' comes under the Concurrent List of the Constitution. Hence, both the Centre and the State government can legislate on the subject. Under constitutional provisions and Supreme Court decisions, where Parliament has chosen to legislate on a subject under the Concurrent List, it has nation-wide application. Hence, any Central legislation on a 'Subject' under the Concurrent List gets precedence over a State legislation on the same aspects, whether supportive or otherwise of the Central law. Such State laws are automatically superseded. The Union Ministry of Environment and Forests (MoEF) is the authority under the law and the Rules of Business of the Government of India, to be in overall charge of 'Animal Welfare'. The ministry is the administrative head of the Animal Welfare Board of India (AWBI) under the 1960 law, and is also empowered to appoint the chairperson and members of the Board.

However, in the matter of the Jallikattu ban, the Board and ministry did 'collude' on occasions, but did 'collide' (in courts and outside) at other times. In the Jallikattu ban affair, however, the Board has displayed a sense of 'autonomy' that is seldom visible in the functioning of any government department or affiliate, barring the Reserve Bank of India (RBI)—which again has reportedly felt constricted by the Executive, from time to time—whichever party is in power, or whichever leader is the Prime Minister and/or Finance Minister at the Centre. As is known, in all such matters and in all matters of such institutions, otherwise 'independent', if it comes to a collision course, the government ends up removing members of the Board under the very same law that empowers it to appoint them in the first place. In the case of the Jallikattu ban-removal in 2017, the AWBI decided not to yield, to what some members thought was a 'political move' aimed at facilitating a review of the ban.

Yet, the Jallikattu ban had its origins neither in the AWBI nor the Blue Cross, nor the Supreme Court, *per se*. Instead, the ban had commenced its chequered career in what was otherwise an innocuous case, though relating to a related issue such as the '*Rekhla* race', or bullock cart race, coincidentally in Tamil Nadu itself. Like with the Jallikattu bulls, the bullocks for Rekhla races, and also the carts are special, and so are the racers, unlike those in load-carts and ploughing fields. Like horse races, where the animal and jockeys are selected and trained for long, so is the case with the Rekhla race.

On 29 March 2006, Justice R Bhanumathi at the southern Madurai Bench of the Madras High Court ordered a ban on Jallikattu and other martial sport events involving bulls and bullocks.

The case did not flow either from any provision of the 1960 law or the 1991 notification of the Centre. Instead, the case before the High Court flowed from a petition filed by one K Muniasamy Thevar of Thannikootam village in Ramanthapuram district, seeking judicial intervention for permission to organise a Rekhla race. Thevar was also the elected vice-president of a local panchayat, under the Constitution. In 2004, Justice F M Ibrahim Kalifulla of the High Court Bench had granted permission for the races. Justices Kalifulla and Bhanumathi (both natives of Tamil Nadu, incidentally) would go on to become Justices of the Supreme Court in their time.

The High Court case came up again in 2004, this time before Justice Bhanumathi. Maybe because the case did not involve the question of animal rights and ban on such sports, neither the petitioner's lawyer, nor those representing the State government, which stopped with the district authorities, had any brief or briefing of any serious kind on the ban issue that the High Court had addressed at the time. As it turned out, the High Court bundled together Jallikattu and other animal sports involving the cattle-head, bringing them alongside Rekhla race, unilaterally and without any immediate provocation or a petition before it.

'Jallikattu is no more fun or *veera vilayattu* (sport of valour and bravery) but a clear violation of animal rights as bulls were subjected to cruelty,' Justice Bhanumathi observed in her 2006 verdict. Even then, the court seemed to concede that Jallikattu used to be 'fun or *veera vilayattu*' earlier. What made the sport unacceptable under the law was not addressed in this case. Only when the Supreme Court was seized of the matter later did the 2014 judgment address such issues. However, counsel appearing for none of the parties seemed to have made any reference to the origin of the High Court case itself, or the 2006 verdict beyond a point, as that was not exactly under judicial review.

Before the Supreme Court was a Tamil Nadu law of 2009, flowing from the 2006 High Court verdict. When the High Court ban came in the way of the conduct of Jallikattu, citing danger to the animal and humans alike, the then DMK government of Tamil Nadu, under Chief Minister M Karunanidhi, enacted the Jallikattu Regulation Act of 2009, with elaborate safety measures and with more stringent punishment than provided for in the PCA Act of 1960. In a way, it aimed at circumventing the ban, implying that the State government and the State Assembly *prima facie* accepted the High Court's observation that Jallikattu was 'no more fun or *veera vilayattu*' and needed regulation.

When moved, the Supreme Court in November 2010 permitted the Tamil Nadu government to allow Jallikattu for five months a year, subject to conditions, much of which flowed from the State's 2009 law and commitment.

However, on 11 July 2011, the MoEF under Union Minister Jairam Ramesh issued a notification including bulls in the list of performing animals under the PCA Act. This meant that bulls could not be trained and exhibited in Jallikattu-like sports, this time including the Rekhla race, too.

Flowing from the MoEF notification of 2011 was a new case in the Supreme Court, which on 7 May 2014, struck down the State law as repugnant to a Central law, though the latter was passed later. In doing so, the court banned the sport completely, also upholding the view of animal activists that the sport was 'inherently cruel'.

Fight or Flight Response

In upholding the MoEF notification of 2011, through the verdict of 7 May 2014, the Supreme Court Bench, comprising Justice K Radhakrishnan and Justice Pinaki Chandra Ghose, cited extensively from the report(s) of the AWBI experts panel, which had monitored almost every aspect of the Jallikattu events in the main, traditional venues.[1] All current references to the ban refer only to this judgment of the Supreme Court.

In their reports to the court, the AWBI experts spoke extensively about the way the Jallikattu bulls should have been handled, and how they were not treated. No stake-holder contested the facts contained in these reports, thus showing the callousness with which the local authorities and bull-owners had treated the affair, knowing full well that the AWBI experts were in their very midst, watching and videographing all that was going on before their very eyes. That even media reports were saying such things even in the Jallikattu events, revived post-protests under the Tamil Nadu law of 2017, should also go

---

[1] Animal Welfare Board of India vs A Nagaraja & Ors Weblink: http://supremecourtofindia.nic.in/FileServer/2016-01-12_1452599675.pdf

a very long way in showing as to what needed doing, and what was not done—and what could still be done, without the ban. The AWBI panel reports, quoted almost verbatim by Justice Radhakrishnan—who wrote the judgment for the Bench with Justice Ghose concurring—in turn quoted foreign experts on animal-psychology and cruelty to animals, convincingly and very well.

Under the sub-head, '*Bulls-Behavioural Ethology*', for instance, the Bench discusses the animal's 'fight or flight response when exposed to a perceived threat' and the like. The threat in this case relates to the environment in which Jallikattu is conducted—massive crowds, pushing and jostling for space, shouting and cheering at the top of their voices, with the blare of the public address system, adding to the confusion that already confounds the animal in a new place.

On the face of it, none could have contested many of the findings unless he or she was also an animal behavioural analyst from a different school of thought. That the experts' report derived much of the theory from western specialists and based their findings and conclusions on such theories, could mean that they were mostly practitioners of those theories and not original theoreticians. If they were original theoreticians, they could and would have theorised about the behaviour patterns of individual gene of cattle-head, in captivity and otherwise, and more so in the Indian context of Indian breeds of bulls. Maybe, the court could have then identified practitioners, to report on the conduct of the Jallikattu animals on a given day and the issues flowing out of them.

An even more basic question of legal propriety and judicial discretion, too, remained. How and why the court relied near-exclusively on the reports of a panel of experts of the AWBI, which was anyway an interested party to the case is unclear. Could the Supreme Court have assembled an independent panel of experts drawn from various agriculture universities and such other institutions from across India, to observe the Jallikattu events and report back?

The finer question however remained—between the law that presumed 'cruelty to animals' and the court's initiative that sought to check if there was 'cruelty' to the Jallikattu bulls in the first place, to see if the ban was applicable to this case in the first place. By extension, it can also be argued that the court might have also concluded that, had the experts' report not cited very many instances of 'cruelty' to the Jallikattu bulls, it might have also ordered the lifting of the ban to the game.

This apart, in the normal course, Supreme Court judgments, and also those of lower courts, often quote extensively from the affidavits and arguments placed by various parties to a case. This is because future appeals and review petitions, if any, rely on the earlier documents cited in courts, to make out a case, one way or the other. The court's time too cannot be wasted, seeking to re-invent the issues that had already been agitated in great detail. The more important purpose for higher courts citing litigants' arguments extensively in their judgment is to put on there cord the facts and circumstances of individual cases.

By convention and otherwise, lower courts are bound by the verdicts of the higher courts, under all circumstances. The larger issues agitated in most cases in the higher courts have future use and reference in cases coming up before lower courts across the country. Unless the lawyers and judges in the lower courts have access to most if not all the important arguments submitted before the higher courts, there can be a mis-representation and/ or misunderstanding of such rulings. This way, lower courts are often seized of the larger issues decided upon by higher judicial fora. It is for this purpose, for decades and centuries now, authorised law journals and legal periodicals have been reproducing all important judgments of the Supreme Court and all High Courts in the country. In recent years, the Supreme

Court and High Courts lose no time in putting up such verdicts on their web-sites web-sites as soon as possible.

However, interestingly, the 2014 Supreme Court verdict did not record the arguments of both sides, enough. Instead, it very heavily reported the observations and recommendations of the AWBI experts' committee, and left it mostly at that. Is it possible that counsel appearing for the pro-Jallikattu, anti-ban parties to the case did not make any argument worthy of the Bench taking note of and mentioning it in some detail in their judgment?

Rectifiable, but...

There is another angle to the experts' panel reports. Most of the specific instances of cruelty to the animals at the Jallikattu events that the panel members had observed and listed out in their reports were rectifiable. If the animal behaviour aspects of the experts' report deal with instances of psychological cruelty to the Jallikattu animal, and the physiological changes sought to be imposed through forcible feeding of intoxicants, their on-the-spot observations related mostly to the way the animals were crowded, ill-fed and left uncared for behind the Vaadi Vasal at three major venues.

If the Bench had passed strong strictures against the State government and local officialdom, who were tasked with the job of ensuring the safety of the Jallikattu bulls, tamers and spectators, it could have changed the situation the very next year.

The court had a better say than otherwise, as the State of Tamil Nadu had specifically promised to enforce such arrangements and supervision—and was going about it in such a callous manner.

Would it then flow that the Bench was overly concerned about imposing the ban more than regulating the game with some of the remaining grey areas, but with maximum guarantees?

The grey areas cited by the AWBI experts and quoted in the Supreme Court verdict included letting or even forcing individual animals loose through the narrow Vaadi Vaasal, and onto a mass of spectators, whom they might not have expected to be faced with, in the first place. The narrowness and the existence of the Vaadi Vaasal is a part of the culture and tradition of Jallikattu, and if that issue needed to be addressed, again the Bench could have asked specific suggestions of the experts panel, or the 'Respondents' (A Nagaraja and others), who had wanted the bull-sport continued/restored.

Culture and Tradition

In a multi-lingual, multi-religious, multi-cultural, and at times multi-ethnic nation such as India with a multiplicity of castes and plurality of sub-regional behaviour patterns, it is unnatural and impractical to expect that Judges of the Supreme Court understand each and every language, their respective history and literature, or all the content and import they are endowed with. The lawyers of various parties to a legal dispute, however, are expected to know them. Designated 'senior counsel' arguing a case before higher judicial forums, comprising the Supreme Court and the high courts, are respected for their command over law, nearer home and afar, and their knowledge of jurisprudence and judicial processes. Advocates of such parties to a dispute from the State or region where the case originates are expected to be conversant with the local customs and traditions, which have validity in law. *Where a State government is a party to a legal dispute, officials briefing those senior counsel are expected to have studied the issues threadbare.*

In the case of Jallikattu, there are issues and questions of customs and tradition. As a nation and people(s), India has had little to go by, in terms of recorded history of bygone millennia. What have been handed down are religious epics and historic legends, until such time recorded history became a practice, if not habit. Some of these epics and legends form a part of language and literature. Lawyers arguing before Judges who may not be conversant with aspects of local culture and tradition, and officials/clients briefing them, are expected to be knowledgeable, even if it is acquired knowledge, and not from personal exposure, association and identification of any kind whatsoever.

In Para 42 of the 2014 judgment, under the sub-head, *'Culture and Tradition'*, the Supreme Court verdict discusses related issues. 'Even the ancient culture and tradition do not support the conduct of Jallikattu or bullock cart race, in the form in which they are being conducted at present...', the judgment reads. 'Welfare and the well-being of the bull is Tamil culture and tradition, they do not approve of infliction of any pain or suffering on the bulls, ...on the other hand, Tamil tradition and culture are to worship the bull and the bull is always considered the vehicle of Lord Shiva.'

In Para 44, the court speaks thus: 'As early as 1500-600 BC in *Isha-Upanishad*, it is professed as follows: *The universe along with its creatures belongs to the land. No creature is superior to any other. Human beings should not be above nature. Let no one species encroach over the rights and privileges of other species.'*

Well said, yes, but *this* is all the concession to texts of religion, history and literature in any language, Indian or foreign, that the judgement has made.

Thus, in the very next Para 45, the court observes, 'In our view, this is the culture and tradition of the country, particularly the State of Tamil Nadu...' *Then the court observed that there was no cultural or religious sanction to Jallikattu (in any form).*

In pronouncing so, in Para 46 the court refers to Section 28 of the Prevention of Cruelty to Animals Act, which has 'taken care of the religious practices of the community, while killing an animal'. The section reads thus: 'Saving as respects manner of killing prescribed by religion: Nothing contained in this

Act shall render it an offence to kill any animal in a manner required by the religion of any community.' The reference is to animal-sacrifice.

Jallikattu does not involve killing, more so any purposeful and intentional killing of the bull, for religious reasons or otherwise. It is yet another saving clause as far as the verdict goes, but unrelated to Jallikattu, that the 1960 Act itself exempts killing of animals for meat from the application of the law.

If the lawyers, especially those representing the respondents, namely, the Jallikattu organisers, the State of Tamil Nadu and the Union Ministry of Environment and Forests (MoEF), had made any mention of religious texts going back to Lord Krishna's bull-taming prowess, and to Tamil literature going back to the Sangam era, the judgment does not mention them, either. It should thus flow that no such mention, or submission, was made.

In seeking to spell out a clearer understanding and idea of 'Jallikattu' as a sport, in Para 16 of the verdict, the Supreme Court observes thus: 'Jallikattu includes *Manjuvirattu*, *Oormaadu*, *Vadamadu*, *Erudhu*, *Vadam*, *Vadi*, and all such events involve taming of the bulls.' The inclusion of two terms here, might have flown from the inadequate understanding of the lawyers who argued the case(s) of the respondents.

Oormaadu refers in common parlance only to the local 'temple bull' or the bull adopted by the village community. The term Oormaadu, or oor-maadu, translates as 'village cow', or the community's animal(s). In some places, it even refers to the cow, and not the bull. The village bull does not have a role in Jallikattu. *But village/temple bulls are released from the Vaadi Vasal first.* By culture and tradition, no tamer ever stands in the way, and literally so. It is a religious sacrilege and defiance of the community to do so—and in that order. The term Oormaadu by itself does not refer to any form of Jallikattu.

Nor does the term *'Erudhu'*, which means a buffalo in Tamil. Any close resemblance to Jallikattu with reference to a buffalo is '*Erudhu virattu*'. Going by the Supreme Court verdict in the case, it looks as if the lawyers arguing the respondents' case in particular should have known their bulls and bull-sports better. This is so, even in spite of the very fact that Justice Radhakrishnan, who wrote the verdict, hails from neighbouring Kerala, and might have got familiar with some Tamil terms in some contexts, but not every term in every context.

Safety and Security

For all this however, the Centre's notification of 7 January 2016, seeking to rectify or reverse the Supreme Court ban of 2014, did have clear-cut instructions, for the State government(s) in particular. In doing so, the Executive Order of the Union of India, Ministry of Environment and Forests (MoEF), laid down conditions to ensure that the bulls are treated properly and not subjected to any cruelty.

The State government followed suit by instructing district collectors ('district magistrates' in some other parts of the country) to follow the instructions. The collectors were also instructed to ensure with the help of the local police, the safety and security of not only the animals but also the bull-tamers and spectators. It was a welcome change and relief as over the previous decades some of the more important and easily accessible Jallikattu venues have begun attracting foreign tourists and those from other parts of the country, and also the State. This means that the crowd potential is not easy for the organisers to assess beforehand and make appropriate seating and security arrangements, even if they want to. All of it also costs a lot of money, which the organisers either do not have or cringe about.

Already, with the 2009 Tamil Nadu law in place, State government officials, including senior police officers, were to be present at Jallikattu venues. Government veterinarians and doctors were to certify that the Jallikattu bulls were in good and non-inebriated condition, and so were the tamers. Both, more especially the tamers, were given coloured vests with serial numbers, for the authorities and audience (though not animals) to identify. Galleries were erected, and police, fire service and medical personnel were directed to be present in good numbers at the venues. *Yet, the political and bureaucratic top-rung failed to personally ensure that these orders were actually implemented sincerely and seriously.* With the result, incidents of cruelty to animals, collapse of galleries and death of tamers and injuries to spectators all continued—reported with unfailing frequency and equal gravity in the local media, as the AWBI experts' team had done of the 2013 events and which were cited in the Supreme Court verdict in May 2014.

Not a Gladiator-type Sport

Jallikattu, or more so the ban, was back in the news in 2016, just days after the 7 January notification of the Centre, removing 'bull' from the 1991 list. People for Ethical Treatment of Animals' (PETA), an international non-government organisation (INGO) and another moved the Supreme Court, just four days later.

On 12 January 2016, only two days before the commencement of the annual Pongal festival, when the first of the season's Jallikattu events were set to begin the Supreme Court stayed the Centre's notification and issued notice to MoEF and the State of Tamil Nadu, for their response on the submissions of the petitioners. On that occasion, a Bench comprising Justice Gopala Gowda and Justice Pinaki Chandra Ghose allowed an in-chamber hearing, but would not alter the spirit of the 2014 judgment. It may be recalled that Justice Ghose was a part of the Division Bench that had pronounced the 2014 verdict.

As pure coincidence would have it, his would become a popular, if not a house-hold name across Tamil Nadu post-Jallikattu, but in an entirely different PCA context. On 14 February, 2017, Justice Ghose would preside over a two-judge Bench with Justice Amitava Roy, to pronounce the historic verdict in the 'Jayalalithaa disproportionate assets case' under the Prevention of Corruption Act (PCA).

By the time the Jallikattu ban was re-imposed in 2016, or the 2016 central notification had been stayed to be precise, the AWBI, the original initiator of the ban move and the earlier case in the Madurai Bench of the Madras High Court too had joined in as a respondent.

In the course of the hearing of the case, the court would observe on 9 November 2016 that India cannot 'import Roman gladiator-type sport'. The fact is that *Jallikattu is not an 'imported' from Rome or anywhere else sport.* Nor was it a 'gladiator-type sport', as wrongly understood outside Tamil Nadu. A gladiator-type sport, if it involved an animal and a human, is closer to the Spanish bull-fight, if at all.

The Jallikattu is a local sport of valour, about which enough evidence has been marshalled. This was followed by the Supreme Court order of 16 November 2016, dismissing the Tamil Nadu government's petition and arguments to lift the ban.

In doing so, a Bench comprising Justices Dipak Misra, since elevated Chief Justice of India, and Rohinton F Nariman declared the Tamil Nadu Regulation of Jallikattu (TNRJ) Act, 2009, as violative of Article 254(1) of the Constitution. The said constitutional provision reads thus: 'If any provision of a law made by the Legislature of a State is repugnant to any provision of a law made by Parliament which Parliament is competent to enact, or to any provision of an existing law with respect to one of the matters enumerated in the Concurrent List, then, subject to the provisions of clause (2), the law made by Parliament, whether passed before or after the law made by the Legislature of such State, or, as the case may be, the existing law, shall prevail and the law made by the Legislature of the State shall, to the extent of the repugnancy, be void.'

The Bench did not seem to have been convinced about the State government's pleas and submissions that Jallikattu was not cruel *per se*, which is what the 1960 law and the 1991 notification addressed. *Where there was physical cruelty, it was a matter of non-enforcement of existing provisions and directives of the governments concerned.* The Apex Court had on 21 January 2017 dismissed similar pleas for re-examination of the 2014 judgement.

'Unfair' to the Bench...

Earlier, a fortnight after the 16 November 2016 order, on 1 December to be precise, the court observed that the Centre could not 'negate' the 2014 verdict and allow the use of bulls in Jallikattu-like events (and going by various other names, as well). Whether they referred to the State government or the Centre, the court's conclusions, if they were so, were in the form of oral observations. The judgment in the pending case had not been pronounced—and would not be pronounced soon.

It was thus that the Jallikattu events of the 2017 Pongal season got stalled. On 9 January 2017, five days or even less ahead of the commencement of the festivities, Tamil Nadu's Chief Minister of just about a month, O Panneerselvam, wrote to Prime Minister Narendra Modi, for the Centre to promulgate an ordinance, to facilitate the conduct of Jallikattu. The three-day Pongal festivities commenced with Bhogi, the massive house-cleaning ritual, on Friday, 13 January.

In between, the State government, more than the Centre (almost as always) seemed to have studied the mood of the population. Through much of the previous months, then Chief Minister Jayalalithaa's long hospitalisation, her controversial death, and the political and constitutional fall-outs, all had damaged the fair name and image of the State, in the nation's eyes.

Just as the State was beginning to recover from it all, the unanticipated and unwelcome Vardha cyclone ravaged the State capital of Chennai and suburbs as never before in living memory. The post-cyclone relief work had re-established the credibility of the State administration as never before in the previous five years and more. The people especially were apprehensive about the government's initiatives after the cyclone, as they had had a very bad experience after the 'Chennai floods' earlier in the year, when Jayalalithaa was Chief Minister and was supposed to be in full control. It also established the tentative, three-time Chief Minister O Panneerselvam as an able administrator, who was also accessible to the bureaucracy and the people alike.

Thus when the ruling AIADMK leadership and the State government were both recovering from the consequences of Jayalalithaa's hospitalisation and exit, no one in power wanted new and/or inherited troubles of any kind on his hand. More importantly, Pannerselvam possibly also wanted to send out a message to party leaders, cadres and the larger population alike that he was not passé as on the two earlier occasions, and as Chief Minister he could get things done by the Centre as much as his '*PuratchchiThalaivi* Amma' could do in her time.

This meant that the State government under Chief Minister Panneerselvam would pressure the Centre to do something about lifting the court-ordered ban that was already in force.

The Centre thus approached the Supreme Court, seeking an early and final verdict on the original case, which involved the challenging of the January 2016 notification of the Union of India facilitating Jallikattu but was stayed subsequently. If the court did not remove the stay of the January 2016 notification, no Jallikattu was possible in the 2017 season, as well.

From a political perspective, the Centre, or the Bharatiya Janata Party (BJP) ruling the Centre and Prime Minister

Narendra Modi's leadership, could either claim credit for the return of Jallikattu to Tamil Nadu, or absolve itself of any blame for not doing enough to restore the sport. It was the same in the case of the Tamil Nadu government, the ruling AIADMK, and Chief Minister Pannerselvam—the latter, to a greater or lesser extent.

Waking up late to the developing situation, the Centre moved the Supreme Court, on 12 January 2017, only a day before *Bhogi* celebrations, for an early verdict in the pending case, on which the Bench had already reserved the orders a month earlier. The mention came up before the Bench, comprising Justices Dipak Misra and R Bhanumathi, while they were hearing another case. The Bench observed that 'it is unfair to ask the Bench to pass an order'.

Justice Bhanumathi, who had ordered the ban first in the Madras High Court back in 2006, recused herself from the case, as is customary in such matters.

In a way, the Supreme Court would stick to its position, not to be pressured into delivering a judgment a week later on 20 January 2017. That's when Attorney-General Mukul Rohatgi approached Justice Dipak Misra with a plea, not to rush through the judgment in the immediate future. There is still no verdict at the time of going to press.

It was in the aftermath of the Jallikattu protests all across Tamil Nadu, that the State government was forced to act in favour of the sport and the State Legislature took the cause upon itself. The Bench had no hesitation in conceding the Centre's submission this time. This would mean that pending the Supreme Court verdict in the case flowing from the previous year's notification of the Centre, the State government could consider doing something legally and constitutionally about restoring the sport, at least in the interim. Educated by the media, the nation was well aware of the drift and the direction of the ongoing processes—tactic, if someone wants to dub it that way.

'Okay' for an Order

In an unprecedented move, of course at the instance of the AIADMK government, the State Assembly met in an afternoon sitting on the opening day of the calendar year's first session. Conventionally, the House disperses for the day after the Governor addresses the session. In the afternoon session this time, the House unanimously passed a Bill moved by Chief Minister Panneerselvam personally, to facilitate the return of Jallikattu this season. This was after the protestors—or, their so-called leaders—refused to first accept the Chief Minister's assurance to get matters sorted out. Later on, Acting Governor Ch Vidyasagar Rao promulgated an ordinance for the purpose, just days before he was to address the State Assembly.

In between, the Chief Minister rushed to Delhi in the midst of continuing protests back home, to confer with the Centre. He sat down with Union Home Minister Rajnath Singh, officials and the law officers of the Centre, to try to find a way out of the Supreme Court's 12 January observations, not to be rushed into pronouncing the verdict in the 2016 case. In these meetings, it was explained to the Tamil Nadu team that the demand of the protestors and the expectations of the State government, for the Centre to promulgate an ordinance to facilitate the sport that very season could not at all be met, as it could be construed as 'contempt of court'. No government at the Centre would and should ignore such a possibility.

Also, what if the court was to pronounce the verdict in the meantime and uphold the ban? Any fresh ordinance or notification by the Centre too would suffer from the same consequences, for the same reasons.

The Centre promised, as an alternative, that New Delhi would seek to convince the court that the verdict could be delayed, and the State government, in whose name no law or order positive to Jallikattu existed at the moment, could take legal and constitutional initiatives in this regard. The Attorney-

General packaged the presentation well for the Supreme Court, which had felt hurt at the hearing a week earlier, when Judges also expressed dismay at the law and order situation that was being caused by the Jallikattu protests in Tamil Nadu.

'The Centre and the State are in talks to find a way out in the matter and our request is that the court should not deliver the judgement for at least a week', the Attorney-General told the Bench. Possibly not unaware of the mounting pressures on the governments at the Centre and in the State, and the social, political and constitutional possibilities, the court also conceded the point. 'Okay' was the one-word response of the court, which in turn set the ball rolling for the conduct of Jallikattu in the 2017 season.

The court looked the other way when Governor Rao first promulgated an ordinance on 21 January, and the State Assembly soon thereafter followed it up with the unanimous passage of the 'Prevention of Cruelty to Animals (Tamil Nadu Amendment) Bill, 2017, moved by Chief Minister Panneerselvam. In doing so, the ordinance and the Bill that followed, sought to amend a Central legislation, the PCA Act of 1960. This is acceptable under the Constitution, where a 'subject' falls under the Concurrent List. Such amendments and modifications had been attempted earlier in relation to specific pieces of legislation that had been inherited from the British era or passed by Parliament as stand-alone legislation in the post-Independence era.

Unlike on many previous occasions, the Centre had no hesitation in forwarding the same for presidential assent. Nor did President Pranab Mukherjee take any time, or seek clarifications of any kind. The fact that the subject came under the Concurrent List of the Constitution, gave the Centre the power to pass law that was binding on all States. It also meant that the State Legislatures too had powers to amend those laws, as applicable to their respective jurisdiction. The fact that the

Union Cabinet under the Prime Minister had no hesitation in commending the said State legislation to the President for his assent, and the latter too had affixed his stamp, could answer one issue that the 2014 judgment had addressed: Where Parliament had passed a specific law, upturning a custom or tradition specifically, the law and not the custom would prevail.

The new TN legislation raised another question, which had more of constitutional import rather than legislative action or inaction: Will the Centre's approval and consequent presidential assent for a State (amendment) law, upturning the spirit and content of a Central legislation, mean that there was no legal case for the courts to interfere? Or, would, if required, Parliament too deemed it fit to pass an amendment law, the spirit and content of which derived from a State amendment law, and court verdicts, existing or future ones, would not count?

Without providing any answers to such questions, the Supreme Court, for the immediate presence, refused to interfere with Tamil Nadu's enabling law, when challenged, this time round. This was in contrast to the immediate stay granted to the Centre's notification of the kind only a year earlier.

Some leading jurists had flagged yet another relevant question in the early days of the Jallikattu protests: 'Should *en masse* public opinion be allowed to hijack the due process of law, legislation-making and judicial pronouncements?' In their eyes, the apex court's latest position was an extension of the concept of 'people taking law into their hands'.

Where from Here

The Judiciary did not give way, or give away, in the first phase of the protests, or pre-protests 2017. It was just the other way round, a fortnight later, when nothing had changed legally, but everything else had changed in reality, on the ground. Any 'stay' on the operation of a new law on a subject on which another court verdict was pending meant that another case, another series of hearing, and another verdict. This is what the new PETA petition on which the Supreme Court has since ordered notice to the State government means.

For the generation that followed late Idi Amin, dictator possible without a parallel in global history in the decades after the two World Wars, Kampala was in the news as the capital of Uganda that he terrorised. Uganda and Kampala remain, but Idi Amin is gone. But there is a 'Kambala' nearer to the Jallikattu land of Tamil Nadu. After the 2017 Tamil Nadu law upturning the Supreme Court ban and facilitating Jallikattu all over again, and possibly taking the cue from Tamil Nadu, neighbouring Karnataka government too promulgated an ordinance, for the return of 'Kambala', the traditional slush-track buffalo race, conducted in the northern districts of the State every year, during the rainy season. Unlike Jallikattu, which is staged on dry ground, the Kambala is conducted on specially-prepared slush-land, often a ploughed field with water added for creating the slush to required consistency (!). Unlike in the Rekhla, where light-weight carts are specially made for the purpose, the animals in Kambala are tied, tied two each, to the ploughshare for the race. The Prevention of Cruelty to Animals (Karnataka Amendment) Ordinance 2017 removes the Kambala buffaloes from the list of 'performing animals' under the PCA Act 1960. As any Ordinance goes, its life is limited to six months, this one ending on 20 January 2018, to be replaced in between by a regular piece of legislation in and by the two Houses of the State legislature.

As with the Jallikattu, PETA moved the Supreme Court, against the Karnataka Ordinance, citing near-similar reasons challenging the Ordinance and thus the restoration of the earlier ban. Apart from possible divergence, if at all any, in matters of physical cruelty and alleged intoxication of animals, the PETA arguments almost always have to run on near-similar grounds when it comes to other aspects of 'cruelty' to animals in terms of animal psychology, *et al.*

In a way, the two cases are inter-linked, whether or not the Supreme Court hears them separately or clubs them together. In its new petition on the new law in the 'Jallikattu case', PETA has attached investigation reports and supportive video-evidence to prove allegations about continued cruelty to the bulls in the Season-2017 sport events conducted in various traditional and non-traditional centre, since February 2017.

According to the PETA petition, the Tamil Nadu Act and the Rules framed under it for its implementation violated the 'five-internationally recognised' animal freedoms, recognised by the World Health Organisation for Animal Health, with India as a member. The 'five freedoms' comprise freedom from hunger, malnutrition and thirst, freedom from fear and distress, from physical and thermal discomfort, and freedom from pain, injury and distress apart from freedom to express normal patterns of behaviour.

Worse still, *even after the State government had promulgated the new law to facilitate the return of Jallikattu with accompanying expressed and impressed commitment to regulate the sport to avoid cruelty to animal, even the revived Season-2017 witnessed the death of five bulls and humans, including a policeman on-duty and spectators, apart from tamers and injuries to close to 2,000 persons (or, 1,948 to be precise).*

Citing investigation reports from Palamedu, Avaniapuram and Alanganallur (all three in Madurai district) and other traditional centres, the PETA petition argued that 'Jallikattu takes advantage of bulls' natural nervousness as prey animals by deliberately placing them in a terrifying situation in which they are forced to run away from those they rightly perceive as dangerous and a threat to their lives'. Taking off from video and photographic evidence, the petition further submitted that *'collapsed bulls were violently forced to their feet instead of being provided veterinary care or rest; bulls sustain broken tails; are stabbed and jabbed with weapons; are hit and jumped upon...'*

According to PETA, 'Such abuse at Jallikattu events leads to severe injuries and even the death of humans and bulls.' Independent of the queries that the court might ask the State government counsel and officials, the latter if summoned, they have a lot to answer in terms of the alleged callousness of the authorities in not ensuring the implementation of the enabling law and the enabled Jallikattu events. Suffice is to point out that it was only, possibly, in the light of such callousness in the implementation of the 2009 Act that the Supreme Court struck down the same and restored the earlier ban.

All of it also depends on the quality of the evidence adduced by PETA and other petitioners/interlocutors, if any, and also the larger question on the legality and constitutionality of the new law. That is to say, there are two broad questions—one pertaining to the WHO-recognised 'five freedoms for animals', and two, the implementation of safety measures for animals and humans, tamers and spectators included. In the case of the latter, the sub-text is this: Will better enforcement or straight ban alone will help?

The Protests: Why

WHEN THE Constitution is so very clear about the powers of the Supreme Court to interpret laws, and by extension make and unmake laws, where was the need, occasion and environment for the population of an entire State to challenge the order of the nation's highest Judicial forum, that too on the streets—and so very openly?

Despite occasional heart-burns, especially over the Cauvery water dispute in recent years and decades, the Tamils as a people are as law-abiding as any other section of the Indian society. This is so even going back to the freedom era when *Periyar* E V Ramaswamy Naicker's Dravidar Kazhagam (DK) confused their socio-political opposition to the Congress Party with the national movement and observed Independence Day as 'black day'. Soon, The self-styled 'exclusive' social movement that the DK claimed to be soon split and the breakaway DMK acquired a political role and relevance, inching towards electoral participation and ruling the State in 1967. The constitutional cooption of what used to be considered an organised 'separatist movement' at the birth of the nation is a red-letter event in the nation's post-Independence history. Even the DMK-sponsored anti-Hindi agitation of the Sixties was in more ways than one a part of this process.

In terms of reach, 'Hindi' as a political issue had been on the anvil for nearly three decades at the very least, before it flared up (again) in the mid-Sixties. In the pre-Independence Thirties, protestors Thalamuthu and Natarajan had died in police custody. Though the elected Madras Presidency Government of Congress 'Prime Minister' C Rajagopalachari, popularly known as Rajaji, attributed other causes for their death, the organisers called them 'martyrs' of the 'anti-Hindi imposition' movement.

The subsequent decades also witnessed periodic protests either against Hindi, or against the 'domination' of the North or the Brahmin leadership, both identified with either Hindi or the Sanskrit 'parent', or against both—pepperd with those against price rise and every-day issues of governance and other factors of incumbency. By the time the anti-Hindi agitation gripped the whole of post-Independence Tamil Nadu of the Sixties, the Dravidian political movement in its new, DMK avatar had been around for a decade and a half. After early reluctance, the party had also faced two elections to the State Assembly and the nation's Parliament. At the time of the anti-Hindi agitation, it had started smelling power in Tamil Nadu, still called 'Madras State'.

The DMK came to power in the State, through the historic Assembly elections of 1967. Just three years earlier, the protests had been the cause of many college/university students losing their lives in police firing. For the first and only time in post-Independence Tamil Nadu, the army had to be called in to control street-violence. By the time the anti-Hindi agitation had engrossed and enveloped the State, the DMK had established a commendable campaign strategy and had commendable strategists at all levels, who also doubled as lower-level electoral organisers.The party also had young, inspiring public speakers, who could 'move mountains through the very power of their Tamil oratory'. The Tamil youth of that generation aspired to acquire similar oratorical skills and identified with these leaders—and by extension, the ideologies that they professed and politics that they practised. Among them were DMK founder Annadurai, actor-politician MGR and Karunanidhi. The followers of the new political creed accepted whatever was on offer, whatever they were asked to do. In a way, it resembled, the days of the freedom movement, when the average Indian youth readily jumped onto the Congress bandwagon.

The anti-Hindi agitation, or the protests against 'imposition' of the language, did involve burning of the relevant constitutional provision, but there was no real defiance of any court order, *per se*. In contrast, the Jallikattu protests were nothing but a demand for restoring the traditional martial sport of the people. It was same as the State's demand over the Cauvery water dispute andthe Mullaperiyar storage issue, and other greater concerns of the Tamil Nadu population. In all such earlier cases, the public protests and political calls for the same were all confined to protesting against the neighbouring State—and their governments, not the people—and these only urged the Centre to do enough. There was no sign whatsoever that even remotely amounted to challenging any order of the Supreme Court, in letter and/or in spirit. Even the Kudankulam protests of the more recent origin did not involve any possible or plausible defiance of judicial verdicts and orders, including interim orders of whatever kind.

Compared to the rest, in the case of the Jallikattu protests, the organisers, if anyone could be identified and even arraigned as such, did not belong to a political party or even led any one of them. There had been those in the past, like those on the Sri Lankan Tamil cause and the Cauvery waters row, when the

State government itself had given protest-calls and also 'enforced' it, so to say. This also meant that the organisers of the protests could be arraigned for 'contempt of court', which when it involved the nation's highest judicial body came with political consequences that were beyond comprehension. Having sworn or vowed to work under the nation's constitutional scheme, no political party or leader, or such other institutional organiser calling for such agitations, could bring himself up to defying, and be seen as defying the Constitution and the Judiciary. It went beyond their apprehensions about consequences or fear of penalty or punishment, including imprisonment for a term. To them, like with the much of the rest of the nation's polity, it was all an inherent article of faith.

The only noticeable exception in this case was/is that of then Uttar Pradesh Chief Minister Kalyan Singh committing to uphold law and order in Ayodhya on 6 December 1992, but not standing by that commitment when the disputed structure was being brought down. After the Supreme Court penalised him with a day-long 'imprisonment', political leaders elsewhere too did learn their lessons. But not necessarily the youthful apolitical/non-political organisers of the Jallikattu protests, as some individuals and groups were seen to be. Anyway, they all belonged to a generation well removed from that of the 'Ayodhya demolition' and Kalyan Singh's day-long imprisonment.

The Ayodhya-linked defiance of court orders apart, Tamil Nadu and especially the citizenry, was also not the first State to do so, even otherwise. The reverse is the truth. The Centre, unwittingly and unintentionally, may have set an unhealthy precedent when both the Modi government and the predecessor Manmohan Singh dispensation, seemingly over looked and ignored successive observations of the Supreme Court of India in the 'Aadhar card case', and at every turn. Not only that, the Centre continued to go ahead with the implementation and/or enforcement of the scheme, in every sector of the administration, and for every use by every citizen of the country, in every which way, even as the Supreme Court ordered its suspension, pending the final disposal of the case. Even now the court is trying get the banks to abide by its ruling, and has also constituted a Constitution Bench to hear the case, where the Centre seems determined to push through the 'digital reform' of the Aadhar variety.

Unlike the Jallikattu, or even the Cauvery water dispute where the average Tamil had a lot and more direct and even more immediate stake, the 'Aadhar card', its implementation or imposition impacts every Indian, all 125 crores, or 1.25 billion. Each one of them sharpens his ears to the local TV news channels every time the word 'Aadhar' is pronounced or anything to do with the Aadhar card is announced. Reading newspapers and understanding them requires a citizen to know reading, if not writing. Viewing the local TV news in the local language, and more so, hearing and listening requires only the faculty of hearing. Native wisdom has endowed our people with a sense of comprehension, at least to the extent that he understands that he does not understand, and to seek clarification from those he thinks in the neighbourhood would know better. With the continual defiance or seeming defiance of the Supreme Court observations in the Aadhar card case, the Centre itself seems to be setting an unhealthy precedent for the people to follow the ruler. It is the reverse of the Sanskrit saying, '*Yatha raja, tatha praja*'. The Tamil equivalent is equally poignant: '*Mannan ev-vazhi, makkalav-vazhi*'. Both mean the same: 'People follow the sovereign'.

In a nation where people have not lost faith in the Judiciary, owing to cultural tradition, historic mooring and socio-constitutional realities, and have greater faith and respect for the Judiciary than any other constitutional institution, in 2016, the Centre's continuing diatribe on the Supreme Court over the appointment and transfer of Judges too took its toll on the people's unassailable faith in the system—where they are already disillusioned with the rest. Every new generation born in the post-Independence era has also been witness to the government of the day at the Centre, clashing with the Supreme Court of India in matters of judicial appointments, elevations and transfers. Independent of justification or otherwise, it happened during Indira Gandhi's time, pre-Emergency. Now, it is happening again, though the comparison should stop here. So people's own respect for the institutions, though not the Constitution, faces constant stresses and strains. The weaker among them get a wrong message, and top it up with their own interpretations and analyses of other events and developments, and arrive at equally avoidable conclusions that are patently wrong.

In a State like Tamil Nadu, the unusually and even more inexplicable long delays in the final disposal of the 'Jayalalithaa assets case' and the '2-G scam cases' all added their own share. Over the past decades, the independent courses that the Cauvery water case with Karnataka and the Mullaperiyar reservoir storage dispute with another neighbour Kerala, have left only a bad taste in the mouth of the average Tamil, even granting the political motivation of his leaders and government in the State. Different Benches of the Apex Court, for instance, admitted, though not always allowed, interlocutory petitions filed by one or the other of the four accused in the Jayalalithaa case, long after a Bench of Brother Judges had ordered a fast-track trial. Less said thus about a Karnataka High Court Judge upturning the trial court's conviction and harsh sentencing of the four accused in the case the better.

As is also known, the average Indian may not know the nuances of constitutional law. But almost each one of them has a fair idea about some common aspects of criminal law(s), especially such as the relevant provisions for granting bail to an accused. The accused is not arrested in most cases. And people may have stood guarantee for those that the courts let out on bail. In the present-day milieu, every village has produced at least half a dozen professionals, including lawyers, who handle the cases of or between the local people, invariably friends or relatives, who all have a fair understanding of the law of the land, their interpretation and enforcement by the Judiciary and implementation by the Executive.

So, when the Supreme Court granted bail to Jayalalithaa and others, when the accused approached it after denial by the Karnataka High Court following the trial court handing down a four-year jail term, questions were freely asked in the Tamil/Tamil Nadu social media. As may be recalled, for a four-year jail term, only the High Court, and not the trial court, could be approached for granting bail. While Justice A C Chandrashekhara denied bail, when approached, later on after full hearing in the appeals case, Justice C R Kumaraswamy acquitted them all. In between, the accused appealed to the Apex Court for bail after a firm 'No' by the High Court.

The social media questions after the Apex Court granting Jayalalithaa and others bail were not at all about the Supreme Court's power and authority in the matter, or the fact of it granting bail, either. It was about the *court granting bail without even ordering notice to the State of Karnataka, the prosecuting agency, that too appointed by the very court years ago.* That much of law, the people have come to know after watching high-decibel talk-shows in local television news channels. Some social media material also referred to the fact that the Supreme Court had long ago directed the Bengaluru trial court to conduct a speedy trial, yet ended up having to hear interlocutory petitions from one or the other accused, the effect of which was to hold up the trial. Suggestions thus came to be made for legislative or judicial processes to ensure that interlocutory petitions, especially to appellate courts, should be clubbed together with the final appeal, in such other cases in the future.

Unfortunately, many in the social media also overlooked the very fact that it was only after the Supreme Court Bench hearing the bail petitions coming down heavily on the accused (especially Jayalalithaa) and also the State government that all violence, public and talk-show criticisms apart from caricaturing of trial Judge Michael de Cunha, all stopped forthwith. The protests across Tamil Nadu, and even within the Karnataka High Court premises and neighbourhoods in Bengaluru, all of which tantamount to 'contempt of court' came to a sudden halt, only after the Supreme Court's caustic observations to the senior counsel for the defence. If someone thought that through street-protests, and (allegedly inflated) number of pro-Jayalalithaa suicides across Tamil Nadu (alone) would help retrieve the legal situation, the higher Judiciary ensured otherwise.

As the Bench observed—rather the Judges went, instead, by the honourable commitment of Jayalalithaa's veteran of a lawyer, respected jurist and Senior Counsel, Fali Nariman—that all protests would stop forthwith and that his client would not stir out of her Poes Garden home, in anyway violating the expressed and implied bail conditions. Incidentally, the AIADMK later distributed Rs 7 crore to the families of 244 suicide victims, amidst days and weeks of street violence since the trial court verdict. This was apart from all the damage caused to public property during the cadre-protests across the State, against the trial court sentence and the High Court's denial of bail.

Contrast this with all the protests against Jallikattu ban yielding to the State government promulgating a facilitating Ordinance and following it up with a regular legislation, and the picture is complete. Only months later, the Supreme Court Bench hearing the 'NEET case' passed severe oral strictures against the Tamil Nadu government, directing it to ensure the restoration of law and order (or, face the—legal and constitutional—consequences). The State government complied in this case and ensured over the days that the anti-

NEET protests, especially after the suicide of one girl, Anitha, did not become an unmanageable law and order situation. In comparison, again, in the 'Jayalalithaa bail case', the protests stopped within minutes of the court ticking off the petitioners, none of whom was in power but were in prison in another State at the time. All of it should speak volumes for the processes.

Ingenious Circumvention

It is all not only about people occupying the highest elected office in the State or even the country. It is also about State governments as institutions, starting with Tamil Nadu. The Madras High Court, for instance, has lost count of the number of cases in which the Tamil Nadu government has stopped bothering about implementing judicial orders, with the result Judges and Benches have been forced to tick off high officials, summoned specifically to the bar of the court, to remind them of something called the 'contempt of court law'.

Not very infrequently, the court has also been compelled to summon senior officials to be present, if only to force them to file their sworn affidavits that had not been done for long. Invariably, in most such cases, either junior officials collect the data and the government legal team puts together the papers for the official concerned to read and affix his signature—or, there are policy decisions that those above him, and at times including him, would have to take and inform the court accordingly. In the post-protests weeks and months after Jallikattu-2017 and even earlier, the High Court thus felt the need to summon high-ranking officers of the civil administration and the police force, whenever they were found wanting in giving due respect to court orders, at times followed by summons.

But there is yet another case in which the State government found what could only be described as ingenious or 'devious' ways to circumvent express orders of the Supreme Court, again after the Jallikattu protests of 2017. In its wisdom, the court passed orders to shut down all liquor shops along all National Highways and State Highways, across the country. The court rationalised that with liquor outlets on main highways, truck and other vehicle drivers were tempted and they tended to consume liquor rather excessively. This in turn contributed to the increasing number of avoidable road accidents, causing numerous deaths and untold miseries to the affected families.

Tamil Nadu is the only State in the country where the State government not only owns and runs retail liquor shops and low-end bars, but also has a monopoly over the retail sale of all liquor brands, Indian and 'foreign', the later covering the likes of whiskey, brandy, beer and wine. Contrast this with the enviable record of the then Madras Presidency under then Prime Minister Rajaji introducing prohibition in pre-Partition India for the first time, and the clock has come more than a full circle. Admittedly, a substantial share of the State's revenue now comes from liquor revenues, in sales income and also taxes and duties.

In the face of unending protests at the height of the 2016 Assembly poll campaign, the ruling AIADMK under late Chief Minister Jayalalithaa was also committed to introducing total prohibition in a phased manner. This was against the rival DMK announcing total prohibition from day one, if elected to power. On returning to office for a continuous second term (and the highest-ever sixth term for any chief minister in the State), Jayalalithaa ordered the closure of 1,000 liquor vends at one-go, and promised more in the coming months. However, she was hospitalised soon enough and passed away. The government of Chief Minister Edappadi K Palanisami that was in office, when the Supreme Court ban came about, had ordered the closure of 500 more liquor shops when it took over the reins.

However, when the Supreme Court order finally came, the State government did not shut down 3,500-odd shops as it was expected to do. If the party and the government were serious about the poll promise, they would have conceded that those shops would have to go sooner or later. So what if the sudden closure of those shops cut a deep hole in the State Treasury? But if the government was serious about the poll commitment, then they should have found out alternatives very long ago, ready for implementation. That was not to be.

Instead, once the court orders came about, the Tamil Nadu government shifted these shops away from the national and State highways, and just moved them into the interiors. This defeated the very purpose of the Supreme Court order, but the State government did not care. However, the local population, especially the women folk in localities wherever the new outlets were put up, were concerned. They protested, and at times attacked the new shops or the chosen buildings, still under preparation or construction. This meant that the State government's ingenious attempt to hoodwink people had failed.

It then looked at an even more dubious option. That was to have the local bodies across the State, starting with the municipal corporations in the cities, starting with capital Chennai, to take over the various national and State highways passing through their jurisdiction for better administration and management. This meant that even in the original sites from where they were sought to be shifted to interior villages, near schools, hospitals and places of worship, none came under the known classification of national or State highways. The liquor outlets could continue to operate from the original shops.

New 'New Year'

There is no denying the dubious distinction of the Dravidian polity in other issues of social, cultural and at times religious relevance. Similar instances can be cited elsewhere, too, but in the case of Tamil Nadu, it was when DMK's Karunanidhi, (as the Chief Minister in his fifth and more recent term, 2006-11 and probably the last one) changed the Tamil New Year celebrations from mid-April to Pongal day, in mid-January.

As per Hindu religious traditions and social customs, the New Year is born with the advent of the Tamil month of '*Chiththirai*', falling on 14/15 April. Not only religious ceremonies and astrological predictions (which Karunanidhi bemoans in others but is said to be secretly practising himself) but even social practices and economic activities often linked to agriculture, especially paddy cultivation, have centred on calculations with Chiththirai as the first month of the Tamil New Year. The change-over was a political message of sorts when pan-Tamil sentiments had remained on the surface and did not go far deep, as used to be the case in the Fifties and the Sixties, though arguments and justifications, quoting Tamil literary references, are being cited to say why the mid-April commencement is only that of the 'Hindu calendar', and not the 'Tamil New Year', whose birth should only be in mid-January.

That Jayalalithaa and the AIADMK, on return to power in 2011, promptly restored the original Tamil New Year, should go without saying. Jayalalithaa's restoration had nothing to do with the 'competitive' Dravidian politics. Instead, it had everything to do with social beliefs and customs that the Tamil community believed in and practised for generations, centuries and millennia. To the limited extent that DMK leaders who may still swear by Karunanidhi's 'calendar reform', which was only a shift of the New Year, nothing more, nor less, they at least should preclude themselves from arguing the case for Jallikattu, based on Tamil customs and traditions.

Early on as Chief Minister in the Seventies, Karunanidhi had also declared Mattu Pongal, or the day after the main Pongal festivities when alone Jallikattu season too commences, as the birth day of Tamil saint-poet Thiruvalluvar. He also introduced the 'Thiruvalluvar Year, or '*aandu*', which still finds mention in all State government notifications and press releases, with no one really taking any notice whatsoever, even years and decades down the line. Unlike the shifting of the Tamil New

Year change-over that Jayalalithaa corrected promptly, neither she, nor her mentor MGR as the AIADMK Chief Minister in their time, did anything to revisit or reverse the new 'Tamil calendar', centred on a non-existent birthday celebration for Thiruvalluvar. This owed mainly to the fact that Tamils did not seek to replace the Gregorian calendar. The fact is that such contrived attempts by the political class in a belated realisation of unexplained and not-so-popular schemes have only taken the seriousness of the 'identity discourse' of the kind that Jallikattu and Jallikattu protests have flagged since. So, when larger and more identifiable issues as Jallikattu becomes the cause, there are still those among the Tamils in the State who see it in a less serious light, and not necessarily for any ideological fault on their part.

There is an urban elitist concept of 'moral standards', which, however, keeps changing from individual to individual, over individual to individual. Given the greater levels of urbanisation that Tamil Nadu has achieved over the past decades—it is the highest in the country at 50-per cent and more in the country—and the speed with which it has been achieved, the political and administrative class have failed to keep up with the unfamiliar concept that they are yet to acknowledge in social transformations and intelligent interpretations to issues and situations and intellectual pursuits that are still believed to remain 'class sensitive'. Unacknowledged by them in context, and unknown to the rest of the country, *the social transformation of rural Tamil Nadu has revived a sagging sense of personal pride in the individual, which takes a collective, community form and shape on occasions like Jallikattu, where the 'collective consciousness' of the people find expression.*

The political class seeks to codify it as directed at the Centre and elsewhere, not towards itself—again, born out of ignorance than arrogance. This consciousness is felt more often on the streets of foreign nations, where a strong community of Tamils from the country work, live and live mostly in isolation as individuals and families, interacting limitedly with fellow-Tamils and fellow-Indians on occasions. In the mid-Nineties, they felt a sense of pride that 'two *veshti*-clad Tamils', DMK Chief Minister Karunanidhi and his electoral ally and infant Tamil Maanila Congress (TMC) founder, the late G K Moopanar, became king-makers at the Centre. It was a return to the days of Tamil/Dravidian (?) glory', through another veshti-clad Tamil—the late Kamaraj—who had presided over Delhi's 'political durbar' as a gentle colossus.

In the years and decades after the Nineties, the very same Tamils felt shamed, and were made to feel ashamed, by reports of Jayalalithaa's birthday celebrations when ministers ate '*mann choru*', or sand as prasad, and by her long secretive hospitalisation that soon reached a new, low levels of a 'Greek tragedy' and worse. So did the sibling-rivalry in rival DMK's 'first family' for a decade and more. In particular, criminal cases involving their own political class, like those against Jayalalithaa and Karunanidhi's daughter Kanimozhi, MP, in the 2-G scam, all made them all bow their heads in shame before fellow-Tamils from elsewhere, especially neighbouring Sri Lanka, in their common workplace, overseas.

Nearer home, they were rubbing shoulders with fellow-Indians in the IT corridors of Bengaluru and Hyderabad, Delhi and Mumbai, where again the story was no different. No one has understood the depth of this aspect of the 'Tamil angst' in shaping the Jallikattu protests, nor have local politicians and administrators, contributors to the same, want to acknowledge it, even if they have understood that it does exist.

The Last Straw

Yet, the immediate provocation for the Tamil protests on Jallikattu, other than the court-imposed ban, rested elsewhere. This flowed from what the ordinary Tamils felt were wanton and callous disrespect of the Supreme Court orders by neighbouring States in matters that were of great concern to Tamil Nadu and its people. In the Cauvery and Mullaperiyar cases, the Supreme Court had invariably given verdicts or passed orders that had upheld Tamil Nadu's case. However, both States, in turn, had 'defied' those verdicts and orders with 'absolute impunity'. Whoever or whichever party was in power at the Centre, and whoever be their alliance partners from Tamil Nadu in the coalition government over the previous decades, nothing came of such court orders.

There can be no denying that the Constitution of any country is made by wise people, for such other wise and law-abiding people to follow and implement. Such submissions about the constitutional niceties and behavioural proprieties by State governments apart, the Tamil people have all along felt hurt and dismayed, discouraged and frustrated. There was thus an overwhelming sense of frustration, bordering on betrayal in some, over the courses that these two cases in particular had taken, more especially in the recent phases and times, closer to Jallikattu-2017.

There was a proverbial last straw, still. It came in the form of the Centre's submission in the Cauvery water case, where the Karnataka government, with the full backing of all parties in that State, both inside and outside the Legislature, had repeatedly declined to 'follow/obey' the Supreme Court's more immediate directions for releasing a limited quantum of water, put at a low 2,000 tmcft at one stage, to Tamil Nadu. The directions on water-released derived from the recommendations of the Cauvery Water Tribunal, appointed by the Centre, as per a court directive, long ago. The Centre had also notified the Tribunal award, and the Supreme Court too had upheld the same. The limited quantities that the Supreme Court ordered through much of the 2016 Cauvery water season were a fraction of the award-commitments for Tamil Nadu, but Karnataka too cited poor rainfall and storage levels in its Cauvery reservoirs, to be of help.

In early October 2016, then Attorney-General Mukul Rohatgi told the Supreme Court so very unexpectedly that Judiciary could not order the Centre to set up the Cauvery Water Management Board (CWMB), as directed earlier. Only days earlier, on 30 September, had the court directed the Centre to do so within four days and report back. To be fair to the court, and also to Tamil Nadu, in a purely legal context, the setting up of the Board was a long-pending recommendation of the Tribunal. The Centre too had acted upon such recommendations in the earlier phases of the case, which has had a nasty habit of showing up at the commencement of every 'Cauvery water season', coinciding with the arrival of the south-west monsoon in June. It is one thing for the Centre to report to the court on the impossibility of the task, given especially Karnataka State's total lack of cooperation in the matter. It is another thing for the Centre to take an unexpected decision—and do so, so late in the day—to tell the nation's highest judicial forum that it did not have the authority in this regard. It is an added fact that the Board was a product of the Centre-initiated processes under the Inter-State River Disputes Act, and the Supreme Court was only seeking to enforce the same.

In a way, the court directive of 30 September 2016 may have provided the Centre with an occasion to tell the Karnataka State that its hands were tied. It had also been a kind of standard operational practice that governments, both at the Centre and in the States, had followed when faced with impossible situations of the kind. It was so under successive regimes at the Centre over the previous decades, drawn as their Prime Ministers and partners were, from different political parties and distinct notions about the larger concept of 'federalism' and 'power-sharing' among the various arms of the Indian State. In doing so, Attorney-General Rohatgi submitted that such a course as the setting up of the Cauvery Water Management Board could be taken up only by the Legislature, and not by the Judiciary. Again, it was just a coincidence that the two cases, on the Cauvery water dispute and the Jallikattu issue, were heard by a Bench headed by Justice Dipak Misra, since elevated as the Chief Justice of India in due course and following the due process.

In the Cauvery Board case, Attorney-General Rohatgi submitted before the Bench that the court should not have asked the Centre to set up the Water Management Board as the main civil appeal by the Karnataka government on the issue was still pending. He also submitted that the Centre was not a party before the Cauvery Water Disputes Tribunal, which alone had recommended the setting up of the Water Management Board involving Cauvery riparian States. 'Since the Central government was not a party to the proceedings before the Tribunal, it did not have opportunity to submit to the Tribunal that the Tribunal will not have any power of recommending the creation of a Board as suggested. Setting up of a Board is part of legislative exercise…' In this context, a petition presented by the Centre 'submitted that constitution of a Board as suggested by the Tribunal and ordered by this court on 20 September is not contemplated by the statute. By setting up of a Board of this nature, the Central government is denuded of its power under the Act of 1956 (the Inter-State River Water Disputes Act) to frame a scheme based on an award which goes through a legislative process by placing thereof before the Parliament and the final say is vested in the Parliament'.

In doing so, the petition was going back on all the purported commitments and natural follow-up initiatives of successive governments at the Centre. Even more, a petition of the kind, for the first time possibly ever, also contended that the Centre is conscious that the 'sanctity' of the court orders must be upheld besides 'dignity and majesty' of the judicial system. Having submitted as much, the petition went on to say that 'in order to make another attempt to defuse the matter and find an amicable solution, the Central government proposes setting up of a High Power Technical Team'. The petition also named the members of the team.

The Karnataka government's defiant stand against the Supreme Court's order on releasing a limited quantum of Cauvery waters from its limited storage, had shocked the Tamil Nadu government and the people, not only for what it said, but also for the way it kept repeating the same *ad nauseum*, without any respect or regard for the 'sanctity, dignity and majesty' the Apex Court had commanded in the post-Independence scheme of things.

The form and content of Karnataka's submissions before the Apex Court, and its protestations outside *per se* did not surprise anyone, more especially in Tamil Nadu, be it the government or the polity or the larger population, keenly following the possibilities of obtaining irrigation waters in the coming days, without having to wait even for weeks, if rains continued to fail (as it was playing truant for consecutive years and seasons, already). The same could not be said of Tamil Nadu's reaction to the Centre's new line of thought in relation to the setting up of the Cauvery Water Management Board, which had been a taken-for-granted position in the past. Whenever the issue had been agitated, predecessor governments at the Centre had let the impression gain ground that they were only waiting for a Supreme Court direction in the matter, given the complexities of the 'federal principles' of the Constitution and the Indian State structures at the implementation level. Independent of the feelings of the State's people and polity in Tamil Nadu, there are those who are apprehensive about the positions that individual State governments and Legislatures might take in legal and constitutional situation of the kind.

As for Tamil Nadu's population and polity, the apprehension was that the party ruling the Centre (the BJP on this occasion, as against the Congress rival on most others in the past) had taken a political view of things, more than abiding by the spirit of the Constitution and the nation's federal scheme. The State Assembly elections are due in Karnataka in early 2018, and the BJP, it was argued, hoped to return to power, after a gap. The party, it was said, would not want to upset the Karnataka voter, especially in the southern Cauvery delta districts. Against this, Tamil Nadu was/is a non-starter still as far as BJP's electoral fortunes are considered, and the BJP, it was believed, could afford to take a political risk of the kind. This was also unlike all previous Tamil assessment of the 'dual game' that they thought 'national parties' in power at the Centre played on the 'Cauvery water dispute' especially, given the latter's electoral concerns in both Tamil Nadu and Karnataka, depending on when polls were due in either or both of them.

On earlier occasions, the Tamils saw the Centre 'balancing (off)' Tamil Nadu's interests for possible political gains for the ruling party in Karnataka. The argument flowed in the reverse when elections were due in Tamil Nadu. But this was the first time that Tamil Nadu felt being left naked and nude before the nation's all-embracing constitutional scheme, that too by the Centre which they had been told was the 'lord protector' of every interest and concern of every stake-holder—and believed as an article of faith, whatever the political differences and ideological dichotomy. It hurt them, it shocked them, as never before—and the angst and helplessness that they felt as citizens was never felt to be understood by other stake-holders in the constitutional set-up that is what India was/is, since Independence.

Defiance, not the Rule

Yet, it is not as if every State in the Union has defied the Apex Court's orders in one instance or the other. Even with regard to the main 'Jallikattu case' in which the Supreme Court had pronounced its verdict in 2014, Maharashtra, too, was involved as party. It had to do with bullock cart races in the State, which again the Centre's 2011 notification ended up banning. The Bombay High Court had upheld the ban, and it was challenged in the Supreme Court, by race-organisers who had moved the High Court in the first place. The State of Maharashtra did not move the Supreme Court, hence did not even join the Supreme Court's proceedings. Following the Jallikattu protests and revival in Tamil Nadu, news reports claimed that Maharashtra too was considering to move the Supreme Court, to try and revive the local bullock-cart races, too.

In the case of Jallikattu and Tamil Nadu, it was wholly different. The State was involved. Yet, it should also be the last such case, where a State's population comes to the streets and demands that the Centre and the State government defy the Jallikattu ban. As people, the Tamil Nadu population could have defied the ban, by organising Jallikattu on their own, in villages, which were anyway in the interior—or, so went some wishful thinking. It is another matter that the State administration especially could not have claimed, if it had come to such a situation, total ignorance or complete absence of advance-alert from its regular and not-so-regular sources, if the higher judiciary were to intervene, even if *post facto*, and charge it with contempt of the court. Tamil Nadu also being the most urbanised State in the country, the State police and civil administration are known to be effective and efficient still, when given the freedom to act. Even without it, in this era of IT boom, social media growth, internet connectivity and mobile telephony, the courts would call it phoney if the State government were to submit that it was totally unaware of the goings-on at the grass-roots level, if such organised sporting events such as Jallikattu were to be conducted in the rural, semi-urban and at times urban areas of the State.

But it was also the social media that was used extensively to make the protests happen in the first place, and spread and strengthen by each passing hour and each passing day. Considering that the Tamils as a people, given even otherwise to greater sensationalism and sentimentalism—or, that has been the stereotypes that the national media has built up over the post-Independence era—came out in the midst of their festivities and holiday mood, should go a long way in making the rest of India ask as to the why of it, rather than stop with asking about the how of it. More importantly, GenNext that has invariably been credited with making merry over long weekends was the one that was doing the unthinkable, so to say. They were standing in the sun during day, and the chill of Chennai's beach-breeze of the wintery months—and elsewhere, too, in the open. While some slept on the beach sands during nights, others stood guard, especially to ensure the safety of the women among them, not all of them friends or relatives of theirs, many of them unknown to them until that day, and possibly from the day after the end of the protests.

Tamil Winter!

True, winter in Tamil Nadu, barring in a few hilly places, is no comparison to that in the plains of the rest of India, barring of course, neighbouring Kerala. Peaking around Pongal-Makar Shankranti festivities across the country, in January 2017, however, it was a 'Tamil winter' of a different, euphemistic kind. Yet, those people accustomed to the dry heat and sweat of the State's celebrated long summer months, was ready to stand in the dew-like conditions that became prevalent and apparent this season, especially. Better or worse still, this generation that had been living an insular life almost since childhood, with their parents focussing their children's attention all the time on marks and scores since their pre-KG and LKG days, was the one that was actually taking the lead. Yes, in the absence of an organisation, and any exposure to the 'organisational' that they were exposed to, either as IT or other professionals, or as young and upcoming managers in human resources, and as MBA students, they were putting their education and expertise to work, on a different and untested plane altogether.

Fair to the point of conceding it, the experience and expertise of the well-oiled machinery, it should be said that the Tamil Nadu police may have been caught completely off-guard. One main reason for such possible failure of intelligence on the part of the State police and the civil administration was that they were yet to level with the likely uses to which technology could be put. This was so despite the fact that the State police has been completely modernised at all levels, including on the IT front. But it is about an attitude, a mindset, too. It is about the over-reliance on technology and not possibly giving enough attention to the conventional forms of information-gathering, like 'human-int', or 'human intelligence', where foot soldiers of the force would fan out, and return with meaningful and 'actionable' intelligence.

There was a second, and a much more important factor. Not only the governments and their intelligence agencies, but even the so-called organisers of the Jallikattu protests, had not obviously anticipated such a public response to their call, which was not exactly a conventional call for rallies and protests of the kind—but sent out by a group of youth through the social media, defying the conventional routes that political and other organisers in their place had institutionalised over years and decades. The intelligence men possibly were concerned more about who were behind such calls, once it became known that such calls were going out. They were also believed to be aware of the ideological background and organisational structure of those who were sending out such social-media calls, but did not seem to have looked ahead to predict or foresee the possibilities. That was also because, even taken as groups, as different from individuals, they did not number too many, and anyway had their place in the Indian scheme. They also had the freedom to express themselves, in a non-violent way that was not anti-national or secessionist in anyway.

In the light of the Supreme Court verdict that the 'Rajiv Gandhi assassination' was not an 'act of terror' even under the then existing law as applied to the case, and its later-day observation that support-calls for banned organisations (like the LTTE) was not an 'act of terror' in the 'Vaiko case' after Tamil Nadu's MDMK leader was arrested by the Jayalalithaa government, also proved to be a dampener of sorts, from a policing perspective. Rather than thinking ahead, alerting and acting ahead, the administrators, including police administrators, seemed to have been conditioned by the past—both of the perceived organisers and their own institutional memory and behaviour patterns as servants of the State—to go only after the events and developments, so to say.

The Protests: When

WHEN IT all began, none expected the Jallikattu protests to assume such proportions, in breadth and width just in a matter of days. Even the organisers, if any, would not have expectedit—and did notexpect such crowds. Rather, there were no organisers or organisations owning up the anti-ban, pro-Jallikattu protests this time round. It is not as if there had not been any protests in the previous years, whenever the conduct of the sport came under the threat of an imminent or extended ban. Those protests were invariably a gathering of sport enthusiasts in the respective villages. The State government took up the matter with the Centre, pass legislation or go to the courts, and the local polity indulged in competitive politics, giving it an avoidable pan-Tamil colour and leave it at that. At best, traditional Jallikattu organisers or 'village *panchayats*' of local headmen, may have given a call for protests of some kind or the other, but nothing of the gigantic proportions of the 2017 State-wide agitations took place.

The first signs of a possible protest, and the possibility of it getting some traction with the State's population, at least in some select centres, became available a few days before the traditional 14-16 January Pongal-Jallikattu season of 2017. On the morning of 8 January, Sunday, some mobile phone-owners woke up to see a message, mentioning a protest on the Marina sands in Chennai that very evening, and urging them to join in, to press the demand for the conduct of the sport later that week. The SMS and WhatsApp messages had come from someone they knew—either a colleague, or a friend or a relative, whether they had cared to store those numbers earlier, or not. Incidentally, not very many people outside a known circle, or known circles had received the 'call', if it could be dubbed so.

Most 'outsiders' to these 'friends circles' did not even know such a thing was happening, be it the protest-call doing the rounds, or the protest, either. The morning of 8 January had opened as a relatively uneventful Sunday. After weeks and months of high tension attending on the late Chief Minister Jayalalithaa's hospitalisation, deteriorating health, later her death after 75 days, and the political high drama(s) that had followed, not many were even in a mood to tune on to TV channels, news or not, for any update on anything spicy. If anything, many had missed it all, until later in the day or the next day, when the local media began catching up with what was still a token demonstration, and nothing more. None of the participants either seemed to have thought of it as a trial-balloon or considered the possibilities of participating in the 'real thing' only a week or so later.

At the Marina on the evening of 8 January, hundreds and thousands—not hundreds of thousands—of weekend revellers had gathered, as usual. The weather in January was pleasant, and families had been visiting the beaches and other places of visitor's interest after months of self-doubt, caused by Jayalalithaa's health condition and later on, by Cyclone Vardha and consequent destruction and disruptions. Among them were some who had (also) responded to the protest-call, for the conduct of Jallikattu. Conservative estimates put the figure at around 5,000. Other, more ambitious estimates, especially the more sympathetic sections of the social media, claimed that up to 20,000 people had participated. Many of the 'participants' came with family members, including infants. Most of the participants were also young, whether single or couple, or as a group of friends. Many, though not all, were living alone in the city, and the young couple among them constituted nucleus families. So, the infant on a Sunday afternoon especially could not have been kept out unless they decided to stay back home, themselves. After all, it was the much-awaited weekly-off for their domestic helps and the child-minders that at least some of them had employed. All of it, however, also indicated the socio-economic class from which many of these protestors came. Most of them were educated and gainfully employed.

Less ambitious

Barring lesser-known politicos from an earlier generation or two, who too had responded to the social media calls from friends and admirers, there were not many grey-haired people in the crowds. It was the first time after the 'Moopanar rebellion' against the ruling Congress leadership of Prime Minister P V Narasimha Rao's intention to join hands with the 'corrupt' Jayalalithaa-led AIADMK in Elections-96 full two decades earlier, preceded by Vaiko-centric 'second split' in the DMK in 1993, that so many young faces had gathered for a 'cause'. Unless someone had taken a closer look, or if he had not understood the Tamil slogans that were being shouted and/or read the placards that were both in Tamil and English, any bystander or passer-by would have assumed that it was one of the 'corporate' campaigns on product-promotion or some social cause or the other, organised by some NGO and/or funded by corporate, as a part of the their 'CSR projects'. A keener observer would have noticed that the campaigners that evening were not wearing the standardised 'uniform' T-shirts and/or caps, customised for individual occasions, with a legend written all across the front and the back. Their children, who too had got used to such sights on Sunday mornings on the Marina especially, would have been looking around for a celebrity (preferably a film-star) for flagging off the event.

None of this paraphernalia was visible, nor was any of it around that evening. Film-stars and politicians would make a beeline for the real event a week later, most of them only to be booed out by the participants. One after another the 'organisers' trooped in, so did their friends and the latter's invitees. Then, they took out what should be considered a less ambitious march from the Gandhi Statue to the 'Triumph of Labour' Statue, both at different points on the same beach, which from end-to-end measured around 13 km. The full length often used to be the distance for 'welfare Marathons', if Sunday morning to-do's could be called so. The selected route for that evening covered only 2 km.

But the more steps the protestors took, more confident the organisers among them became. At the closing venue, more people had joined them, and even more had stopped by to take a look—and also stay back a few more minutes to assimilate what was happening. Later that evening, the social media got busier than in the morning, or the previous evening. More pictures of the evening's rally began doing the rounds, and more people than those who had sent out the invites for the rally were sending the pictures around. The Tamil TV news channels especially were adding the much needed pep, and talk-show time to spread the message. The average guy who had given himself and his TV set rest through the day, if he had switched on his favourite news channel by dinner-time the evening's event was there with his supper. A day later, TV talk-shows discussed the psychology and pathology, and whatever other '-ology' was available to dissect the protests, making them more popular.

It was not only in Chennai. On day one, picking up or sharing the WhatsApp and/or SMS messaging style, counterparts in the temple-town of Madurai also sent out calls for a similar protest/rally, demanding the conduct of Jallikattu. Among the bigger cities, Madurai is central to the sport in the State, and more so in the southern region, where the city is located. Protestors gathered in equal, if not more numbers, in Madurai, but it did not stop there. Over the next couple of days, symbolic protests came to be organised in other cities, towns and villages across the State, demanding Jalliattu. The culprit, if it all it could be called so, or the enabler, if that's the word, was the social media. Yet, the organisers remained unnamed, and unknown. They would remain mostly so until after the final, big protests a week later. Rather, the 'real organisers' of the bigger protests, especially in Chennai,still remained outside the pale of identification and recognition for the average common man, at times including those that had participated in those protests for one hour and more, or for one day and more.

Some later-in-the-day social media claims on the day the 'symbolic protest' said that at some local churche(s) in the vicinity, the 'Jallikattu issue' had formed a part of the Sunday morning. The claims could not be denied as most such reports did not name any church. Nor did those reports prove the claim/charge beyond reasonable doubt. But this added a new twist, which however went promptly unnoticed—and rightly so. Unlike in States like neighbouring Kerala, where for instance, the Christian community celebrates the annual harvest festival of *Thiru Onam* in the Malayalam month of *Chingham* (August-September), the equivalent Pongal festivities in Tamil Nadu have mostly remained a Hindu religious affair.

As Justice Bhanumathi had observed in her 2006 High Court judgment banning Jallikattu, the sport was 'fun' on the one hand and a 'veera vilayattu,' or a sport of valour on the other. Barring the oormaadu, or the local temple bull, whose progress should not be stopped, every other animal coming out of the Vaadi Vaasal was fair game. It was so even after some villages, especially in southern Kanyakumari district, began celebrating Pongal as a community event over the past decade and more, involving all religions. However, Jallikattu is not known to Kanyakumari district (though later after the protests began, the district bordering neighbouring Kerala, of which it was also a part until 1956, would join in, all the same).

Religion and Religious Beliefs

In villages where Jallikattuhas been in vogue, the local temple bull is the first animal to be presented at the *Vaadi Vaasal*, but stopping it is believed to bring the curse of Gods on the person concerned and the village concerned, alike. That is the only religion-related part of Jallikattu. If local Christian or Muslim communities had ever organised Jallikattu likewise, there are no records or publicity. In their case, however, the same rules regarding oor-maadu is followed. Overall, organisers, animal owners and bull-tamers are all mostly religious, even otherwise. Considering that taming a bull in some venues is a prestigious affair, there will always be prayers for the good wishes of the gods. The animal at times gores tamers, and they face the risk of being gored as much as others. There again, prayers are in order. Yet, most owners and tamers are Hindus by religion, and have invariably belonged to the martial three-sect Mukkulathore caste(s) Traditionally, the sport was also confined to the vicinity of Madurai and Tiruchi cities, far away from the epicentre of the 8 January protests. Not by design, but more by accident, Chennai and the Marina also became the epicentre of the main protests a week or so later, drawing mutual strength and sustenance from others of the kind.

If, hence, reports of church sermons in favour of Jallikattu in Chennai were true and had also triggered some queries and interest, they were all submerged in the festive mood of the week after, and were washed away in the tsunami that the main protests became. By the time the protests ended, and did so violently, especially in Chennai again, some of these issues were flagged again in sections of the social media. They were neither taken too seriously, nor were they acted upon, one way or the other. The sum total of such allegations, as they had to be called thus in the absence of concrete evidence to the contrary, was that various peripheral groups had taken an extraordinary interest in the protests, both before it became a mass event, and as it began winding down following the State Assembly passing a Bill facilitating the conduct of Jallikattuin 2017 without further delay.

This time, however, the religious element—it could apply to all religions at the local levels—was more evident in one other factor. Speaking on TV and to the print media, local women in villagers where Jallikattu had to be stopped last year owing to the Supreme Court ban, were seen declaring that the rains had failed the region only because the discontinuance of the sport, as the gods were upset and cursed the local population. It is a common belief in almost every religion and caste-groupings across the country, that gods do punish wrong-doings and wrong-doers. In this *Kali Yug*, god too does not reserve the punishment to a future birth in which Hinduism believes. The punishment is instant, in the very same birth. To them, non-conduct of Jallikattu, whether it owed to the ban or not, was wrong-doing.

As the main protests began spreading from one village to another, from one district to another, and from one region to another, this message also kept spreading. Yet, no one was known to have asked anyone why in the years, decades and centuries when Jallikattu had not faced any problems, the rains had failed, still. But then, these are harsh and hard beliefs, which cannot be and should not be over-rationalised. It only ends up as the questioner mocking at the beliefs of his fellow villagers and countrymen, which no system or no religion relishes. Nor do the believers like and respect such an approach.

Not Paid-for Crowd

Just like the 8 January 'token protests' or 'symbolic protests' demanding Jallikattu this year, even the main agitation a week later began without much preparation, organisation or 'notification', seeking people's participation—or, at least in ways known to the rest and/or in ways the rest had known. Time used to be when gathering a million party cadres at a venue for political rallies in Tamil Nadu was not a great difficulty. Yet, months of preparations and publicity went into them. Even the rally-venue (invariably political party conferences) would be competitively decorated, so as to draw media attention and cadre appreciation, apart from political rivals and apolitical onlookers in large numbers. The night decoration of the massive venues (invariably thatched *pandals*) with colourful lamps has always remained a talk of the town concerned and across the State. This enthused their party counterparts and rivals to do betterso as to win a word of appreciation from their leaderships concerned.

As the new millennia approached and the new century commenced, gone were the days when even the most popular of political parties and the most charismatic of political or even religious leaders could command a crowd of even a hundred thousand on a regular basis. A few thousands were in order, anything above that would gather only ahead of election-time, or if the crowd had been paid-for even otherwise. In this environment, for the Jallikattu protests (rather than the protestors) to collect anywhere between half a million to one million participants in Chennai alone was not only astonishing but also astounding.

Definitely, they were not paid-for crowds.

It did not stop with the numbers. Political rallies are generally held in a single venue if it were to attract large crowds. But the Jallikattu rallies got organised simultaneously in different parts of the State. Unlike political rallies, there were no prior preparations running to hundreds of thousands of rupees, no formal venue with decoration and facilitation for food, shelter and transportation. Why, there were not even any formal invitations plastered all across the State—like 'Kamaraj calls...', 'Annadurai calls...', '*Kalaignar* calls...' (in the name of DMK's Karunanidhi), or '*Puratchchi Thalaivar* calls...' or '*Puratchchi Thalavi* calls...', the latter two referring to AIADMK's M G Ramachandran and Jayalalithaa, respectively, in their time. Nor had the organisers arranged for rows after rows of chairs, tons of food, and thousands of litres of drinking water (more when the political party concerned was in power and could command the resources of the government for the purpose). In the Jallikattu protests, the participants came on their own, some thoughtfully brought food for themselves, and some others brought at least bottles of drinking water for the protestors sleeping in the open air of the venue, overnight. A stage did come when sympathetic store owners and traders' associations would distribute cartons of drinking water bottles, and other sympathisers, biscuits, cakes and fruits.

In some pockets of the Marina protests, packets/cartons of dry fruits too had found their way, to feed and re-energise the protestors and organisers alike. By this time, some of the so-called organisers and even protesting youth had become identifiable and had decided to stay back through day and night—or, at least for the most part. It was no different elsewhere, too, where again, protestors from across the neighbourhood had gathered. Men and women, young and old came, bringing with them their aged parents and/or young children, including infants. To them all, it was fun of a kind but emotional all the same. More to the point, it was a picnic with a greater purpose than ever before, and possibly ever after. It was no different in other venues, especially those that had traditionally hosted Jallikattu.

'Ground Zero' pilgrimage

It was thus that students and other youthful participants in Palamedu, Alanganallur and Avaniyapuram, down south, closer to Madurai, gave out their names and native places on TV cameras—at times they were from Chennai, where the largest protest was already well under way. They declared that they had come all the way, be it from Chennai or Vellore in the North, or Coimbatore or Dharmapuri in the West, to what they called was the 'Ground Zero' of Jallikattu, a term that 9/11 in the distant US city of New York had contributed to the English lexicon a full decade and a half ago.

Many of them confessed that they were on a pilgrimage to those hallowed centres of Jallikattu, though on a normal day, on a normal street, one would not have expected such a reaction from such an age-group on such an eminently forgettable issue. Did they have friends or relatives in those villages where they had joined the local protestors? 'No,' the girls especially said emphatically. 'We came here because we wanted to be here. We wanted to tell our next generations that we were here at this critical phase of our own times.' But where were they the previous day? They were staying either with their families in their native places for Pongal festivities or in their college hostels, or work-place. It was an instantaneous—and at times momentous—decision that they had taken, to travel to these villages whose name some of them might not have even heard of 24 hours earlier, but chose to identify with in the 'larger pan-Tamil cause', which was however dear to them.

What made the protest proper a picnic of sorts was this. Traditionally, the third day of the Pongal celebrations is called the 'Kaanum Pongal'. Translated, it literally means an occasion for visiting friends and relatives, to seek the blessings of elders and exchange greetings and pleasantries with others. Traditionally, it had also included people visiting places of interest in the neighbourhood and beyond, where they could meet with such other friends and relatives—or, total strangers, with whom they would exchange pleasantries and at times food, as well. It has also been a village custom, taken to the urban centres, including metropolitan Chennai (earlier Madras), for people with all family members, young and old, to take food and water, for the whole day, and have an 'eat-out' in the place or places they visit.

In Chennai, Marina has been among the favourite spots, so are the local now shifted to suburban Vandalur, public parks, including private amusement parks, which charge an entrance fee. Every village in the State has its common meeting place, or temple tanks or river-banks, and every town and city, their own venues serving such purposes over years and decades. It is like in any other State or region in the country, and elsewhere, too. In Chennai, Marina being a favourite 'Kannum Pongal' venue and meeting-point, even people who had come from the rest of the city, or even suburbs, joined the protests willingly. They had brought food for the family, and did not think twice to share it with the youth, who were in the age-group of their own sons and daughters. All of it fitted with not only the traditions of the day, but also with the larger Indian customs of sharing food and caring for all, a forgotten custom in the fast-paced life of the present day and generation.

Positive Conspiracy

A combination of factors thus 'conspired' and positively so for most parts, to make the Jallikattu protests possible, and a grand success until violence involving the police and sections of the 'protestors' visited on the venue on the last day—after identifiable leaders of the State-wide Jallikattu movement had declared it 'purposeful' and announced its conclusion. It is still questionable if they were the real organisers of the protests, especially on the Marina sands, or if there were any 'real organisers' at all, in the real sense of the term. For, no organisers had claimed ownership of the protests until controversy started setting in and the government, especially in the State, wanted someone to talk to and negotiate with. To that extent, definitely, yes, those that the government talked to had been involved with the pro-Jallikattu demand over the previous years, as well. Some others were relatively popular in their own right, and that gave them an edge in terms of relative face-recognition.

It was however an entirely different matter if the massive crowds was ready to abide by the call of those celebrities, if they could be called and considered so, for concluding the protests. This was especially so after the State Assembly had passed an enabling Bill, over-riding the Supreme Court's earlier directions, at least for the present. The same went for veterans in the fields of law and public persons with ideological moorings, who welcomed the decision of the State government and the initiative/cooperation of the Centre. They too sought to intervene and explain the salient features of the new legislation.

Inspirational, Intuitive

The conviction for withdrawing the protests—or from the protests—came as intuitively for most participants as their decision to participate in the protests had been inspirational. Those sections of the protestors, especially in Chennai and a few other centres, who refused to withdraw were neither clear on what more did they want, and what kind of assurance/reassurance could convince them after the State Assembly had unanimously passed the enabling Bill, and the Centre had very clearly indicated its willingness to ensure presidential assent for the same without any further loss of time. There were also equally convincing assurances that the Centre would try and ensure that the Judiciary did not intervene this time round.

The fact of police intervention and its contribution to the withdrawal of most protestors from among those that had stayed back, especially in the Marina venue, after the majority had withdrawn also highlighted the absence of formal organisers with a formal leadership—to guide them on the stage and time for stepping back.

It is not that the unexpected and unprecedented success of the protests had gone to the head of the organisers. Instead, whoever remained at the Marina venue after the rest—equally, if not more, sincere though less serious participants—had left were only proving their critics right. The criticism all along had been that those who were really behind sending out the early social media calls for joining the protests either had an ideological or a political agenda, or both.

In the early hours and days of the main protests in particular, a new story doing the rounds attributed the social media reach and spread also to a section of the ruling AIADMK, which was facing internal troubles within the party and purported 'external pressures' from the ruling BJP at the Centre, reportedly to do their bidding in the post-Jayalalithaa political environment. Names did get an occasional mention in private conversations and in the social media itself. But this again did not prove anything, one way or the other.

The motives of the residual protestors in Chennai were claimed to have been anti-national, and their methods aimed at provoking the police especially to come down violently on the peaceful protestors—and also take the blame for the same. As the events and developments of the last hours proved, despite the police acting or reacting to violence, that too in an equally violent way, the provocation for the latter remained to be debated and decided upon.

The State government has appointed a one-man Commission to probe the violence that attended during the end-game of the protests in Chennai. Justice S Rajeswaran, a retired Judge of the Madras High Court, has been named under the Commission of Inquiry Act, for the purpose. At the time of writing, the probe report, whenever presented to the State government, is expected to throw light on the why's and wherefores of the violence, which also brought a bad name to what had otherwise remained one of the most peaceful and most participatory and self-inspiring protests with great community participation that India has seen since Independence. As is done on such occasions, the government started with an initial three-month term for the Commission but has since extended it by three months at a time, justified in turn by the vast turf that the probe has to cover, in geographical terms of where all the Jallikattu protests were held, and especially where they ended in violence or tension–and also the issues that needed addressing for a comprehensive understanding of it all. The question is, if the Rajeswaran Commission will be able to submit its report by mid-November 2017, the State government had extended the Commission's term by another three months, ending 31 January 2018. This would mean that the Commission's report and recommendations may not be ready well in time ahead of the 2018 Jallikattu season commencing in mid-January, for the authorities concerned to study, understand and implement recommendations that are considered worth, if only to try and avoid a repetition of the previous year's events, incidents and episodes.

The Protests: How

WHEN THE main Jallikattu protests began, or happened, it was unlike anything that had been planned, anticipated or hoped-for. Unlike the 8 January 'trial balloon' of a protest, if it could still be called so, the main protests had their origins in Palamedu, one of the traditional venues of Jallikattu, rather *the venue* where the first of the major sport events of the season takes place every year. Unlike elsewhere, the Palamedu Jallikattu happens on the very afternoon of the day of Pongal. Elsewhere, it would be the next day, or the day after 'Mattu Pongal', and 'Kaanum Pongal', respectively. As the Supreme Court itself had taken into account, according to the local customs and traditions in the matter, it would at times extend up to four or five months in the first half of the Gregorian calendar. That way, Mattu Pongal itself was/is all about celebrating the cow, or maadu in Tamil—and by extension, the bull—and thanking and worshipping the animal for all the benefits and benevolence that it has conferred on human beings.

It is a unique celebration of cattle-heads as never done anywhere else in the country, even by those communities that worship the Cow as '*Maa* Lakshmi', the Hindu goddess of wealth. To think that the same people who celebrate and worship the animal only hours earlier will take great pains to derive vicarious pleasure, happiness and merriment by putting the very animals to and through pain and cruelty in the name of Jallikattu should be hard to stomach. This is truer of people of Palamedu, where the piety and peace of the Pongal day of worshiphas to be followed by the Maattu Pongal the next day, with the Jallikattu in between the two—all of it within two days. At least the intention is not there, though the practices may have denigrated into cruelty of some kind, or even one kind or the other.

But that is where the final January protests too began—at Palamedu. Yet, it was only in the Marina, Chennai, that it took real good shape, and a day later. For the Palamedu protest came just a day after the Supreme Court had sharply rebuked and said 'that it found no reason to hear the Union of India on the subject', when the Attorney-General was on his feet.

Would a favourable hearing by the Supreme Court have helped in diffusing the ground-climate in southern Tamil Nadu, from the next day on? It was doubtful, and it would have been doubtful even on that very day if Jallikattu events had not been staged in Tamil Nadu in this year (2017), and an indication to the same was not made available on Friday the 13th, that is 13 January 2017. When the Supreme Court's mind was known and an indication to its mood too came across to drawing rooms across Tamil Nadu, through television news channels, the decision had been made—or was being taken, individually as well as collectively, in the hearts and minds of the people of Tamil Nadu.

Reactive, not Pro-active

So, when the Palamedu protests happened in the afternoon of Pongal Day, Saturday, 14 January 2017, it also provided the cue for a State-wide protest. Having tasted victory—limited but unexpected—only earlier in the week on Sunday, 8 January, the organisers in Chennai and elsewhere got back to work and put together their own teams of social media activists. Unlike on the earlier occasion, this time round there was better coordination, better communication, and better organisation (if, sending out WhatsApp messages from one's own house or work-place can be considered one).

Yet, the first batch of protestors on the first day of the protests on the Marina sands did not number beyond 50. Some have put the figure as low as 38, to be precise. In between, protest-calls had gone out in Avaniyapuram and Alanganallur. The poor handling of the emerging law and order (L&O) situation at the protest venues in some places was believed to have angered the local population to come out in larger numbers than might have been thought possible. Chennai was no different. But weeks and months later it is still doubtful if the State government in particular had a full picture of the situation that was emerging, or was likely to emerge.

With the result, the government's reaction politically, and the police action on the law and order front were more reactive than pro-active. It helped the protests gather both momentum and strength with each passing hour, but after a point it became clear that any intervention of the kind, especially thoughtless interventions, could have brought more people to the protests, or triggered more protests to erupt in newer places and venues than already. There were even reports and analyses about the State government, especially the emerging/existing faction identified with then Chief Minister O Panneerselvam (OPS) within the ruling AIADMK, sympathising with the protestors' cause, if not their methods. There were also additional/opposing reports that other factions within the ruling party, with greater say in and influence over the State's entrenched administrative and police set-up, were out to embarrass, and sabotage the Chief Minister's genuine efforts at finding a solution acceptable to the protestors, whose numbers were growing, nonetheless.

As two-time Chief Minister earlier, Panneerselvam had made himself a butt of all political and not-so-political jokes in the State as the ready-made stop-gap that was dependable and loyal, and nothing more. However, after assuming office as Chief Minister on the night of Jayalalithaa's death in hospital, on 5 December 2016, he had started showing silent signs of breaking from his own past, and past image, as well. For any Chief Minister in his place, reporting to a non-politician in Jayalalithaa's live-in confidante, V K Sasikala Natarjan and her diverse and divided family members, the year-end Cyclone Vardha that ravaged the State capital would have been nightmarish. Much of it would have also gone against the 'oath of secrecy' that the Chief Minister and his ministerial colleagues had taken while assuming office.

Challenge to Opportunity

As things turned out, OPS converted the challenge of managing the post-Vardha ground situation into a personal opportunity, and the opportunity into an occasion to prove his leadership qualities (which none thought he had possessed all along). It was the kind of popularity that came his way within the first weeks of becoming Chief Minister. Both the party cadres and public at large started respecting him, for his clear-cut strategy, free-access to the people and visible freedom for the officials to act, when required. More importantly, the senior bureaucracy, or sections thereof that was tired of inaction on the part of the Jayalalithaa leadership, even when she had not been hospitalised, saw in Pannerselvam, a new hope for the State, and a new leader whom they thought deserved their support and cooperation.

The entrenched political leadership of the party under Sasikala could have none of it, and pat possibly came the decision to let Panneerselvam cook himself in the soup that the Jallikattu issue was fast becoming. They had equally entrenched leaderships in sections of the civil service and the State police force. These sections, it was said, would not respect the Chief Minister, who was still settling down and was seeking to tear himself away from the apron-strings of the emerging Sasikala leadership of the party, and the entrenched family control over the party and the government, even when Jayalalithaa was alive, around and relatively active.

Over the decades, there was developing also a genuine concern for the larger Tamil cause among the civil servants and the police force in the State. Even many non-Tamil officials in the Tamil Nadu cadre of the Indian Administrative Service (IAS) and Indian Police Service (IPS) had begun acknowledging the spirit and justification behind the larger pan-Tamil cause, though they may have a larger distaste for the 'competitive nature' of the State's Dravidian polity. If corruption was the issue, parts of the officialdom had also got decayed through a mutual osmosis process! The politicians alone were not to be blamed. But the pan-Tamil identity, rather identification with the larger pan-Tamil cause, was rampant in the ranks of the uniformed services. It was equally so in other services of the government. Just as it was gaining silent momentum elsewhere, the issue(s)—it was not just one issue of Jallikattu but a cumulative of various issues over a period of time—were obtaining traction from within the government ranks, uniformed and not. Nowhere else was it as evident for a long time as in the Jallikattu protests, when they began. In some venues, as it turned out, TV channels showed police men and junior officers in uniform, swearing by Jallikattu for the whole world to see.

No cause to Act

For all this however, the police did not have a cause to act in the early days of the State-wide protests, as violence was neither on the ground, nor in the air. Unless the police, acting on their own or on the directions of the State government, had tried to stop the protestors from gathering in different venues across the State, there was no way, they could have stopped the protestors on the streets, while proceeding to self-designated rally venues. Two, there was confusion at the administrative-level, both political and bureaucratic, including the police brass, on what was unfolding and how to handle a protest that was massive and at the same time peaceful, so there was no direction for the men on the ground to disperse or otherwise discourage the crowds from gathering. Three, there was genuine sympathy for the larger cause that the protestors were flagging, namely, the 'forced alienation' of pan-Tamil social and political identity that in the eyes of most Tamils had suffered over the previous years and decades. Four, and as important as the rest, a generation of parents had appeared on the scene, who were protective and respectful of their teen-age children's thinking and thought process.

Before the Jallikattu protests in 2017, the 15-day Opposition Congress (O)-led State-wide *Satyagraha* of 1972 was the last peaceful agitation of the kind to have been as much successful. That agitation was against the alleged wrong-doings of the Karunanidhi-led DMK government in the State. One should not overlook the presence and reach of the political organisation that had made it possible. It also meant that a lot of planning, funding, organisation and consultations with the ranks and also the State authorities had preceded them, at times on a daily/hourly basis. Yet, at no place can that agitation, or any other of the kind, violent or peaceful, claim to have attracted hundreds of thousands of participants as the Jallikattu protests brought into the Marina sands in Chennai in 2017.

Came Indira Gandhi's Emergency of the mid-Seventies and much of the campus-driven protest-initiatives of the kind came to a sudden halt, as much in the State as elsewhere in the country.In between, much of the rest of North India, since identified as the 'cow belt', had witnessed unprecedented student protests for the first time since Independence. Dubbed the 'JP movement' after the late socialist leader, Jayaprakash Narayan, who was the inspirational force behind the anti-Indira protests, it would produce new-generation leaders, who would go on to rule the country and the States. The list included present-day Prime Minister Narendra Modi, and the likes of Nitish Kumar, Lalu Yadav, Sharad Yadav and Ramvilas Paswan (all Bihar), Mulayam Singh Yadav (Uttar Pradesh), and the late S Jaipal Reddy and M Venkaiah Naidu (Andhra Pradesh). However, Tamil Nadu was not in the list.So, the Jallikattu protests was also the first one of this magnitude in Tamil Nadu after the anti-Hindi agitation and the Kamaraj-led Satyagraha, both within a matter of six or seven years from each other, when so many students gathered across the State, and also in the same venue, or specified venues. Again, unlike other intervening agitations of the kind like those on the Cauvery water dispute and the Sri Lankan ethnic issue, this was apolitical and remained apolitical till the end.

All of it also meant that unlike the past—be it the days of the freedom movement across the country or the anti-Hindi agitation nearer home in the State—there was no question of parents standing in the way of children getting involved with agitations and police. If anything, most parents saw their children's participation only on the television news channels, or got to hear from them, *post facto*. There was also no doubt in the minds of these young participants, who were the starting-point of the agitation across the State, that their parents would not stand in the way. The fact that most of them were gainfully employed and were respected by peers for what they knew, also worked on their collective psyche. By keeping away politicians and other partisan interests from their movement—which it became on its own from day two of the main protests—the youthful organisers ensured that there would be an overflow of sympathy and support for their cause, more demonstrable than any time in the past. Of course, the organisers' angst was all about politicians purportedly serving only their partisan electoral interests by misleading the State's population on larger pan-Tamil political causes, which actually had larger societal and/or socio-economic dimensions. But by choosing to keep them all away, the organisers had actually, and possibly without predicting the dynamics, had opened up the flood-gates for larger participation.

No Quick-mix

For most of the participants, and those outside, it was the first time since the anti-Hindi agitation that an 'outlet' presented itself to vent their ire, the angst that had remained mostly bottled up in the past. One possible reason was the anxieties about fear gripping the population whenever and wherever such protests had been planned and/or planted through the previous decade and more. Be it on the Cauvery water dispute, or on the Mullaperiyar storage issue, or on the Sri Lankan ethnic cause, or the more recent 'Kudankulam agitation' against nuclear-power, each one of the public agitations had a political organiser. It would put off the rest, and even the apolitical sympathiser of the cause. Compared to them all, the 'fishers' issue' involving neighbouring Sri Lanka, Sri Lankan waters, Sri Lankan Tamil fishers and the Sri Lanka Navy (SLN) was an orphaned cause, so to say. The fishers took pride that they were children of the seas, and there was disconnect between them and their concerns and cause on the one side, and the hinterland population and polity on the other. There isn't enough beingsaid about the fishermen's protests along the south-central Tamil

Nadu coast, against the arrest and/or killing by Sri Lanka Navy personnel, yet.

On issues like Kudankulam, even when the original organisers were apolitical, or claimed to be so—and there was nothing to disprove the claim—the quick mix of the political class meant that neutral observer-sympathisers had problems identifying with the agitation, though not necessarily the cause. The protests drew a lot of sympathy and support despite the fact that the State was reeling under long hours of power-cut during the period, at times up to 16-18 hours per day in many industrial areas as also towns and villages. The early day violence, involving police intervention, also may have put off people from sympathy protests elsewhere in the State. This was despite the sharp, anti-national rhetoric of most speakers, including some of the important organisers of the Kudankulam protests, both in the village and elsewhere in the State, including capital Chennai.

The Kudankulam protests were known as much for the organisational skills as for the larger cause. After a point, it became clear that as much as winning over the cause through peaceful protests, at least a section of the organisers were too deeply interested in consistently and continuously embarrassing the governments of the nation, and the nation as a whole. Once again, it was possibly the delayed realisation of the section of the innocent protestors that they were also being used as a tool in a larger process about which they did not have much clue, either in the beginning or later on, that seemed to have contributed to the protests fizzling out, ultimately.

It is purely a coincidence that elements from the local Church were also seen being active in the anti-nuclear protests in Kudankulam and adjoining coastal villages, where violence and use of 'country-made bombs' to settle group rivalry issues was not uncommon. Of course, neither the Kudankulam protest leaders, nor the Church had anything to do with that kind of violence, which also did not erupt ultimately, but the State government's apprehensions in this regard too were for real.

The 'Kudankulam protests' notwithstanding, in the months and years following, there have been a surfeit of local protests on local and not-so-localised issues across the State, all of them thankfully non-violent but very well organised.Then, there were the not-so-infrequent and near-ubiquitous lawyers' protests on a variety of issues and on court premises across the State, which often involved pan-Tamil causes, rhetoric and at times violence, or anticipation of inevitable violence. Anyway, such protests were confined to a select section of the State's 'elite', and to the court premises, where the common man had no *locus standi* to be seen protesting, if challenged and/or arrested by the police or other authorities.

The unexpected death of Sasi Perumal(60), while climbing up a mobile transmission tower as a part of his peaceful campaign for total prohibition, on 31 July 2015, lent greater momentum, depth and reach to a genuine cause, which went far beyond political branding of any kind. But in the weeks and months that followed Sasi Perumal's avoidable yet accidental death, and running up to the State Assembly elections in May 2016, such protests were mostly localised, with visibly left-leaning organisations, lending leadership. More recently, most anti-demonetisation protests in the State, too, were noticeable for the participation and leadership of left-leaning organisations.

No Cares, No Worries

Thus, there was a multiplicity of circumstances, adopting a similar, if not the same modus and methods, that made the Jallikaattu protests, click. Until late in the day, the protestors, outside of Chennai's Marina, did not raise any anti-national slogans, or slogans that could be construed as anti-national so far as the motives and motivation of at least those sections of the protestors and organisers went. Elsewhere, the 'flags' of the

LTTE, and a few other organisation banned under law across the country, were visible in the early hours, but sympathetic TV media editors seemed to have cut them all out of vision. Later on, better sense seemed to have prevailed, with the result, no visible signs of ideological identification of any section of the protestors or organisers were on display at the venues. No speeches were made in most venues. Even where they were made, it was confined only to the history of the Jallikattu case and a case for Jallikattu, and the historicity of the martial sport from time immemorial.

What was as surprising as the protests and the crowds that gathered was the willingness of the participants to be shown up on television cameras. Many of them were gainfully employed in the IT sector, with opportunities and past occasions of travelling abroad on overseas visas from host countries. Their employers should have been concerned about the future eligibility of some of these boys and girls for obtaining visas for short-duration for on-site work on behalf of the Indian private sector corporations that had been awarded software contracts. Those in the know would suspect that visa officials of host nations in Chennai and the rest of India too would have liked to take a closer look at the faces of protestors that the television news channels had started showing through the day and night, at times with sound-bytes.

There were also among the protestors, students in their final or penultimate semester in professional courses, who had already obtained job-promises in campus interviews. Most other youthful participants in the protests were waiting to be interviewed on campus for jobs when their time was to come up in the next three or six months. Then, there was an emerging and unnoticed group of professional college students, whose sole aim still was not to get into jobs that related to their educational qualification but the civil services, with the main aim of 'serving the society' and 'giving back the society in our time what the society had given us'.

Their numbers were not small, either. They were all there in the protests, not only in Chennai, but in what in IT industry parlance in the State had come to be described as 'Tier-II' cities like Coimbatore, Madurai and Tiruchi. Tamil Nadu has a proliferation of engineering and other professional colleges across the State, with the result, the protesting students would have belonged to even the smallest of hamlets in an isolated hill-top, with no access to urban centres or even urbanised villages. Everywhere the youth joined with enthusiasm and fervour that had not been on display for decades now and for a cause that they only understood more emotionally than rationally—though many others in the groups could rationally and forcefully explain and argue their cause and case.

But none of the youthful protestors was worried, none was perturbed. Whether they had applied their minds to such possibilities as denial of visas, or of jobs, was unclear—and would remain so. Possibly, they did not know the possibilities of visa officers and police officers having to do a duty of checking the background of the people wanting to visit their countries, or take up a government job, whether at the Centre or in the State government. Possibly, they knew and still ignored it. Either way, it did not matter to them. There were enough participants who knew the rules of the game. There were enough parents who were in government service and knew it even better. To 'em all, it just did not matter. What mattered was the angst of the average Tamil, the pride of all Tamils.

Pay-back Time

It was thus that an unknown element known as the 'pride of the overseas Tamil' came on board and on display this time, and unlike any time in the past. Time had been when over the past decade especially, Tamils from India in jobs, with or without citizenship in the host countries, would join pan-Tamil protests in the cause of the 'Sri Lankan Tamil' population, organised by the Sri Lankan migrant Tamil population in those countries. The Tamils from India overseas also influenced their families and villages to pressure State-level political parties and individual leaders of every political party, to come out openly against the Sri Lankan State, government and the armed forces, and even more so on the side of the Sri Lankan Tamil minorities in the island-nation, even if it meant courting the dreaded LTTE.

It was kind of pay-back time for the Sri Lankan Tamil community in particular, to stand up for a cause that had become closer to their brethren from the 'Indian motherland'. Egged on by the example set by the Sri Lankan Tamils over the past decade, the Tamils from India, and their cultural organisations and community associations across many parts of the world organised Jallikattu protests, as if by cue, and almost from day two or three of the Tamil Nadu protests.

The overseas protests had become higher in numbers and larger in participation over the following weekend, 21-22 January, Saturday and Sunday, when alone those working and living in other countries, got time to participate in public programmes. That was as far as the West went. In the Gulf nations, it was the preceding Friday holiday for the local employers that had gathered the crowds for protests by overseas Indians. Whether true or not, pictures also appeared in the social media of pro-Jallikattu protests in Russia and China, unlikely venues otherwise, owing to a variety of social and political reasons. But in the Gulf countries where a lot of Tamils from India and Sri Lanka worked, and so also in the US, Canada, Australia and across Europe, where the two communities shared bread, the protests were well-attended. In countries like South Africa, Malaysia and neighbouring Sri Lanka, where the Indian-origin Tamils had lived for long, the protests had a deeper meaning. In Sri Lanka, Tamil politicians were, however, cautious not to identify with the larger pan-Tamil cause across the Palk Strait, lest it should be misunderstood, misconstrued or misinterpreted by 'Sinhala nationalist' rivals. Hence, the emotive linkages from Sri Lanka was less on display, but there was no denying the fact that both Tamil and Sinhala politicians, and also the Tamil masses, were following it all on local television channels, and on Indian TV channels beamed from across the seas.

It is another matter that a Tamil politician from Sri Lanka's Upcountry region—with no links to the LTTE or the Sri Lankan Tamil cause—would field his well-looked-after bull in the famous Alanganallur Jallikattu competition, when it became possible under the new Tamil Nadu law, with the Supreme Court, too, looking the other way, post-protests. Senthil Thondaman is a scion of the famed Thondaman family of political leaders among the Tamils of recent Indian origin, or Upcountry Tamils as generation of indentured labour imported from India by the common British ruler, were known. He is the grand-son of the late Soumiyamurthy Thondaman, who was considered the 'Father of the Upcountry Tamils' in post-Independence Sri Lanka. Senthil's uncle, Arumugan Thondaman, was a minister in successive governments in Sri Lanka, barring the present one. Senthil's bull won at AlanganallurJallikattu, post-protests, and he became the proud owner of a Maruti car, presented by the organisers, to the owner of the best-maintained animal(s). The two also appeared in other Jallikattu venues in the State, later on.

The Violence

THE STORY of Tamil Nadu's 'Jallikattu Protests *circa* 2017' would not be complete without some mention of the violence that marked the end-game in the main agitation theatre at Chennai since pre-dawn hours and well into the pre-noon part of that day. Every time the unprecedented success of the Jallikattu protests, the massive attendance and the 'positive outcome' are mentioned in the future, the violence part will be an avoidable but inevitable add-on, or a foot-note, or both. In the year of its happening, it marked the end-note, without which the protests would have had only a happy ending—followed by the happier ending of Jallikattu proper in the days and weeks that followed.

There is no denying that the police too was involved in the violence. Television footage, and also some possibly edited and exaggerated versions in the social media, showed police alone in bad light. But there were others, possibly limited in footage and content, which blamed the other side, the group of residual protestors, who had decided to stay put at the Marina venue even after most others had left the previous evening, convinced about the success of their collective project and celebrating the success. After all, the protests had made the new enabling State law for facilitating Jallikattu here and now inevitable, with the Centre playing an understanding partner in the federal scheme, and the Supreme Court too acknowledging the reality of the existing and emerging situation, if nothing more. The question arises, had it not been for the protests, any State legislation of the kind would have had as 'smooth' (?) a passage as this one had even if its application might end up getting limited to a single year!

Forgotten 'Inauguration'

Worse still for these residual protestors on the Marina, in most rural villages and traditional venues of Jallikattu—the latter, if any—the local protests had ended quietly. Those protests were mostly spearheaded not by 'faceless' youth as in Chennai but by the village headmen, who had organised Jallikattu over the previous years, too, and as community leaders, during the times of their forebears, as well. They too went back home without any fuss or complaints, after discussing and debating the issues and the consequences involved among themselves. They invited the urban youth to come back to view the sporting event, when held in the days that followed. Some local organisers even announced tentative dates for the local events even as they all were going back home, celebrating the success of their demonstrations.

As with the commencement of the protests, the concluding part also got full television news coverage. At the commencement of the protests, the 'national channels' especially and some regional news bulletins, too, had missed out, starting with the import of what at the time looked like an innocuous social media announcement/invite for the protests. The celebratory conclusion of the protests made instant news for them all too.

Thus, when the protests ended and there was hope of Jallikattu being staged in 2017 itself, the news was all over the place, and overseas, too, owing to the large media attention that it had attracted, only weeks after the news of Chief Minister Jayalalithaa's death, and to Cyclone Vardha, in between.

Through that week, not just to the local media and the Tamil social media, all across the country, Jallikattu became the hot topic. The national media even forgot their staple news diet in Prime Minister Narendra Modi, the Uttar Pradesh Assembly elections, and US President Donald Trump's 20 January Inauguration. By then the residual group in the Marina, and their leaders, self-styled or otherwise, had also established ground-level contact with counterparts in other parts of the State, especially traditional Jallikattu centres. There were even doubts if some of the urban youth who had joined local protests elsewhere, had actually been a part of the faceless organisers at the Marina—and were in constant touch. But no evidence was available, after all, as with other claims and charges that would be thrown up through the second half of the protests.

Seeds of Suspicions

If anything, these claims and counter-claims, charges and counter-charges relating to the identity, and social and ideological background of some sections of the participants in the protests, especially at the Marina, became the subject of off-line conversations, as well. It was also the ones that triggered social media discourses, and sowed seeds of suspicion in the minds of a majority of participants, who were innocent, and a large number of bystanders, who were ignorant, about the identity of these faceless groups and their nameless leaders. These varied groups, and their various leaders, were sighted only on the Marina venue, that too, deep inside the crowds. They were mostly unavailable to TV cameras and for sound-bytes, as should have been the case in the normal course, for them to talk to the people, appeal for their sympathy and support, and explain their cause at every stage.

That way, their silence after a point, and their unwillingness to show up, and own up the protests, too, hurt their known and established cause, which was the demand for legalising and staging Jallikattu from this year on, after a break.

Instead, it only 'exposed' their 'hidden cause', though no one knew what it was, who they were, or what (all) their motives were. This also affected the decision to prolong the protests adversely. There were no known consultations with the mass of participants, nor was any known attempt made to assess the mood of these common people before a decision was taken to continue with the protests. The same applied to the self-styled core-group's acceptance, or non-acceptance of the promises of the governments in the State and the Centre, as they came, accompanied first by a Jallikattu-facilitating Ordinance, followed immediately by the due passage of the Tamil Nadu Assembly's enabling Bill, with public promise of immediate assent from the President of India, for it to be made law.

Wallowing possibly in their success, both unprecedented and unexpected, the core-group, if any could be called so, clearly overlooked one basic lesson in organisational skills. There were believed to be more than one core-group, linked in some way but independent otherwise. Each one of them had a common agenda to make the protest a success, and also prolong the 'agony' (?) as far and as long as possible. Going beyond focussing the collective energies of the masses against the political leadership and even the governments in the State and at the Centre as institutions, using the protests to embarrass the Indian Establishment and the State structures seemed to emerge as one of the undeclared goals. Yet, going by their individual ideologies, each one of them had a sub text. Rather, the Jallikattu protest was a common sub-text to their individual main goals.

Even the collective position and consequent posturing of wanting to upset the existing Indian scheme went only as far as methodologies went. Leave aside government pressure, which was not uncommon under such circumstances, or the increasing presence of policemen, also aimed at possibly sending out a message to all those gathered, the 'organisers' forgot that their own 'tools of communication' to the masses outside could be used in more ways than one. Rather, it could serve twin-purposes, without anyone having to take any great extra effort or initiative. That should include the State government, and the State and Central agencies, which some loosely claimed were 'spreading misinformation' through the social media—against the continuance of protests. But the reverse in terms of 'mis-information' was truer. More importantly, the 'core groups' forgot that the right-thinking people who had supported their larger and identifiable cause, were both thinking people and right-thinking, still.

One such mis-information related to the police planning/plotting to target the girls among the protesting youth. Conversely, there were also the equally exciting social media rumours that the core-groups were trying to use the women among the protestors as 'human shields'. In this case, the unsaid sub-text was that if the police did not attack the girls, then the core groups could take their undefined, yet, not-so-undefined immediate goal(s), to the next level. If the police did not budge, then the 'brutal attacks' on these hapless girls would have been used to besmirch the Indian State system even more.

The Probe

VARIOUS VERSIONS exist as to the cause of the 'Marina violence', and the legally-constituted Justice S Rajeswaran Commission is seized of the matter. The State government ordered the independent probe under the Commissions of Inquiry Act, after the vocal and identifiable political Opposition charged the Chennai City Police with forcibly and violently removing the peaceful protestors from the Marina, and going after them deep into neighbouring fishers' colonies and other residential areas, hitting them to the point of causing bleeding injuries and fractures in some 'victims'. Though not *sub judice, per se*, the commission of inquiry, and also the separate police investigations that have been ordered, alone can bring out the truth, whole or partial. The police investigations, as with other instances and cases of the kind, will revolve around the actual events—and 'criminal conspiracy', if any, behind the violence.

The Rajeswaran Commission can be expected to come out with the greater truths pertaining to allegations that the police had resorted to unbridled violence, and had attacked bystanders, and residents of a local fishermen's colony, abutting the Marina beach and forming a part thereof. The last time the fishers were provoked into blocking the main thoroughfare leading up to the State Secretariat and the Madras High Court, among other important government offices, there was violence and police firing not far away from the State Police Headquarters. That was when the late M G Ramachandran was in power. There was fishers' violence again when Jayalalithaa was in power. These had nothing to do with MGR's filmi image as '*Meenava Nanban*', or 'friend of the fishers', be it in the film by the same title released in 1977, the year he became Chief Minister, or '*Padagotti*' ('Boat-man') in1964. It is also the title of an MGR movie.

Sections of the local media, and more so, sections of the social media with no legal accountability *per se*, also claimed with 'photographic evidence' and 'video evidence' of a woman in police uniform torching vehicles, as if to provide justification for 'retaliatory violence' by the cops, if only to restore law and order. Such allegations also claimed that policemen/ police women in uniform had set fire to the Ice House police station, not far away from the large Marina stretches and in the heart of the over-crowded residential locality of Triplicane. Names of some police personnel also found their way onto the social media, but nothing was conclusive.The police did not deny the former allegation of a woman in uniform setting fire to an auto-rickshaw, but did describe the second episode graphically, indicating that a local mob had outnumbered the police personnel on duty in the police station episode. The police station is not on the protestors' route by any stretch of imagination, and the episode had the signature of pre-meditated vandalism written all over it, going by some of the social media visuals and claims.

It is not entirely unlikely that the police investigations will cover allegations against fellow cops, if it is true. No progress in the investigations has been made thus far. It is not unlikely that they may commence/recommence after the probe panel presents its report to the government. It is equally not unlikely that the probe panel may itself be used to cool frayed tempers, all round, and giving the police investigations, and follow-up action(s), if any, a slow death and quiet burial, as is often the case in this State and elsewhere in the country, top-down. If police personnel are proved to be involved in day-light arson, the responsibility could then have to be fixed at appropriate levels of the hierarchy. But then, whatever the police investigations show up in this or other cases is sure to be challenged by supporters and sympathisers of the 'core groups', and possibly also the political Opposition. Here again, the Rajeswaran Commission may have relatively greater credibility than the police, unless the CBI as a 'rank outsider' (!) is brought in. This does not seem to be happening.

The political Opposition and other critics of the police action also seem wanting to leave it there, at least for now. If the State government then desires and decides, fresh criminal investigations can be started against all those that the Rajeswaran Commission finds as 'guilty' of violence, directly or otherwise. The list can include police personnel at different levels. This has been the past practice across the country in most, if not all such cases, where a probe under the Commissions of Inquiry Act is ordered. Be it as it may, a Commission of Inquiry under the law is neither a judicial office, nor is it an investigation agency, like the police. It is only a 'fact-finding' mission, where the 'evidentiary value' rested on the probability of the possibility rather than the possibility of the same. For proceedings before the courts of law, in cases of the kind relating to violence of the kind, the thumb-rule is 'innocent until proved guilty', unless circumstantial and corroboratory evidence is over-whelming.

Deeper Insights

Of equal, if not greater importance and import, would be the Rajeswaran's Commission's customary findings on the events and developments that had contributed to the Jallikattu protests in the first place. The Terms of Reference of the Commission states as much, in Para 3 (i): 'To enquire into the causes and circumstances leading to the law and order disturbances on 23-01-2017 including damages to public and private properties.'[2] Though the official notification is not very clear if the commission should also look at the larger picture, it is not unlikely that based on the evidence adduced, Justice Rajeswaran may also come up with the run-up to the protests, which alone made the violence since the early hours of Monday, 23 January, possible, though totally unnecessary and even more avoidable, even if the agitation itself might not have been.

The Commission's recommendations, if any, in this regard, should give an insight for governments, law-makers and law-enforcers alike, on the deeper psyche of a large section of the population vide the nation's size and diversity, so as to apply correctives—not only in the case of Tamil Nadu but also in and for the rest of the country.

As may be pointed out, Para 3 (iv) of the Terms of Reference, enjoins upon the Commission, 'to recommend measures to prevent the recurrence of such incidents in future'. Though not mentioned specifically in the Terms of Reference, the panel, either through a public, 'publishable' report, or a 'Confidential' part thereof, can–and will—also thus need to throw greater insights into elements against whom there was near-conclusive or suggestive evidence about mischief-making, conspiracy against mischief-making, both leading to violence. Even more important of them all will be the commission's findings, if any, about efforts by sections of the protestors and the social media groups that had supposedly given out the early calls for the protests in the first place, most especially in Chennai and

---

2 Tamil Nadu Government Gazette Notification: http://www.stationeryprinting.tn.gov.in/extraordinary/2017/23_Ex_II_2.pdf

on the sprawling sands of the Marina. There are allegations of open attempts at alienating the participants—or, who were willing to listen—from the nation, and turn them against the Indian nation. The names of some peripheral groups of different ideological faiths got free mention in a section of the social media. Visuals from the Marina venue also contributed.

The question is, if some or all of it can attract action under those codes/Acts and sections of the law aimed at curbing and punishing anti-national activities, including promoting 'sedition' and 'secession'. Or, if there was collusion among various sections and organisations with an ideological base, each to its own at one level, but possibly coming together, in the name of a cause—but which cause and whose cause—could be another matter for the inquiry commission to ponder over. In doing so, the commission's probe, if not the criminal investigations, can well seek to establish the truth or otherwise of church sermons calling for the Jallikattu protests. So should the source of the 'belief', freely aired by the social media, linking failure of rains to the non-conduct of Jallikattu, leading to *saamikuththam*, or 'curse of gods'. True, the 'curse of gods' lines originated not in the Marina site of the violence. But there is a collective influence of such campaigns on the psyche of the protestors, especially when the protests were spread across different venues across several locations.

In the absence of previous experience in the handling either violence of those levels that erupted unexpectedly, that too in the midst of a large peaceful protest of the kind, which again had taken the government by surprise, accompanied by scientifically-spread and even more 'scientifically thought-out' rumour-mongering of the kind, the State government, it can be said at this distance in time, did not seem to know how to handle the agitations against Hindi in the Sixties. The authorities have learnt a lot since, and the establishment of human rights commissions and NGOs working in the field all have helped to some extent. The social media, which was not known during the anti-Hindi agitation, is now cutting both ways, and even more. Likewise, the probe panel can also go into claims/allegations about some local residents in the immediate vicinity being paid money to create trouble, or to provide food and water to the protestors, or to provide them night-shelter during the days of the protests—and also give them 'cover' from the police during those hours of violence, claiming the youth as relatives or friends visiting them during the festival season.

Yet, there was no denying the truth of identifiable groups with identifiable pictures, posters, flags and slogans appearing or presenting themselves as such at the protest venue once the crowds had gathered. Though not many people in the crowd could identify them, there was visible signs of bonhomie among individual sections within an identifiable/specific area on the vast Marina sands. As some social media pictures claimed, there were left-leaning groups, at times called Naxalites, in different shades of red, Islamic fundamentalist groups, proclaiming themselves as such, and pan-Tamil groups, including groups that had customarily identified themselves with Sri Lanka's Liberation Tigers of Tamil Eelam (LTTE), another banned outfit under the Indian laws.

In the normal course, and but for the violence of 23 January, it would have been a proud claim that Jallikattu as a social custom, had the potential to bring together various sections of the society, divided as some of them otherwise might have been, on a common cause. By extension, it could have also been argued that the State-wide protests in the name of Jallikattu was an expression of the *Tamil angst*, and the long-felt and deep-seated hurt against neglect and alienation from the Union, which needed to be arrested. If it finds some substance in such constructs about hurt, angst and alienation, the Commission can be expected to outline, though not exhaustively, and touch upon the causes and also recommend specific methods to arrest and reverse such alienation. Originally given three months to finish its work, the Commission has got further extensions, as the scope of its hearings needed for Justice Rajeswaran to visit protest venues outside of Chennai, too, and hear out representations from different stake-holders, interest-groups and interested individuals. The latest extension puts the date for submission of report as 31 January 2017, but there is no knowing if the probe panel will require, and get further extensions, and if so, for how long.

New Consensus

A lot of it will depend on evidence that is adduced before the Commission, especially by State and Central agencies that are considered repositories of classified information of the kind. From that could also flow, and flow backward, either by this Commission or otherwise, a detailed probe into the network of organisations that are at it, now and earlier. There could also be evidence to the possibilities of failures on the part of Central and State governments, their arms and agencies, in arresting and reversing the trends, if any, early on. For instance, the governments might have to ask themselves as to why such widespread angst and alienation in a State that is considered one with a population that is mostly literate and mainly educated and thus enlightened, with jobs and lifestyles that have made Tamil Nadu the most urbanised one in the country as a whole.

These are all political issues arising out of a social milieu and economic environment, for which solutions have to be found on the political and politico administrative plains—but also quick and fast. These issues have to be identified honestly, and solutions found and implemented with sincerity. In the existing political environment in the State, there can still be some hope of evolving a new 'political consensus' as different from 'political competition'—and built upon, too. Such issues involve concerns, both real and emotional, relating to ethnicity, identify and economic prosperity—be it on the Sri Lankan ethnic issue, war and violence, or on river water disputes with neighbouring States, or other issues like nation-wide common entrance examination.

In doing so, there is a need and scope for the officialdom (and more so the political class) to identify and implement methodologies that are effective on the ground, without skirting issues too much and too often, with immediate aspects of policing ending up side-lining, side-stepping and over-riding the larger cause and issue. It needs to be understood that whether thought-out or not, such 'interventionist' tactics and/or strategies, whether through law and/or legal forums, or by those involving law and order situations, cannot be an eternal solution to what then also becomes an emotional issue, as well. Real problems require real solutions, and that needs to be found at every turn without piling them up for the future—when it could well explode on the face, without notice, without stoppage and without even a cause or circumstance justifying such an explosive situation.

It is in this context, protests like the earlier one in Kudankulam and on the issue that it highlighted needs to be studied in its entirety. It was not only a law and order issue, just as it should not be considered as one only with a noble cause. The truth lies in between, if one were to consider the options for development that the State and its population, already in the take-off stage of growth and prosperity, in toto. The same applies to post-Jallikattu protests, which again involves questions of development alongside environmental concerns and livelihood options. Governments in the State and at the Centre have to concede that they cannot any more take unilateral decisions on such projects and evolve a constitutional scheme of sorts that makes the 'affected population' not only beneficiaries in whatever form (including jobs and incomes) but also participants in such decision-making.

Those that complain about these protests in Tamil Nadu need to look at the nation's 'development-related' decision-making history over the previous decades and more. In States like West Bengal and Odhisa, Chattisgarh and Jharkhand, the local population came up in arms against coal and mineral mining, industry projects like pith-head power-plants and car-making, and succeeded in the governments concerned reviewing their earlier decision and stalling/stopping them, too. It is only a global trend that has caught on with the 'globalised Indian', too. If government reports are to be believed, Maoist and such other movements have been behind many such protests and criticism. It may also be true, but there is a price that the nation is now paying for the 'collective neglect' that the politico-administrative class had heaped upon hapless sections of the population.

The 'exploitation' is now being initiated by the other end of the stick, which however needs to be contained and curtailed, but the adopted methods cannot be the same as used to be in a pre-globalised, least-connected India of the past. Maybe, strengthening the constitutionally-mandated panchayati raj bodies may have a better and more responsible role to play in such matters. States like Kerala are said to have achieved some success in this direction. Maybe, the Union of India that made it possible, and the State governments that grudgingly acknowledged a constitutional status for the local bodies without actually conferring on them any constitutionally-approved rights and powers, responsibilities and accountability, should undertake a collective re-look, going beyond mere sloganeering.

Compared to other recent protests of the kind in Tamil Nadu, barring the Sri Lankan ethnic issue, most of the rest involved questions on 'Development *vs* Environment'. Yet, most of them ended up attracting and admitting the political class—with the likes of Kudankulam protest leader/

organiser Udayakumar entering the electoral fray himself before long, purchasing little or no support from the voter. It is a lesson for those of the kind. Udayakumar's electoral defeat did not mean that the people did not support the cause that he stood for. It only meant that they respected him for his apolitical stand on a issue that he thought was dear to him and should be so for the people of village and the State as a whole. When he crossed the invisible Rubicon, he lost not only the electoral battle but also the war that he had been fighting before it. In continuation and possibly comparison, too, the Jallikattu protests was one other that was an out-and-out apolitical affair, with political leaders and parties being denied even participation rights. Who denied them the right to participation is a question that the other, ordinary participants in the protests, should ask themselves now, from this distance in time.

After all, the Marina protests, unlike those in many other parts of the State, did not have an identifiable leadership, organiser, or central command on the field. Yet, whenever a political face showed up, the young among the protestors resorted to slogan-shouting and shooed them away. So were film-stars, who in the past had organised protests on varied issues as the Sri Lankan ethnic war and violence and the Cauvery water dispute—on their own, individually or through their organisations. Granting that the politicians had an electoral axe to kind, and also granting that they had not done enough for the causes that were behind the Tamil angst, why were the film personalities denied a role or even entry at times from participation? Did someone among the protestors want to ensure that not only politicians and film stars did not try to hijack their event, but also wanted to direct the protests in a particular way than the common participants had known or anticipated?

Hidden Agendas

At the end of the day, the 'core group' even declined to accept the conciliatory voice of second-line film-star and film-maker, Raghava Lawrence, who despite his broken arm, had come first to express his solidarity and later on to negotiate with the protestors on the futility of continuing it. Likewise, why was Hip-hop Tamizha Aadhi, the music composer, who had circulated a video-song on the Jallikattu demand early on during the protests, denied his role in mediation? Rather, why did the faceless core group decline the conciliatory efforts initiated by Aadhi, who was possibly closest to a part-recognisable face from among the youthful majority among the protestors, for the authorities to approach and talk, too? Also,why did the 'core group(s)' positioned in distant Chennai, and not necessarily belonging to the 'Jallikattu country', not accept the negotiating rights of traditional Jallikattu organisers, from their parental generations, when they alone may have had the authority to talk about the martial art-form, if not on the protests and on behalf of the protestors? Among them, there might have also been older people with adequate experience in negotiating on such issues, and taking it all to a quick and logical conclusion before the protestors were allowed to tire themselves out.

Was there a 'hidden agenda' or separate 'agendas', if not 'separatist agendas', of diverse and diversified groups from within the core group(s), which definitely united in the process of the protest but not necessarily on the end and the goal(s)? Also, alongside, how is it that the police that was seen as being sympathetic to the cause, with individual policemen coming out openly, and in their uniforms, before TV news cameras, or on the social media, affirming their support for the protests and the Jallikattu 'turn against' the protestors overnight? Did the police become privy to some information that the common man did not possess, then and even now? If so, was such information too sensitive for the police and the government to share with the people at large?

Police under Pressure

Yet, there is no denying that the police and the government as institutions were under tremendous pressure, almost from the early hours of the protests, especially on the 'closing day' of 23 January. It was more so in the case of the Chennai venue, but other cities and towns should not be left out either. After all, the nation's Republic Day, 26 January, was only days away.

The Marina has been the customary venue of the annual Republic Day celebrations, comprising flag-hoisting and Parade by the nation's tri-Services, contingents of State police and local school children. With Tamil Nadu having an Acting Governor, Ch Vidhyasagar Rao, and he having to do the honours in Maharashtra, his main jurisdictional State, Panneerselvam became the first Chief Minister of the State, to take the salute at the Republic Day celebrations in Chennai. Since the early days of the DMK regime in the State, this honour for the Chief Minister had remained only for the Independence Day, from the ramparts of Fort St George, the seat of power in Tamil Nadu. This honour for the Chief Minister would be extended to other States, too, in due course, but the Republic Day honours were strictly gubernatorial in nature, the right passing onto the Chief Justice of the State in case the Governor's post was vacant and not held by an Acting Governor, as was the case now in Tamil Nadu. In the districts, the protest-venues and the Republic Day parade venues may or may not have been the same. But with so much tension in the air, it would have looked incongruous for the district administration and the police force to behave as if everything was normal and nothing was amiss, just around the corner and for days together.

If the State government, and to a lesser extent, the Centre, had worked overtime to find a solution to the Jallikattu row, which would satisfy Tamil Nadu's population, and also the polity, it also owed to their urgency to have the Marina readied for the Republic Day Parade, Panneerselvam or not. If the parade could not be held there, that too after the cause for the protests had been removed, it would have been a blot on Tamil Nadu and a stigma on the State authorities, no matter the explanations and excuses. Reports had claimed that the authorities were looking at alternate venues, but the Marina, in front of the Gandhi statute, was the place to hold the Republic Day Parade. When the protests were already winding down to a close, there was thus no reason or justification over the 21-22 January week-end, for the State government to consider shifting the function away from the traditional venue. It would have only given rise to questions, if someone in the protests, some members of some of the 'core group(s)' at the very least were as much interested in forcing the State authorities to shift the Republic Day venue as to having Jallikattu back, and/or forcing the police to act and react in the way they ended up doing on the Marina and in some other venues on 23 January.

Unclear or Motivated?

There is also no knowing if the State administration and police were alive to the possibilities of the protests in the first place, and/or such protests having a quick and wide-spread reach and massive participation? Was there also any possible prediction, based on inputs, if any, and preparation thereof, to face the determination of the faceless core group(s), for keeping the protests as peaceful as possible, as long as possible, so as to attract the maximum support, and all across Tamil Nadu, with massive reach across the country and elsewhere as well? If so, were they not aware of the possibility of violence, and unavoidable police action to clear the protests, once a decision had been made, and the government too had been satisfied that whatever needed to be done, and whatever could be done, had been done to stage Jallikattu all over again?

Barring the local protests for drinking water or other civic facilities, or localised agitations, especially outside liquor shops, demanding total prohibition, in all major campaigns like in Kudankulam and Marina (Jallikattu), the organisers, visible or not, did not know how to begin it but they must have known when to end it. It is unclear if the Marina core group(s) did not know how to end it, or did not want to end it. Or, was this indecision also written into the script at the drawing-board level, if any, with possibilities, if not desirability of violence built into it? Yes, residual issues would always remain, as in Jallikattu protests. But on issues like Kudankulam, they did not and could not see the fulfilment of their demands, either. Yet, the anti-nuclear protests fizzled out as the organisers hit road-blocks, some of them of their own making. Whether those demands were as justified as was being made out to be, were valid or not and what alternatives did the organisers have even later on—to nuclear power-generation—to meet the development demands of an entire nation, and Tamil Nadu in particular, are issues the protest did not delve into.

That way, even some of the pan-Tamil protests of the previous years in Tamil Nadu, especially post-war in Sri Lanka, also did not end conclusively. They ended up fizzling out, instead, as the organisers were either unclear about their goals and tactics, wedded more to ideologies than realities.

In the post-Lankan war issues, the rest of the crowd was not as driven as some of the organisers. If they too were noticed, it was for their determination not to involve politicians, not to allow the political class to hijack the protests, and mostly spending from their pockets and using innovative methods like the social media to send out their calls and update sympathisers and supporters outside the country, too, for them to get emotionally involved—and, 'integrated', too. It is this kind of 'integration' that the Jallikaattu protests, especially that on the Marina, too achieved, but to what end over the medium and the long-term, might also be a question hanging in the air, for adequate answers and responses from the state of India and the Indian State of Tamil Nadu, their respective governments and populations put together and coming together. These questions need to be raised, addressed, and responses found and implemented in right earnest, if a repeat of the same is not to be witnessed, either in Tamil Nadu or elsewhere in the country.

Shrewder Minds...

Whether or not the State and Chennai City Police administrations and also the governments were caught napping over the imminence of the protest, its length, width and depth before hand, or even halfway through it, they did prepare themselves for a peaceful closure in time. By that time, the authorities seemed to have had a better assessment of the existing and emerging situation(s) in Chennai, at the very least. Clearly, by choosing Chennai and the Marina as the epicentre of Jallikattu protests this time, as against other protests over other pan-Tamil issues, the youthful yet unidentified organisers had clearly captured the nation's imagination, by capturing the imagination of the national media, first. Thus, ensuring a peaceful conclusion to a peaceful protest, in which they did not have any role or contribution, also became a necessity for the City Police in particular.

Definitely, there was propaganda advantage in choosing a metropolitan city as the epicentre of a State-wide protest that had its roots still in the rural setting and culture. First and foremost from the propaganda angle, the national and regional media were readily accessible, and the latter too could access the protests and protest leaders, directly or otherwise, even to be updated on what to expect next. Two, the transit population in a city is always more, especially during long festival holidays, and they for sure would also carry the message of the protests, and how the protestors had brought the city to a standstill. If shutting down a city is the measure of the success rate of a protest and also reflects justification for protestor demands, then that too was there. More importantly, in protests of the Jallikattu kind, the leadership of the agitation automatically passes on to local elders, even if they are apolitical and this particular protest itself had been started by the local youth. In an urban milieu, there were greater chances of the leadership and command-control staying with the original organisers, wherever there was not an organised and readily identifiable leadership at commencement. Clearly, all these mattered to the core group, or core groups, to be precise.

It is also this *post facto* assessment of the protest that begs the question if shrewder minds than acknowledged had worked, and worked over time, to keep it all low-profile without identifiable and questionable organising leadership, and yet draw national and international attention, for precisely the same reasons apart from the core cause itself. Looking from another angle, there had been Jallikattu protests in traditional venues and other rural centres in previous years, too, but without much mass involvement and national/international attention. The very idea of shifting the main base to the State capital, to the sprawling sands of Marina, made all the difference this time, and also raised all related questions, including the successful handling of the personal ablution demands and requirements of female participants, came to be met as hours and days rolled on.

Invisible, but...

Maybe because of the prevailing public mood and condition, or because they had other inputs and intelligence, the City Police administration was brought under the care and control of four senior officials in the rank of Additional Director-General of Police (ADGP), under whom, scores of officials in the rank of

Inspector-General (IG) and Deputy Inspector-General (DIG) coordinated the ground efforts for maintaining a peaceful conclusion to the protests. Already, the office of the Chennai Metropolitan Police Commissioner was then being held by an officer in the rank of Director-General of Police (DGP), with and under whom an impressive list of Joint Commissioners, Deputy Commissioners and Assistant Commissioners were/are ranking officers.However, there were reports that many high-ranking police officials were conspicuous by their absence from the protest venues, when they were peaceful and later when the situation was tense first, and violent, not very long after. Ahead of the final show-down at Marina, there were reports of tension and violence flowing from the Jallikattu protests in difference parts of Chennai and suburbs. Some of it was being attributed to youth who were returning from a successful demonstration in the Marina. Given the early mood of the protestors, especially the majority of innocent commoners, the question arises if the presence, appearance and appeal by senior officials would have changed the mood for the better, even early on.

Even when the government decided to brief the protestors across the State, only middle-level police officials were chosen to deliver the message, engage the protestors in convincing conversation. They did a good job of it nonetheless. Yet, it was a 'police job' all through, and the rest of the State bureaucracy, it appears in hindsight, was possibly made to sit back and stop with the drafting of the new Bill and other procedural issues. The question then arises as to why the government did not deploy more senior police officials for the task? The question also begs the answer why senior bureaucrats did not engage with the protestors on the site(s), to brief them about the new law and the finality of Jallikattu being staged, once the formality of presidential assent for the State Bill had been obtained.

Better or worse still, when so many ranking officials were said to have been in charge of controlling Law and Order, arising out of the dispersal of the Marina protestors, how come so much violence was allowed, and was allowed to spread to outside the beach area, and spill over to residential localities on the other side of the main thoroughfare? There were also reports of violence, including vehicle-burning, supposedly involving early returnees from the Marina venue. Or, was there specific and actionable intelligence that the Marina venue had become the gathering place for all kinds of militant outfits and their silent followers, that the police feared the worst after a time? As much as there were sympathetic supporters for the protests from within the uniformed services—and some of them appeared in their uniforms, too, before TV cameras—there should have been others, less conspicuous and often in civvies, who should havehad their noses to the ground, and felt that all was not going to end as well as they had begun?

Large Indian Market

Such doubts and suspicions, if any, too, is not without substance. After all, throughout the protest period of close to a week, and even a day or two more, at every turn, new elements got thrown into the media and social media discourse. On one day, as if to widen the scope of protests and at the same time, keep it still linked to the Jallikattu issue, there were claims that the court petitions for the ban were all along at rendering native species of bulls redundant to maintain, with the conventional care attaching to them, so that imported cows, and those produced locally through artificial insemination, could dominate the Indian dairy scene. In this era after the economic reforms India has become a 'large market' for the western world. With that also came protests against genetically-modified seeds, attempts at corporatisation of plain-land agriculture, entry of MNCs and even the Indian private sector into retail-trade, especially in farm produce. Replacing Indian cattle-heads with imported animals, mostly through artificial insemination, with the aim to render local animal-species extinct, captured the imagination of the local population, in relatively better-educated Tamil Nadu. No data was sought or provided, however, other than claims to the contrary.

Even without it, politically-motivated strands of protestors started introducing and including PETA as among the enemies of Jallikattu, going far beyond their publicised positions on the subject. PETA became a bad name overnight, so did Pepsi and Coke, as without anyone's knowledge, the Jallikattu protestor websites were calling for their immediate ban. Some protestors were even shown breaking bottles of these 'imported' drinks and the drinking water-bottles sold by them. Suddenly, some associations of retail traders in the State also claimed to have decided on stopping the sale of 'imported soft drinks' from1 March 2017, once their existing stocks had been sold out. Whether or not the self-imposed trade-ban got enforced, at least in the immediate period, neighbourhood stores in parts of Chennai reported a sudden fall in sale.

Whether the demand for a ban on PETA, and the no-sale decision against Pepsi and Coke, had any logical link to the demand for restoring Jallikattu is unclear still. Whether or not the violent end to the Marina protests were an accident or an after-thought, if not premeditated, the anti-PETA and anti-Coke/Pepsi protests seemed to have crept into the Jallikattu movement only midway through the week-long protests. As with the rest, these campaigns too started with the social media. To be fair, if it can be so, a new group of youth seemed to be joining the protest, like any other enthusiastic onlooker or participant. Thus began the sudden sloganeering on these issues. If the faceless core-groups had an ideological orientation of a different kind, this group of protestors too had an air of 'neo-nationalism' attaching to them.

Whether at least the Marina protests were a comprehensive, goal-oriented demonstration for a common cause that went ideologically awry after a point, or it became an 'umbrella platform' for multiple ideological and interest groups to pitch in, in the name of a common cause, if only to exploit the situation is debatable. Either way, there were early path-finders and late entrants with their limited vision and unlimited 'ideological' vision for the nation and the State, which serve neither, over the short, medium and long terms. Anyway, that was also not their innate idea and purpose.

If PETA were to be banned as among those who had been consistently moving the courts against permitting Jallikattu, the main petitioner or respondent before the Supreme Court had always been the Animal Welfare Board of India (AWBI), a creature of the Indian laws and a creation of the Government of India, which alone appointed its chairperson and members. Even the exhaustive on-site medical report of sorts on which the Supreme Court had relied so heavily in its 2014 judgment had been prepared by AWBI experts, not anyone from PETA. Since then, however, PETA is the petitioner in the now-pending Supreme Court case against the post-protests 2017 Tamil Nadu law, facilitating Jallikattu.

As over-doing the criticism of the anti-ban groups, pro-Jallikattu sections of the social media also brought in the name of Justice Radhakrishnan, who had delivered the Supreme Court's 2014 judgment, banning Jallikattu permanently. As it turned out, he got to be honoured by PETA, post-retirement. Pro-Jallikattu sections of the social media activists wanted Radhakrishnan to return the honour. Someone even moved the Supreme Court in this regard. So did the such pro-Jallikattu enthusiasts/propagandists want film-stars who had earlier carried the PETA message, to apologise to the people of the State.

Hijacked, or What?

The question still remains—and the Commission of Inquiry may have some if not all the answers—if the so-called perpetrators of violence had (at all) infiltrated and hijacked the peaceful protests halfway through, or were they (among) the faceless organisers, in the first place, those that had sent out the social media calls for people to gather on the Marina, and from which alone local calls for protests went out elsewhere in the State? The truth seems to lie in between, and in that truth will also be the clues to why violence, how violence, and what for the violence?

If such assumptions were true, Marina was also possibly the only venue all across Tamil Nadu where all so-called militant groups had converged, to protest together, where also many of those who had not been known, or had been known but not seen in public, were showing up (though not to TV cameras). If they were all there, and smelt a possible police scheme to isolate them as individuals and groups, and apprehend them for the purpose or investigation and interrogation, was the subsequent violence (also) a ruse for those 'gang leaders' to slip through the mob and make good their escape? It is not unlikely that the names of photographs of some of them are already in the files of the State Intelligence, including the anti-terror Q-branch, and these persons had not been seen or sighted for long. If provoking violence beyond what the police might have been prepared for with all the advance preparations, was also aimed at forcing the government to go slow with possible arrests and launching court cases against individuals associated with violence and other acts of criminality from the past, it is unlikely that much will be heard of such processes in public, unless those thus apprehended want a propaganda advantage of their 'current plight', whenever.

The Angst

INDEPENDENT OF questions as to what caused the violence, or what even caused the Jallikattu protests and contributed to their success, the hurt and angst of the Tamil population in the country cannot be under-estimated or dismissed as nothing more than a self-inflicted fantasy, the like of which or worse things other sections and States in the Indian Union had suffered in their time—and/or continue to do so, now and possibly into the future, too. Yet, there is also an urgent need for the Tamils in the country, whether in Tamil Nadu or elsewhere, to look at issues individually and address them collectively, rather than take up issues collectively, brand them as hurting 'Tamil sentiments' and 'Tamil pride' and/or Tamil socio-cultural ethos, and seek to address them at the level of the individual, by internalising the hurt and angst—and give it a collective expression. The highlight issue was a fast-receding cultural tradition, yes, but the underlying concerns were/are real and immediate.

This is because there are layers and layers of issues and concerns for the individuals that some seek to be pushed under the carpet—or, over it—as 'Tamil identity' and 'Tamil hurt'. In doing so, they also seek to confuse Tamil political, social and economic identities as one, though deep inside,none is ready to give up on the other, or give one up for the sake of the other. From an 'India Collective', the Tamils are to seek a 'Tamil national' identity or a 'Tamil ethnic identity', or a mix of them both. Whatever the reason and purpose, it can cut not in just one or two ways, but in very many ways.

This exclusive 'identity' identification had begun at the turn of Independence, perhaps even earlier. For contemporary historic reasons of those days, the 'Dravidian political identity' had sort of superseded the 'pan-Indian socio-political, national identity' that Gandhiji's brand of freedom movement sought to espouse as a larger cause. Suffice is to point out that the 'Dravidian polity', in the form of Justice Party, had come to power in 1920 in what was then Madras Presidency, a year ahead of Gandhiji taking the national movement to the masses. Though founded in 1885, the Congress became a popular political force only after Gandhiji took it to the masses from 1920 onwards.

The Justice Party first, and the self-respect movement of *Periyar* E V Ramaswami Naicker later on, and the divided Dravidian polity with the DMK parent as the fountain-head, all stood for a socio-political vision and an accompanying politico-economic mission that subsumed the larger 'nationalist' mission-vision of the freedom movement, post-Independence Congress, and those of the ruling BJP at the Centre, for now. It cannot be called the seed and source for the emergence of 'Tamil angst', or 'pan-Tamil' identity, a hundred year hence, or much earlier. But the Tamil socio-political awareness and enlightenment was there, to be seen, felt and imbibed, if that's what was wanted, even through the first-quarter of the

20th century. Rather, the angst of the times was the cause of the emergence of the 'regional' political movement *vis a vis* the nationalist cause, both of varying hues over the past 100 years. It is thus that the inherent region-centric angst became the source and strength of centripetal politics in each of the four southern States earlier than in much of the rest of pre-and post-Independence India. But the Indian constitutional scheme ensured that they all still remained the centrifugal force.

'Identity' Coalitions

In what is now the south Indian State of Tamil Nadu, this angst of the time became the unacknowledged under-pinning cause for the founding of the South India Liberal Foundation (SILF), and it came to be known popularly by the name of its mouth-piece,as *'Justice'* Party. Socio-economic equity and equality became the basic tenet of the new party, which was more of a social force, until the advent of the Montagu-Chelmsford Reforms, and the consequent elections to provincial legislatures, set up under the Government of India Act of 1919. With the Indian National Congress boycotting the elections, as part of its Non-Cooperation Movement, the Justice Party formed the government in the elections that followed. By 1921, the Madras Presidency government came up with what is known as the 'First Communal GO', followed by a 'Second Communal GO' in 1924, and a Third Communal GO by a non-Justice Party administration in 1927, providing for reservations in government jobs, based on castes and religions. So much so even indirect elections for the mayoralty of the then Madras Municipal Corporation was held on a caste-based rotational-basis, year after each year. It was to ensure that non-upper castes also had their mayor. Later, the rotational scheme alone ensured that the upper castes, starting with the numerically miniscule Brahmin community, too benefited from this quota system.

The rules of the game were changed in the Nineties when the then Tamil Nadu government under DMK Chief Minister M Karunanidhi introduced the application of the much-delayed Constitution Seventy-Fourth and Seventy-Fifth Amendments, reviving the elected Council of the Madras Corporation after three decades. Hence, thepresent caste-independent direct elections to the Chennai mayoralty.

The Justice Party government of the Twenties of the last century followed upon the 'reservations' scheme of 1921-24, with the takeover of most, if not all Hindu temples in the presidency, identifying the administration in some cases, and priesthood with the upper-caste Brahmin community. However, as a 'single agenda' party, targeting the uppermost caste Brahmin community in terms of political administration of every kind, the Justice Party soon left behind an electoral vacuum, which a up and coming Congress Party with the freedom movement as its central piece hijacked sooner than the various stake-holders were ready for.

From the top-half, the non-Brahmin upper-castes started losing their political relevance to the newly-evolved Brahmin-Harijan-women combine of Gandhiji's Congress, which was already on the upswing. However, the Justice Party's socio-economic relevance and dominance took a more direct anti-Brahmin shape, hiding in it their in-born anti-Dalit social intolerance so very cleverly. From the bottom half, there emerged, as a consequence of the 'Harijan upswing', political-awakening among the 'intermediary castes'. It was a combination that continued to hold sway over regional politics in later-day Tamil Nadu, for most parts. The emergence of a new 'identify coalition' inspired by Gandhiji, coupled with the fast-tracked achievements of the Justice Party government on the electoral promises from 1920 on, led to the party losing political relevance faster than the founders were ready to accept and re-adjust themselves to the new realities.

The re-adjustment came a decade and more later, after the Congress won and lost power in a matter of two years, 1937-39. *'Periyar'* EVR re-worked the Justice Party movement, to suit the times and also the new challenges. Thus was born his rationalist, 'Self-Respect Movement'. The movement took a new name as 'Dravidar Kazhagam' (DK), and was unabashed in its frontal criticism and attacks on the Brahmin community, and also the symbols and symbolisms associated with the latter. It was a straight-from-the-heart, straight-to-the-heart approach of the *Mahatma* that Periyar had localised, to suit local socio-political conditions, using local idioms and identifiable symbolisms. Thus, everything identified with the priestly Brahmin community, from Sanskrit, (hence Hindi), temples and gods, including religious scriptures, deities and idols, all became targets of Periyar's attacks, both verbal and physical.

Third Coming!

The arrival of Independence and the advent of a non-Brahmin, at times non-Brahminical leadership of the dominant Congress Party, first in the Madras Presidency, and later on in the post-Independence Madras State (now, Tamil Nadu) might have delayed the arrival—rather, the return—of Dravidian polity to the centre-stage of regional politics, which had become even more 'identity-driven' than already. As in the decade immediately before the advent of Independence, the Dravidian movement had 'alien' people in the 'Aryan' Brahmins, their language, Sanskrit and Hindi, (as propagated by the proponents), temples, reservations and every social and political symbol of Brahmins as issues to fight over, for equal rights and more. It is not about the right or wrong of it, which was also not disputable at least at the time it all began. It was about the cause and the symbolic identity issues, which ended up engraving an indelible 'Tamil' historic, cultural, social and political identity in whole generations of populations.

Periyar and his Dravidar Kazhagam had a substantial following, independent of the reasons, justifications, and causes, if any. What is even more inspiring was the way post-Independence Madras State (later renamed as Tamil Nadu) adapted itself to change, and how the dominant Dravidian political ideology allowed itself to be absorbed in the larger Indian national identity and cause. Yet, that could only delay the 'third coming' of the Dravidian polity, which was slowly losing the anti-Brahmin tag to a more pertinent, pro-Tamil, and later, pan-Tamil tag.

In political terms, it might have been different; in electoral terms unexpected, but the attendant social transformation was smooth and silent. From within the 'upper caste-dominated' Congress leadership emerged Kamaraj, a backward Nadar, as the Chief Minister, who stayed on in power for ten years till 1964, before going national as president of the Indian National Congress, still ruling the Centre and most Indian States, including Tamil Nadu. In socio-political terms, Kamaraj's elevation stalled the 'third coming', or early return, of the pan-Tamil Dravidian polity. If a Kamaraj had not risen at the time, considering that the Dravidian political movement was not yet ready, physically and otherwise, to displace the Congress at the helm, one would have been invented.

Inspiration *vs* Aspiration

Between Independence and the elevation of Kamaraj within the dominant, ruling Congress hierarchy in the State, the Dravidian polity too was going through cataclysmic changes. Or, at least that was how some interpreted the DK's boycott of the nation's Independence Day and the subsequent (though not consequent) split within what was then a social movement, into a political party with the name and title, 'Dravida Munnetra Kazhagam' (DMK).

The anti-Hindi agitation, the rice scarcity, and the rising prices all got a 'North-South' divide tag attending on them, too. Barring 'Hindi imposition', which could have and should have waited, much of the issues flagged under the slogan, *'Vadakku vaazhkirathu, Therku theikirathu'* ('North is progressing, South is diminishing') did not have much truth in them. Under the post-Independence Congress regime (1947-67), and more so during the 1954-67 period, there was all-round progress across the present-day Tamil Nadu, in terms of new industries, irrigation and hydro-power projects, new schools and hospitals, free education and free noon-meal scheme for school children, new roads, more buses and power-lines, and unprecedented infusion of Central government funds and projects in every conceivable sector of growth, industry and development—and jobs in the non-agrarian, new-generation industrial sector, which had become an unavoidable necessity for a variety of social and economic realities, all round.

However, given the dangerously undefined aspirations of an already educated and relatively enlightened population, the people's expectations in post-Independence Tamil Nadu was more than what the government(s) of the day could meet. People learnt not to appreciate what they had compared to what their parental generation had. They aspired only for what they did not have. Or, so went an argument. If so, this was so across most of British India, especially in the erstwhile Madras Presidency, where the early arrival of the British East India Company, had changed the political and revenue realities, and socio-political moorings so very completely. The people too wanted all of it, here and now and not be satisfied with some of it now, and some of it later on. It is this inherent inability of the socio-political and politico-administrative systems of the time, and the inherent inability of the Independence era central leadership (of the Congress) to be more definite about what was possible and what was not that the political Opposition in the Dravidian polity, especially the DMK, began exploring and exploiting to the hilt.

When the DMK came to power in 1967, in areas where the previous governments could not meet the people's undefined aspirations, the State was already in the take-off stage. So, the DMK government could take it off from there, and be able to meet much of the societal aspirations, which had formed the centre-piece of their political and electoral agenda and promises. Thus, for everything that the government did in other parts of the country, in terms of the language issue, public distribution system (PDS), prices and supplies, and alsosocial sector advancements as reservations inhigher education and jobs for more communities and castes long before the Mandal Commission report made it possible, the 'Dravidian polity' could claim authorship, though not exclusive ownership.Why, even for a nationally-acclaimed and globally-recommended social welfare scheme like free noon meal for school children by the Kamaraj regime of the Fifties, revived and upgraded as a full-fledged government programme with hundred per cent budget allocation when MGR was in power, the copyright was with Tamil Nadu.

New Challenges

Yet, there was a time between the Seventies and possibly the Nineties, when there was less and less talk of 'pan-Tamil identities' and goals, with most aspirations and consequent expectations and demands of different layers of the local population being met to substantial satisfaction. The trickle-down effect of socio-political transformation and upward mobility that the 'Dravidian social movement' had triggered, starting from the Justice Party's days, was all too visible, though it was violently divisive in terms of social mobility, be it vertical or horizontal, or both. The inevitability of such transformation brought with it, new challenges on the socio-political front, which was less studied or followed, especially by the competing political leaderships of the day. It was not without reason. This was also because there was less of competition, less of available political alternatives. Again, long before the rest of the nation began hearing about the 'TINA factor' ('There Is No Alternative', to the *status quo*), Tamil Nadu had experienced it, was practising it.

The attainment of the social, political and/or socio-political goals of individual political entity, from the Congress to the DMK and later the breakaway AIADMK, and later on to caste-identity parties like the PMK, VCK and PuthiyaTamizhagam, and their inevitable electoral coalitions send out contradictory signals to the self and the other, all at once. On the one hand, the two 'Dravidian majors' the DMK and the AIADMK, had come to dominate the State polity. But in ideological terms, or even in terms of social identity, they had out-lived their political utility for their one-time constituencies.

If anything, the early DMK rule had rendered its own ideologies irrelevant through rampant execution of expressed commitments on the social, political and economic fronts, especially after coming to power. The breakaway AIADMK, from 1972 on, did not have any ideological moorings or claims to call its own. Apart from personality issues, the DMK split itself became possible as an idea only because the parent party had sort of outlived its ideological relevance, utility and purpose. It was like the Congress as a one-issue umbrella organisation fighting for freedom, becoming instantly irrelevant once that goal was achieved.

In the existing Tamil Nadu context, *Periyar* EVR and his DK had hoped to keep their concepts continually relevant as a social uplift movement by staying out of electoral politics. But their followers in the Dravida Munndera Kazhagam (DMK) and its founder, the late C N Annadurai, set themselves a political goal of winning elections and forming government. The goal having been achieved, there was only so much of their socio-economic agenda that they could deliver upon, before becoming increasingly irrelevant—and ready to go their ways.

If personality issues and ego-clashes caused those splits, it was only to be expected. Like Kamaraj and the Congress before them, an MGR would have been invented, if not born already. So would have been an AIADMK, by whatever name called. Politics and personalities apart, through the period from Seventies to the Nineties, the Dravidian political identity got itself submerged in the emergent Dravidian politico-administrative identity, the latter being able to 'deliver' on their promises and the people's aspirations, all of them from the past. The greater the achievements of the Dravidian party in power, be it the DMK or the AIADMK, the greater became their own future promises and the futuristic aspirations of their constituencies. This only fed more aspirations and fed on even more aspirations.

Undefined, Un-refined

The problem with people's 'aspirations' is that it remains undefined, and more so un-refined even if relative clarity emerges as to what (all) it stood for, in a given space and time. It is like the blind men and the elephant. As long as there is a general element of discontent among the masses, and as long as there is a leader or an organisation that has the right mix of imagination, cadre-strength and staying-power, it is bound to feed on the people's aspirations and also feed them, in turn. Individually, people begin to connect with the generalised promises of these leaders, which is mostly the promise of change precededby condemnation of the existing Establishment, established norms and systems or the established political leadership. It depends on what the 'replacement' has to offer, not even in terms of promises, but only in terms of feeding the aspirations of people.

Whether it made economic sense or not, in the Tamil Nadu of the Nineties and afterwards, the rival Dravidian parties did meet most of their socio-economic commitments, both put down on paper before and after elections, and also those that the former inspired, either at the political or social level, for them to evolve on their own steam. Issues of reservations, rural roads and education, poor-housing and unsuccessful PDS scheme had all been addressed. With the result, the Nineties, for instance, would see a craving for schools licensed by the Central Board of Secondary Education (CBSE), whose curriculum standards became a social status symbol even in remote villages of Tamil Nadu, compared to the State Board(s). So was the new-found craving for 'English medium education' from kindergarten upwards, with a dash of Hindi-learning, in a State that had fought 'Hindi imposition' only decades earlier.

By the time the new millennia was set to commence, Tamil Nadu had met much, if not all of its self-desired and self-infused goals in terms of socio-economic and socio-political churning process that it had set for itself since the commencement of the twentieth century. Some might still argue that but for the intervening freedom movement, it might have been completed earlier. The truth is that but for the freedom movement and Independence for the Nation, much, if not all of it would and could not have even taken off.

Since the Nineties, the Dravidian political 'super-powers' too found themselves outliving their carefully carved out political agendas and social commitments. This happened mainly owing to their achievements and contributions while in power. This meant that in the absence of electoral competition, and/or political reach and staying-capacity of such competitors, the DMK and the AIADMK themselves ended up as being a shadow of their original ideological self. Rather, the DMK lost its ideological relevance. For the AIADMK, fighting corruption was its only politico-electoral corner-stone.

Under Jayalalithaa in the Nineties, the AIADMK too became synonymous with 'corruption' and lawlessness that party founder MGR had fought in his time (and won!) against the DMK parent under Karunanidhi. This again meant that they needed to try and retain their old and original cadre-force even while adapting to attract the new-generation voters bereft of the 'isms' of the past.

If they are electorally relevant still, even if they are construed as not having much more to offer in terms of political ideology or even welfare concepts, it is because and only because they are already there, and there is none in sight who has either the cadre-strength, staying-power or patience. This, again, is not without reason.

In the post-economic reforms of electoral politics all across the country, cost of contesting elections and winning them has become disproportionately costly. Floating, running and 'maintaining' a political party from grassroots-level upwards requires deep pockets, which most new entrants do not have. The 'change' is what they have to offer the voters, but they end up changing in between from being the 'new' to the 'old' ways of older parties because that is what politics in Dravidian Tamil Nadu has come to. No, it is not about corruption alone. It is as much about the achievements and contributions of the 'Dravidian political administration', with the result, the individual has fewer aspirations at the personal-level than what's already on offer without he even asking for many, if not most of them. What he needs, thus, he is unable to identify and is unsure of demanding.

Political One-upmanship

This, in turn, has led to a situation in contemporary Tamil Nadu that political one-upmanship has become the order of the day. It does not stop with what one 'Dravidian major' offers in its election manifesto, or in its Budget while in power.

'Social welfare' and subsidy-driven welfare being the same sides of the same coin for both the DMK and the AIADMK, their competition has gone on to seeking to fix the other on the question of 'who has betrayed Tamils and Tamil Nadu (more than the other)', while in power. It is in this context, the history of the Cauvery water dispute with neighbouring Karnataka, the Sri Lankan Tamil ethnic issue, and also the Sri Lankan ethnic issue, the decisive 'Eelam War IV' and the Katchchativu Accords, all involving neighbouring Sri Lanka, have acquired dimensions that were not known to have existed until recently—and not certainly so deep in the Tamil psyche in Tamil Nadu.

Even at the time India was negotiating and signing the first of the two Katchchativu Accords with neighbouring Sri Lanka in 1974, not only the ruling DMK in the State and the Opposition AIADMK under MGR, but even the Congress Party, under the late Kamaraj, had raised its voice. Though Kamaraj had parted company with then Prime Minister Indira Gandhi-led majority faction of the ruling Congress at the national-level, his voice carried credibility all across. Likewise, on the issue of 'Hindi imposition' Congress Ministers from Tamil Nadu (then Madras State) had raised their voice in the Sixties. It was not pooh-poohed as play-acting, as some of the later-day protests by the government parties in the State came to be dubbed. The list included MGR's day-long fasting on the Sri Lankan ethnic issue, Jaya's fasting for three days on the 'Cauvery water dispute', and Karunanidhi's fast that lasted only a few hours on cease-fire in Sri Lanka in May 2009. They were all Chief Ministers at the time, but the political credibility, or the credibility of the political class, was already at a low in the State, more than at the national-level, that the people received all these stage-shows with a lot of cynicism.

During the long periods of socio-political transformation of Tamil Nadu, something was happening at the grassroots-level without anyone knowing or noticing. Even those who had known or noticed them could not care less. It was the increasing ignorance of the younger generation about history, contemporary and otherwise. In its quest for technical and professional education, so as to benefit at the level of the individual from the benefits of the socio-economic reforms from the Nehruvian days till the completion of the Dravidian agenda in power, *the State had lost its sense of history, without anyone noticing it, or anyone wanting toacknowledge it.*

Barring an ideology-oriented political leader like Karunanidhi (for whom too, ideology had become a convenient deflective mechanism, over the years), no one cared about history, contemporary or otherwise. Suffice is to point out that political parties and even most charismatic leaders like MGR and Jayalalithaa relied on their speech-writers and statement-drafters to give them points to counter Karunanidhi's arguments, whether in the State Assembly, or in election campaigns, or plain and simple statement-wars. Ironically, the period also saw a spurt in the number of professional colleges and private schools, more in the rural sector than possibly in the urban areas of the State. They were mostly owned and/or promoted by ideology-driven political leaders from the past, who had settled down for a comfortable business of commercialisation of higher education in 'Dravidian Tamil Nadu'.

Downturn Reaction

This has had a downturn reaction, of schools and parents insisting on their children focussing all their attention to the study of science subjects, neglecting history and other humanities subjects so very completely. Children in Tamil Nadu are still discouraged to watch news channels or read newspapers, other than an occasional cricket-related stuff. All of it has meant that in this 'IT era', when information is king, and information is available at the finger-tips and literally so, there is as many ways to feed on the ignorance of the ignorant youth, many of whom have missed their aspiration-based avocation, whatever that be.

When these 'only technically educated' youth look back from their cocooned IT offices, all that they get to know is what the social media has to offer. Unknown to itself, this generation has thus created a situation wherein even left-leaning political parties that used to pride in their cadres coming from the poor and the downtrodden are unable to attract audience to their public programmes, if the latter are not provided with chairs– even in the midst of paddy fields and farm lands. The dignity that the socio-economic reforms of the previous decades had instilled in them has made the new-generation youth limited in knowledge of their own surroundings, with the result, there is no knowing the history of their own land, or that of a specific issue, or the reason and reasoning behind the decisions that were taken and in ways they were taken.

All of this has led to a situation in the past few years when history and politics, sociology and social realities, fed through the internet and the social media, have become the near-exclusive tool for learning and assimilating ideas, arguments and 'concepts', if any. Google is their sole source of information, and Wikipedia is the Gita, the Bible and all religious texts rolled into one. It is generally overlooked thatWikipedia itself is a volunteer-driven effort and at every stage and turn, the voluminous website tells the reader that some aspects of a claim made in the text are yet to be sourced or sworn to credibility. With the result, Goebbels-ism too has had a field-day—of lies when told repeatedly becoming truth, or is believed to be the truth, no questions asked or no understanding needed.

This is true of many, if not all of everything Indian. In States like Tamil Nadu with relatively higher levels of literacy, education, and consequent 'enlightenment' and urbanisation—which is a two-way street—there are local versions of all of it and more, when compared to the national scene and edition. But do national editions exist? They do. Better or worse still, the authorship for the application of the new-world, new-generation tools lie elsewhere, not in States like Tamil Nadu. But the content-material is bettered and tested in the State. So deploying a tool tested elsewhere for its success became easier and quicker in the contemporary Tamil Nadu socio-economic and socio-political contexts. But for a generation ever open to the world but closed inside, the sources for verifying, double-checking facts as made available through the social media is next to nil. If there were any, they belonged to the same generation and the very same 'closed club' where he or she is already an active member! But then, the *Angst* was not a product of the same, but the Jallikattu protests were a result of it all—and more!

Vaadi Vaasal to Neduvasal

FOR ALL the angst, protests and even violence, Jallikattu had been forgotten within the first weeks of the restoration of the animal sport across Tamil Nadu. People went back to their work and routine, the media in search of other sensations, issues and concerns, of which there is no dearth in the State (and thus contributing not only the publicised but also hidden causes of the angst). The social media too is driven by causes and fed by those behind such. Was it so, is it so? The answer to this query is both yes and no. Yes, because Jallikattu has been consigned to annual memories, to be possibly revived and revisited the next year, and the years after.

Would anyone have cared for Jallikattu as a pride of the Tamils the world over but for the ban, accompanied by other elements of hurt to the 'Tamil pride', is a million-dollar question. Or, will the 'core group' of protestors (whoever they were all) and the participants in those protests soon insist on staging the sport on the Marina sands—or in all conventional, rural venues—in the years to come, starting with *circa* 2018, just one year down the line from the original version and edition? The State government might see a tourism marketing-opportunity in it, considering especially that for years now an annual Pongal Trade Fair is being held not far away, at the Island Grounds, in Chennai city.

Over the past so many decades, Jallikattu, like the annual Chennai Music Festival season in December, has attracted tourists from near and afar. There are also those foreign tourists who land in Chennai for the music festival, then travel to other parts of India, especially south India, or even neighbouring Sri Lanka or Maldives for a holiday, and return in time for the Jallikattu season, before returning home. A few, especially Indians overseas, that too Tamils, add the annual Thyagaraja Music Festival in the temple-town of Thiruvaiyaru, again falling in January-February, to their itinerary, or at times replace Jallikattu with it, or *vice versa*, depending on their other commitments and interests. In such a scenario, giving wider coverage to the Marina sporting event, the local media will surely start flagging nagging questions on animal safety, and that of the viewers, especially tourists from outside the country and the State. After all, they were the ones who had flagged issues of animal safety in the first place, and provided space for animal enthusiasts, only to forget it all when the pro-Jallikattu protests became a mass movement. Maybe, they too had not thought about the possibility of their earlier coverage, contributing to the ban.

A lot can depend on how the pending Supreme Court case (at the time of writing) takes shape, as and when. For, even keeping the case alive without a final decision on the new, Tamil Nadu law of 2017, can well facilitate the conduct of Jallikattu in the year(s) to come.

In the past, judicial stay on the ban, ordered by the Centre, had facilitated the conduct of the sport. A clear and final picture can emerge when and only when the Supreme Court pronounces the final verdict—in this case, or any other(s) that may follow. So can Executive orders, either of the State or the Central government, or of both. To the 'no' part of the answer is the question, whether the angst-protests have ended after all. In the normal course, the welling and swelling of public dissatisfaction, including disaffection, end up as spent-out once the immediate cause and concerns are addressed. It will take a similar bundling up of such other issues and concerns, aspirations and failures, to motivate the masses to repeat the 2017 show.

In India, as elsewhere, such signals and symbols to social revolutions, if the latter can be called so, happens in every new generation. It is as much in Tamil Nadu, too. Rather, it takes a new generation to find expression for the pent-up emotions to find socio-political space and acquire adequate pace, as well. A 'generation' in context is around 20-30 years, or so. It is thus that the Justice Party revolution of the early Twenties of the previous century was followed by the freedom struggle and the Independence-induced socio-political and economy-driven industrial revolution since the Seventies. The anti-Hindi agitation followed in the Sixties, and so on. The current period was thus ripe for a revolution and for the pent-up angst of our times to find public expression. The Jallikattu protests happened. It fitted the time scale.

Trickle-down Effect

Rather than seeing the possible end to the angst-induced protests, the process has percolated to the lower, village-levels. They have broadened to cover other aspects of social and community life and living, wherever and whenever the governments at the Centre and/or in the State is seen as taking unilateral decisions impacting on local trade and life, land, water and air. Call it the trickle-down effect of democracy or whatever, but it has been so as with other aspects of the greater concept and goal, including socio-economic uplift through the electoral process.

If the Jallikattu protests focussed at the Vaadi Vaasal of the the sport arenas across the State, the immediate next venue for a new cause and a new protest was Neduvasal, a village in south-central Pudukottai district. Within weeks of the conclusion of the Jallikattu protests, the locals in Neduvasal began protesting against what they alleged was the 'unilateral decision' of the governments at the Centre and the State to license exploration for hydro-carbons in the village. The work had commenced some years earlier but was suspended after similar protests, but much limited in scale and publicity. The villagers and their protest leaders said that extraction of hydro-carbons would convert the Cauvery delta (or whatever remained of the same after the eruption of the legal and political issues involving neighbouring Karnataka) a piece of parched land, where nothing grew afterwards. It was an expression of the local people's angst, but in the mood set off by the Jallikattu agitation only weeks earlier, soon political party leaders, environmental activists and all supporters of the bull-taming sport, began taking an interest in the Neduvasal protests.

The Jallikattu protests, especially its size and consequent/subsequent success, helped focus media attention on a relatively greater degree than earlier, on the Neduvasal protests, too. Like the larger-scale Jallikattu protests, the Neduvasal demonstrations too were in the making for long. The governments and government agencies had lost sight of the issues involved and the possibilities –including the possibilities of ideological elements giving it all a harsh and un-yielding touch, and within no time, again. The Jallikattu protests had made it possible, and its success too as plausible. The Neduvasal protests were/are not the only one of its kind, either. Before Neduvasal, there had been similar protests against methane projects, and against the laying of underground pipelines for transporting and supplying imported natural gas to industrial areas in the southern parts of the State, with possible home supplies for kitchen-use.

Ahead of the protests against hydrocarbon-centric projects, there was also a protest about locating a neutrino project along the Western Ghats. According to experts in the field, the India Neutrino Observatory (INO) has the potential to become as famous as CERN's particle physics lab, including the possibility of throwing up Nobel Prize winners from the nation/State. The loss of the project to another State could well be a loss of prestige and pride for Tamil Nadu in the future, too. It is another matter that the first detection of neutrinos, produced by cosmic rays, occurred in an experiment conducted at the public sector Kolar Gold Fields (KGF) in neighbouring Karnataka, as far back as 1965. Ironically, social and political champions of river-water issues in Tamil Nadu, especially the Mullaperiyar storage dispute with neighbouring Kerala, appealed to successive chief ministers there, not to grant environmental clearance for the INO project, proposed to be located across the inter-State border. They argued that the INO could affect the health of the Mullaperiyar dam, which was what the continuing dispute was all about—and this argument was buttressed by the farmers, political parties and successive governments in the State.

Before all this and more, the first signs of public protests for a public project of a massive kind happened in Kudankulam, further down in southern Tamil Nadu, against the Russian-made nuclear power-plants. That captured the imagination of the media and other activist groups, alike. But unknown mostly outside the State and remembered by even the locals was the protest against the private sector Tata titanium project in southern Tirunelveli and Tuticorin districts, in 2007. Considering that the Tatas were then facing deeper trouble in West Bengal over the 'Nano' car project in Singur, both the promoters as also the State government (then under DMK Chief Minister Karunanidhi) thought it wise to shelve the Rs 12,000-crore project, covering 10,000 acres of land, for sand-mining and separation of rare minerals.

Unlike in Singur, or even the later-day Kundankulam and Jallikattu protests, none attributed an ideological angle or involvement against the Tata's mineral-separation project in Tamil Nadu. There were the genuine concerns of the landowners and farmers, and even fishers, as with Kudankulam later. There were also reports of locals-centric commercial rivalry taking its toll on the Tata project. But there were no reports of ideological groups getting involved, or seeking to exploit the emerging and existing situation. It might have also owed to the possible conviction that by backing or joining the protests, they could end up conferring greater respectability and credibility to what had become a commercial battle.

Not far away from the locale emerged the Kudankulam demonstrations of 2011, dubbed the 'mother of all protests in Tamil Nadu' until the Jallikattu protests, six years on. It was in fact the third in a series of anti-Kudankulam protests over the previous two decades and more. On those occasions, there were specific issues over price compensation for private lands acquired for the project, diversion of irrigation waters for human consumption in the proposed Kudankulam township and the like. Though the local Church was known to be involved, no one attributed any ideological involvement. Nuclear safety, or safety from possible nuclear-leaks and bigger accidents, would gain greater currency only in the new millennia in Kudankulam, though long before the Fukushima tragedy in Japan, Chernobyl in the erstwhile Soviet Union and the Five-mile Island leak in the US had made it to the headlines.

Determined Few

Post-Jallikattu and even post-Neduvasal protests (suspended and revived time and again after promises from the Centre and State governments—that did, or did not, convince the local leaderships), there came the anti-NEET protests against nation-wide common entrance examination for medical college admissions, citing quality as the lone cause and justification. Doubts persisted in the 'Dravidian polity' if it was yet another ploy of the Centre (independent of the party in power up there) to dilute the nation's 'federal structure' more than already.

For the youth that had led and participated in larger numbers, the Supreme Court's intervention and insistent in the matter seemed to be providing the proverbial red rag. It all came to a head-on when a rural girl student, Anita, from a poor family, committed suicide, reportedly after failing in the NEET examination, with which the State government could not but cooperate with after the Supreme Court started taking a more serious view than in earlier years and occasions. Daughter of a head-load worker, Anita had scored well in her State Board Plus-Two examinations, and this was also cited by the pro-NEET lobby within the State to deride the Tamil Nadu school curriculum and examination system.

The death of Anita, who had travelled up to Delhi, after filing an interlocutory petition in the case and had to return home without being heard, whipped up sentiments very similar to those of the Jallikattu protests, but it has also taken the angst to a lower level of the present generation youth, to school-leavers and those just below them. Though not wanting to join issue on the streets as it also ultimately involved the future of their children, their limited opportunity to join medical colleges, the socio-political class that the Jallikattu propped up may not give up, at least from within. It has consequences that might erupt like the Jallikaattu protests on a distant day, over an entirely different issue.

The interim period since the successful Jallikatatu protests also saw Tamil Nadu farmers—or, at least a vocal and imaginative section thereof—taking their agitation for better prices for their produce and other governmental aid, assistance and subisidies, to the capital city, not Chennai but Delhi. In the past, protestors from Tamil Nadu gathering at Delhi either had a political message or belonged mostly to political parties. Their protests too were confined mostly to the 'Sri Lankan Tamil issue'. The protestors were often addressed by political leaders and parliamentarians, cutting mostly across party lines and regional-divide. It was more in the nature of expressing solidarity with another regional/peripheral party from another State, especially, the politically 'hyper-sensitive' Tamil Nadu, more so in the coalition era in national politics and power-sharing.

In the past, most farmers' protest at Jantar Mantar, the rally-point in the national capital and larger marches, had related to farmers from the neighbouring States of Uttar Pradesh and Haryana, Punjab and Rajasthan. Whether organised by political parties or farmers' organisations, they used to be invariably huge and large. In comparison, the Tamil Nadu farmers' protests, commencing by mid-March 2017 had fewer participants but the determination of the organisers was obvious. In Delhi, the Tamil Nadu protestors were highlighting the plight of the farming community in the south Indian State, which was suffering the worst drought in 140 years.

The immediate cause and provocation derived from a series of farmers' suicides, caused by farm loans, and private and at times nationalised banks sending in hired thugs to recover tractors and other farm equipment, in lieu of the credit amount. This had led to a loss of face in the community, and loss of the bread-winner for the immediate family. It should agitate anyone under the circumstances, and fellow-farmers in Tamil Nadu are agitated, too—as counterparts elsewhere in the country, when their own brethren met with a similar fate. Depending on different parts of the State, the farmers had faced irrigation problems, caused mainly by the Cauvery water dispute with Karnataka or the Mullaperiyar storage-level issue with Kerala.

Lately, other river water/storage disputes too had emerged *viz* Kerala on the one hand and Andhra Pradesh, on the other—the latter pertaining to the waters of the river Palar in the northern districts of Tamil Nadu.

The angst however flowed immediately from the indifference of the State administration especially, as throughout much of the previous year it was tied down either to the Assembly polls of May 2016, or the subsequent hospitalisation of then Chief Minister Jayalalithaa, or both. Even when facing the Assembly elections, which proved to be tougher than earlier, Chief Minister Jayalalithaa's health did not permit her to apply her time and energyto address various pending and mounting issues of routine administration. Nor did she trust her political/ bureaucratic aides enough, to give them a free hand and take spot decisions.

But sympathy for an ailing leader (about whose 'true condition', the local media—and more so, the social media—continued to speculate, at times derisively), and the cultural empathy that you do not embarrass/harass someone in her place when she was ailing meant that the angst was allowed to pile up, too, with no relief in sight. So when after Jaya's death on 5 December 2016, her ruling AIADMK especially staged high and unbecoming battles of succession, the public mood got disrupted as never before in recent times. The Jallikattu protests happened. If Jallikattu as an issue was not available at the time, something else would have meandered its way into the collective Tamil Nadu psyche of the time and found near-similar expression.

Yet, in the case of farmers, the inspiration for the Delhi protests however flowed from the Jallikattu protests, and the Neduvasal-like agitations, later on. They had repeatedly agitated over their various causes throughout the preceding year or two, but with no relief whatsoever. What went mostly unnoticed for even viewers of the Delhi farmers' protests on the local television news channels was that most participants, especially in the early days, came from the older generation. Their grey hair and burdened demeanour were striking, compared to the youthful bounce that even TV viewers could touch and feel during the Jallikattu rallies. The green shawls that the Delhi protestors carried on their shoulders or used to tie around their heads, or cover their body as protection from the unfamiliar, dehydrating Delhi sun, were not known to many among the agitated Tamil youth of relatively recent origins. Even the older generation that had seen it in their younger days had forgotten it.

Tamil Nadu has had a strong farmers' movement in the early Seventies, with a strong presence and participation in the western and southern districts. The year 2017 marks the birth centenary of the farmer leader from those days, the late G Narayanaswamy Naidu. In the Seventies, there were long drawn-out, massive protests, leading to the police opening fire, in which activists had been killed. The protests of those times are remembered not just for the issues that it flagged or the solutions that it offered/found. It is remembered even more for the classic comment of the late M G Ramachandran, who was then the treasurer of the ruling DMK in the State. 'When police open fire, only bullets fly out...Do you expect rose petals to fall from them?' he was reported to have counter-questioned a newsman at the time. Over time, the protests fizzled out, especially after the farmers' movement got politicised, making it easier for the traditional political class to weaken it from within and without. But the protestors remained.

In the past, whenever the 'competitive Dravidian polity' of Tamil Nadu played out in distant Delhi, Tamil students in the national capital identifying with either the ideology, party or leader would add to the numbers, either out of commitment, identification or admiration. For instance, apart from political parties, big and small, a group fashioning itself as 'Marxist-

Periyarist', for instance, has a vocal and at times substantial presence on the Delhi campus, especially in terms of providing an ideological mooring and identity. It is a combination of Marxist ideology and 'pan-Tamil, self-respect' movement, identified with the late Periyar, the great Tamil social reformer of the twentieth century. Followers held Periyar on par with, or at times more than Gandhiji. On occasions, other Tamils sharing the ideology or views of the protestors, or coming from their leaders' community or village/town too would join in to add numbers and verve to various Delhi protests staged by Tamil Nadu leaders from time to time.

Before the farmers' protests, Delhi Tamils had come together on the issue of Jallikattu protests. Earlier, too, many of the activists among them used to be known as coming together in many, if not most, anti-Establishment protests. Such protests have been against the campus Establishment, the politico-administrative Establishment at the Centre or back home in Tamil Nadu, or even in a neighbouring State like Karnataka/Kerala or a neighbourhood nation like Sri Lanka. Throughout the past decade and more, and even at the peak of the Kudankulam or the 'Sri Lankan ethnic issue', there was no instance of massive participation, as was the case during the Jallikattu protests.

In the case of the farmers' protests, they had a larger and more imminent issue with which every Tamil could identify and seek remedies/justice without fail and further loss of time. They had started off with highlighting their plight, a direct or not-so-direct, immediate indictment of the State government, for the rest of India also to see. There was definitely an anti-Centre stance, which is what had forced them to move over to Delhi and meet up with ministers and parliamentarians from across the country who were/are interested in farmers' welfare. At least initially, the Delhi media was amused by the farmers putting the skulls of those that had committed suicide over the past year or so on display in Delhi than anything more immediate and relevant. But when the Centre announced a relief package worth Rs 2000-plus crores for the State's farmers as against nearly Rs 40,000 crores sought by the Tamil Nadu government, as drought and floods relief for and from the previous year, they had had enough of it—or, so would it seem. The Centre's detailed explanations that it was only an initial payment under a particular head, borne by a particular ministry, and the rest would follow in due course, did not sell.

That the Centre had maintained stoic silence throughout the preceding months had also given raise to suspicions that the BJP leadership was playing politics with their plight and future, in the unfolding post-Jayalalithaa politico-electoral scenario back home. The Centre itself did not find the time and/or the need to explain to them that the package was only one part of the relief amount in a convincing manner. State BJP leaders, who had waxed eloquent on several issues from the past on TV talk-shows, and blaming them all on either the alternating Dravidian party government in the State, or the preceding Congress-UPA regime at the Centre, had lost whatever little credibility and hope that 'Modi care' had been able to build around the party.

Suffice is to point out that at the height of the Jallikattu protests, BJP's Union Minister of State from Tamil Nadu, Pon Radhakrishnan, ended up having to publicly apologise to the protesting population that he had not been able to fulfil his commitment to have the sport staged this year, too. But none cared to take notice, or appreciate him for the relative honesty that politicians were not known to display. Not that the protestors or the larger population had taken any of the promises made by any politician, representing the State or the Central government, the ruling party or the Opposition, on any issue seriously. At least their opponents and critics would remember and seek to recall, if only to try and embarrass them.

In the case of Pon Radhakrishnan's public apology, barring brief reportage in the print and electronic media, no one cared to take notice. The social media that was abuzz with pro-protests news, information, calls and analyses in favour of Jallikattu, if at all, only made fun/pun of the Minister's plight, not hailed him for his honesty and relative sincerity, if it was any.

Troubled Waters

Even as the Delhi farmers' protests were unfolding, and the Neduvasal-type of rallies were spreading to other villages that were expected to be affected by hydrocarbon projects of the kind, the fishers in the State were up in arms, once again against the killing of a brother, K Brijto, 21, reportedly at the hands of the Sri Lanka Navy (SLN). The issue refused to die down, even after promises by the governments and Ministers at the Centre and in the State. However, such interventions alone helped ease the tension, for the striking fishers and Brijto's family members to accept his body after the mandatory *post mortem* examination. A full week had elapsed by then. Though the protests were suspended, the fishers did not formally withdraw the stir. Nor did the arrest of Tamil Nadu fishers by the Sri Lanka Navy, or that of their trawlers (banned in the two countries) stop—indicating future stirs, fishing-boycotts and the like can be anticipated, as over the past years and decades.

Today, in the post-Jallikattu protests mood, the State's fishers have found a critical mass to take forward their agitations of the kind in the future, with greater traction with the hinterland youth and masses than over the past several years and at least two decades. Throughout the past, the State's fishers had found some sympathy with the people living around them, who might have also missed the fish on their dining table and plates.

They did find sympathy and ready support from the political class of the State, which had not missed any opportunity to embarrass one another, harass the Centre or target the neighbouring Sri Lanka, especially its military (navy in this case), on whatever issue that came their way. To 'em all, the fishers issue was more a tool for their political progression rather than to be viewed as a greater cause for which imminent solutions had to be found. The Jallikattu protests had fanned a new traction, and this time unlike in the past, there was greater and faster empathy and sympathy for the fishers, which could be touched and felt, elsewhere across the State, too. Yet, the fact remained that it was not as much as in the case of the Jallikattu protests, though the problems and concerns there were more real and live and livelihood-threatening than in the case of any other.

Kalam, *Kant-h*?

INCREDIBLE BUT true. That it should be happening in an 'enlightened' State such as Tamil Nadu. There is no denying the State's scholarship or its greater contribution to social reforms, social justice and social welfare—political and administrative initiatives and policy-formulations that should have achieved the set goals long ago, and sub-served the motives and motivation that had necessitated and made it all possible in the first place. It is hence inexplicable, too—but true, again. According to some recent studies, Tamil Nadu accounted for most protests and agitations for any State in the country, over a five-year period, 2009-14. The *India Spend* study claimed that at 109,548 the State accounted for nearly 25 per cent of all protests across the country during the period. It was nearly three times the number of agitations that the second-placed Punjab witnessed (40,513) during the period. It was the height of Sri Lanka's conclusive 'Eelam War IV', starting with 2009 and included the years when the UNHRC at Geneva was seized of the 'war crimes probe' in the country.

Any study will also show that it was also the period (possibly starting with the year 2007-08) that Tamils as an 'ethnic group' had protested on any issue in a big way wherever they lived than during any time in the past. In Tamil Nadu, these protests were accompanied and/or followed by those on the Kudankulam issue, the fishers' concerns, the Cauvery and Mullaperiyar disputes, and a host of other issues, from the poor/non-supply of drinking water in individual localities, power-cuts and the like. A year after the study concluded, the State was seized of the 'liquor ban' protests in various localities, in the run-up to the 2016 Assembly elections, which naturally did find its way into the study. For the massiveness of the protests, the Jallikattu rallies out-beat the Kudankulam agitation, which was confined mostly to the villages around the locality though at times smaller ones were staged in urban centres, including Chennai, Madurai etc.

Yet, most of these protests were not without an air of discomfort, bordering at times on suspicion, about the real players behind the organisation, or their real motives. None seemed to have been willing to come forward to prove their credentials other than to run down their critics, that too conveniently through the social media. In the case of the Jallikattu protests, for instance, the organisers, real or imaginary, seemed unwilling to accept victory and concede their own success. They wanted the protest to continue, if only on the weak plea that the governments could still go back on their public commitments and legislative initiative, with all political parties standing by it. It can be argued that they were disillusioned by the precedents from the past, even on the Jallikattu issue—which alone had forced Minister PonRadhakrishnanto apologise in public.

In the past, on the issue of 'Hindi imposition', then Union Minister from the State, O V Alagesan, quit the government of

Prime Minister Lal Bahadur Shastri, owning up responsibility for not being able to convince his leadership, as promised. Alagesan's resignation did not set the Cooum, or the Cauvery or the Vaigai or the Palar on fire, the anti-Hindi agitation had done it already. The resignation did not even douse the flames. But the angst and disillusionment in Pon Radhakrishnan's time was so very complete that no one even bothered to demand that he quit. Nor would they have been moved, either, if he had quit, or the entire State government, then under Chief Minister O Panneerselvam, had done so. They might have been surprised, and pleasantly so, as no one expects governments even in politically-alive States like Tamil Nadu to quit office on principle, or for a 'principle'. None of it would have shocked the protestors or the people at large into stunned silence. Such was/is the credibility of the political class, especially since Jayalalithaa's hospitalisation and subsequent death, that anything would have been *passé*. Nothing would have taunted them, leave aside daunted them.

The political class was/is afraid that it was/is a twin-edged sword that could hurt them, as much. The non-political class of protestors, and the real power(s) behind those protests, seemed travelling in a different plane altogether. They were clearly working for a continued stalemate, which alone they seemed wishing for, all the time. So even when most protestors returned home, satisfied with the promise made by the governments in the State and at the Centre, and the initiatives that they two had taken together or separately, the core group(s) would not leave until they had sent out a violent message, as well.

Could the violence have been avoided? Yes. Why was it not so in practice? The police (alone) were not to blame. There were those that were determined to end the protests in violence. They wanted it, they got it—or, so it seems. But did the protests, its theme and the larger participants and the national/international audience seek/deserve it? NO.

Right Place, Right Time

Looked at rationally and logically, nothing explains the success of the Jallikattu protests. Nothing else explains the need and spread of the Chennai violence that followed. Vandals set fire to police vehicles even some distance away from the Marina venue, in whose neighbourhoods, however, the cops stood accused of burning their own vehicles and those of others. It is for the Justice Rajeswaran Commission to find the truth (as only commissions of inquiry under the relevant law are tasked too, but have seldom found the whole truth and nothing but the truth). The hope is that this one will go in for the culprits of violence, and go behind and beyond the culprits to pinpoint the causes and *cause celebre*, not only of the violence but also of the need and justification for the Jallikattu protests in the first place. If nothing else, Tamil Nadu needs to know. The nation should know.

If the pent-up Tamil feelings and sentiments triggered the success of the Jallikattu protests, did anyone foresee the possibilities and triggered it by calling for the mass movement? Did Jallikattu issue happen at the right place at the right time? Or, was it an accident of everyday events that it got the better of the Tamil Nadu population and their better judgement(s)? After all, over the past year and more, there had not been any governance worth it, and more so after Jayalalithaa's hospitalisation.

A people who had prided themselves as the soldiers of Periyar's 'Self-Respect Movement' until not very long ago were being treated contemptuously to an everyday sight of political veterans falling at the feet of their *'Amma'* (when they might not have done to their biological mothers, in a long time), every now and again, and senior civil servants, described as the 'steel-frame' of the inherited Indian Establishment, showing no signs of any steel or frame in them, individually and collectively. It is another matter that they all remain the same in other States and the Centre, too. It got institutionalised in Indira Gandhi's time, if not that of Jawaharlal Nehru, and continued under Vajpayee's coalition set-up with some if's and but's, but has become a fine-art again in Prime Minister Modi's time now, whether or not he likes it or wants it. But Tamils and Tamil Nadu want to be thought of differently, and act differently, too, but to the outside world but not within, and from within.

Apolitical Vision

Despite all this and worse, if there is one person who has influenced, or inspired, to be precise, the present-day Tamil Nadu youth, it is former President A P J Abdul Kalam. It may be more, or less, the same way in much of the rest of the country–other than those that continue to look up to the likes of Bill Gates and George Soros for such inspiration. The average Tamil youth could actually relate to Kalam, his means, mission and vision, not only for the nation but also for them all at the level of the individual. Before Kalam, yes, Gandhiji and Jaya Prakash Narayan (JP) in their respective times and circumstances had influenced the nation's youth.

Nearer home in Tamil Nadu, Periyar, and social-reformist counterparts elsewhere played a role, bigger or smaller in comparison. Closer to our times, Anna Hazare did stir up the conscience of the nation's youth. None of them barring Kalam held any political office. Yet, barring Kalam, there was a political content to everyone's mission and vision. At a time when the rest of the nation's youth were being inspired by political issues that Anna Hazare represented and by political leaders like Narendra Modi, their counterparts in Tamil Nadu drew inspiration near-exclusively from Abdul Kalam. It was more so in his role and contributions as a technocrat, not as a former President, but whose rags-to-respect story through sincerity and dedication, simplicity and brevity stood him apart. He did not make political sense, because he did not talk politics, but he made greater sense as he was talking precisely that.

Kalam did hold a political office, and the nation's highest one at that, but his mission and vision for the nation's youth was apolitical. There was no politics of any kind whatsoever in his speeches, writings or interactions with the students and youth, across the country, and their cousins and country-cousins, whenever he travelled overseas. In the case of the Tamil youth, they readily identified with the man, as one of them, and as the pride of all Tamils. They all did hear about Indra Nooyi and Sundar Pichai, yes, and a host of other young Tamils doing great things in corporate America and the rest of the world, but immediate identification with them invariably stopped with the urban, urbane sections of the State's youth. For the rest of them all, young and old, men and women, poor and rich, they can still all imagine themselves in Kalam's shoes, or slippers, or whatever he had or did not have as he grew up to what all he became.

Yet, when Kalam, from among the most respected scientific administrators of the country, sought to explain that the Kudankulam project was not dangerous, the non-committed youth alone heard and also listened to him. The protestors pooh-poohed him, as they seemed worried more about carrying forward their agenda than finding the truth, the whole truth and nothing but the truth. With their fingers to the people's pulse, political parties in the State that were sympathetic to the protestors' cause, were wary of commenting on Kalam, leave alone joining issue with him.

Yet, at Kalam's unexpected death in 2015, the whole of Tamil Nadu wept with his family, as had happened only in the case of Annadurai, Kamaraj, MGR and Jayalalithaa before and after him. Barring Kamaraj, who was a former Chief Minister, the other three were in office when they died. They were also reigning supreme as political party leaders with a massive cadre-base—and a larger support-base that owed to the social and welfare schemes that they had initiated, or represented, or both. Truth be acknowledged, Kalam's death touched many people at a more personal level though they may have seen him only on the television screen.

Before Kalam's time, earlier generation of young Tamils, still shaking off their rural background and knowledge and understanding gathered from the upbringing that accompanied it, drew inspiration from the likes of the late Dr M S Udayamurthy (1927-2013), who in contemporary terms could be described as a 'self-improvement *guru*' of his times. A native of the tail-end Nagapattinam district in the Cauvery course, Udayamurthy acquired a doctorate in chemical engineering from the US, worked there, and returned to promote environmental causes across the State. In the process, he ended up addressing youth across the State on issues that impacted them the most in the Seventies and Eighties, thus becoming a 'motivational speaker' of his time, who was possibly better in Tamil than in English–or, as good as in Tamil as in English, a rare quality this in contemporary Tamils, then or since, mostly. Udayamurthy later founded the '*Makkal Sakthi Iyakkam*', or the 'People's power movement', but his unsure approach to take on the established polity in the historic Elections-1996, ended the sojourn. His long illness also proved a dampener. Incidentally, for the generation before Udayamurthy, there were the likes of 'Tamizh-vaanan' (1921-77), who even while writing detective novels in Tamil, set in overseas locales, gave a lot of self-improvement tit-bits to the readers of his youth magazine, '*Kalkandu*'. Born Lakshmanan Ramanathan Chettiar, his trade-mark cap and dark-glasses, made him a mix of ideas and imageries that the youth of that time needed to identify with, living as they did in the midst of the over-heated political atmosphere of the 'anti-Hindi' generation and years, too.

Off-screen Admission

But in Kalam's own time, or even starting off earlier than the great man came to be recognised so much across his own native State, another man who did influence the Tamil youth of his times (rather at its non-commercialised peak) was 'super-star' Rajnikanth. Long before the rest of the nation's film-goers discovered him, and paid up huge premium for the 'first-day-first-show' ticket of his movies (bilingual or dubbed in their respective languages), the Tamil youth had found in the man a simplicity, sincerity and honesty that others before him had seemingly lacked. It is Rajni's off-screen admission of 'guilt' (if it was any) that made up his huge fan-following from the Eighties and the Nineties, leading up to his super-stardom, first within the Tamil film industry and later on at the national-level, too. Before Rajnikanth and the more enlightened film-goers of his time, film-fans were fighting each other, having to choose between M G Ramachandran and Sivaji Ganesan. Of them, MGR took his mass-following to the DMK party to which he belonged and to the AIADMK, when he floated it. Sivaji Ganesan—the title identified with the Maratha warrior-king, which role too he portrayed on stage and on the screen, later on—had a fan-following cutting across political loyalties, yet he derived more from the Congress Party than the other way round.

But after they both suddenly left the scene—first out of mutual competition and even more out of the new-generation film-goer getting increasingly tired of their ageing faces and type-cast roles in stereotyped scripts—there was a gap that no one was able to fill. Most, including Rajnikanth, did not even pretend to attempt. For, Kamalahaasan, the up and coming local boy, was an iconoclast in word and action—who would go places as a film actor and film-maker, but not your super-star material, at least not yet. Rajnikanth too came up as an iconoclast but the new-generation youth, coming from an untested socio-economic background, could readily identify with the man. He was possibly the first Tamil film actor in decades uninfected by the screen presence of MGR or Sivaji for the new-generation fans to feel fresh about the man they saw on-screen. His sleight-of-hand, on-screen tricks like throwing the cigarette in the air and catching it with the lips, made him readily recognisable for the older generation and even more identifiable for the younger. But it was his off-screen lines like 'I like to drink hard arrack ('*pattai charayam*', in Tamil) in my leisure time' and his freely referring to the mental stress that he was rumoured to have gone through under work-pressure made him likable than being disliked by a conservative society that was learning and beginning to shed at least some of its age-old inhibitions.

Before Rajni's times, MGR especially would not only be the eternal do-gooder on-screen, but would also be shown as divining ways to avoid consuming liquor or smoking cigarettes in his films—unlike Sivaji, who did not go out of the way to deny the character what the script demanded. As with MGR's, Rajni's films from the Nineties on began carrying an occasional and oftentimes forcibly scripted-in political message, but then off-screen, people were equally convinced that he was too good a human being to allow himself to be drawn in, into active politics.

Of course, in Rajnikanth's time, there was already the up and coming Kamalahaasan, who had started off as a child artiste, and often got compared with Sivaji Ganesan for histrionic talents and MGR for his eye for technical details and 'production value', especially as he swung between semi-arty stuff and commercial cinema. For the average film-goer of the time, Kamalahaasan was a class apart, and Rajnikanth was readily identifiable. Even as Rajnikanth was moving up the ladder, not only in the film world but also in personal life, as sounding more philosophical and spiritual than anyone would have credited someone in his place with, the common man came to relate to the likes of Vijaykanth and Vijay, who in their times and respective generations got to be identified as 'poor film-producers' Rajnikanth'. But they too would move up the ladder, with Vijaykanth also trying his hand in direct politics by launching a political party of his own. The Desiya Murpokku Dravidar Kazhagam (DMDK) did not go places after the early promise because relating to the common man as a film actor and political leader are two different things.

Idealising, Idolising

To the twenty-first century Tamil youth, who has idolised Abdul Kalam, without having to put out his idols in a State where even film-stars had temples built for them in an earlier generation or two, public agitations and violence should have been an anathema. This should have been so, even granting that they had only resorted to self-preservation of their community identity and acted in self-defence against police highhandedness (alleged or real). All of Kalam's self-help advice was about self-improvement, and for greater identification with the Indian nation and Indian nationhood, without getting caught within the narrow confines of identity politics of every kind. If alive, Kalam might have identified as readily with Jallikattu as a martial sport as much as he would have most definitely eschewed and censured street-protests, leading up to violence, in the name of greater Tamil identity and angst.

In Kalam, there was a man who grew over and above the circumstances into which he had been born, and grew out of it all by himself—not when he became the President of the Union but at every step and every turn, leading up to the mighty steps of the Rashtrapati Bhavan. Those steps that he walked were decorated and embellished by his own academic and scientific successes that also made his nation greater than when he had arrived and had later stepped into the realm of space and nuclear technology and administration—as the likes of Sarvepelli

Radhakrishnan and Zakir Hussain, among others, had done in their own ways, when they walked the same steps, one as a world-renown philosopher and the other as an educationist, both academics in their own right. In Kalam, the nation had its first technocrat-President ahead of having aeconomist-Prime Minister in Manmohan Singh a few years later. Yet, when the 'village boy' from a fishing hamlet, sought to reassure the local people that the Kudankulam nuclear power-project would not harm them or hurt their livelihoods, the fisherfolk allowed themselves to be guided and at times controlled by people whose genuineness and scholarship were no patch on his. The same was the case in terms of Jallikattu and Jallikattu protests, too. No marks for guessing up to what point would have Kalambeen with them if he were alive, and wouldhe have said what they were doing was wrong.

To select a contemporary contrast for comparison, Rajnikanth did not possess an inspirational personality when he arrived. If anything, for a film hero of his times, he was among the least impressive, by looks, colour of the skin and diction, leave alone his language skills when it came to the local lingo, Tamil. He was still the Marathi Shivajirao Gaekwad from neighbouring Karnataka, but a bus conductor who would make it big. Yet, Rajnikanth was also yet another straight-from-the-heart public speaker at least when he arrived, and sounded as genuine as they come–and as philosophical and spiritual as he climbed up the filmi ladder. What more, here was a man whose rags-to-riches story might have also inspired a few youth, most of whom were as unemployable as they were mostly unemployed.

Yet, when Rajni decided to go to Sri Lanka in the post-Jallikattu phase of March 2017, to participate in a public function organised by the producers of his upcoming multi-lingual film extravaganza *'2.0'*, to present newly-built houses to 150 families of Tamil war-victims in the island-nation, sections in Tamil Nadu did erupt in anger. They had all along been complaining that India was not doing enough, though none of them were known to have donated a penny or paise to the Sri Lankan Tamil rehabilitation efforts, other than through words, which were mostly counter-productive. They were protesting that the film-producer, himself a Sri Lankan Tamil, had alleged business dealings with family members of war-time Sri Lankan President, Percy Mahinda Rajapaksa.

The repeated denials of the producer had fallen on deaf ears this time as on an earlier occasion. More importantly, no Sri Lankan Tamil society organisation or polity had expressed reservations to a fellow-member of the community providing those homes through a family charity. Maybe, weary of war, violence and even post-war political diatribes from all sides, for the Sri Lankan Tamil population, in those regions still limping back from decades of war-devastation, the presence of Rajnikanth perhaps electrified them.

Rajnikanth did cancel his Sri Lanka visit, heeding to pressures from nearer home, but then, he also said in his statement announcing the cancellation, how he had planned to take up the even more troubling issue of 'fishers' problem' with the Sri Lankan leaders, starting with incumbent President, Maithiripala Sirisena. It was not that at one meeting of the kind—or, even more—Rajnikanth would have been able to end any or all of the crises of the ethnic and fishers' kind, but then his presence and the international media attention that it would have generated would have been the kind of awareness that those that had protested his visit had been seeking all along–not that they did not know it, either. The question is thus not what Kalam or Rajnikanth could have done, but what they could not have done with those that were all the time flagging pan-Tamil causes but would not like to hear other views.

This, of course, does not answer questions on whether protestors would have listened—even if it had come from a Kalam here, or a Rajnikanth there, or, even together—at the time of Kudankulam or Cauvery/Mullaperiyar issues. Kalam had attempted to drive some sense and woefully failed on the Kudankulam front—or, was betrayed. In the case of Rajnikanth, it was the Sri Lankan Tamil cause, where he was coming out openly for the first time, with a positive gesture, which could have actually inspired others of the ilk, too. Though the Tamil Nadu voter did hail him and stood by him when he called for them to vote out the Jayalalithaa-led AIADMK regime when most film personalities of the kind preferred to look and act distant from what all were unfolding before their very eyes, as their electoral behaviour proved in subsequent polls of 1998 and afterwards, they backed his political judgment only as long as he reflected their mood and sentiments—not otherwise.

This might be a contrast from the days of MGR, who was riding both the filmi and political boats at the same time, jumped from one to the other, and cruised along very comfortably. Yet, whenever the question of the super-star entering direct politics arises, the Tamil voter still pauses to recall his famous one-liner from Elections-96: Even god cannot save Tamil Nadu, if these people were to return to power (*...Ivanga meendum aatchichi-kku vanthall, Tamizh-Nattai Aandavanalum kapparra mudiyadhu).* But a generation down the line, the Tamil voter has become more discerning in such matters, too. It however has nothing to do with Rajnikanth all along, and the likes of Kamalahaasan in more recent, post-Jallikattu times though no really linked to the same, talking politically sensitive issues. In a way, they need to relate to their fans' overall personality and larger concerns than the other way round. It may or may not have anything to do with the stars' decision to enter direct politics on a later day, but on issues such as brigand Veerappan's abduction of then Kannada film icon Rajkumar, the Cauvery water dispute and more recently political corruption, which Kamalahaasan (too) has since taken up the two-way communication is complete.

Nation Needs to Know...

BEFORE TAMIL Nadu's Jallikattu protests, the nation had been treated to massive, popular agitations of the kind in distant Delhi, when Anna Hazare gave the call. It was against political corruption of the highest order, at the highest of administration, or as what the people eitherbelieved or were made to believe. The protest leaders, starting with Hazare, did not name names, cite cases or even episodes, and not certainly figures. That job had already been done by the political Opposition and the media, some more than the others, but all of it within the four walls of democratic norms, rights and duties. Team Anna only gave an apolitical touch to the process, especially for those lacking mental clarity and moral justification to take the protest plunge.

After a point, the discerning from among the media observers and others did not miss the point, when slogans shouted at the Delhi venue especially had a unique mixture that had been forgotten since the days of the post-Emergency revival of democracy and free-speech. From one corner of the Anna protests would emerge slogans like *Vande Mataram*, identified with the centre-right RSS-BJP, Hindutva combine. From the other end could be heard the counter-slogan (!), *Inquilab, zindabad,* identified even more with the nation's centre-left communist parties. At that point, these conflicting political forces also lacked the moral authority required to swing in the fence-sitters while a third, *aam aadmi* grouping of common men and women, too, was seeking to exploit the emerging vacuum.Caught in the middle was Anna Hazare, whose chief commissars of the time, in Arvind Kejriwal and Kiran Bedi, would go their political ways. If he was wise to it even then, Anna did not express it. If he was ignorant of their possible machinations even at the time, he conceded it, or so it seems. At the end of it all, Anna Hazare packed up and went back to native Maharashtra even as leading members of Team Anna thrived in politics and public life, where they had not actually and directly belonged until coming under the favourable gaze of the 'mentor', who eventually disowned them.

Disappear as Fast

In Tamil Nadu, too, where Anna Hazare's call reverberated to positive public vibes, especially among the enlightened youth, there did emerge political aspirants, who again would not be able to stay together for long after—even when their electoral appeal (or, that of the cause that they had flagged) did produce a certain, though limited, ripple. They split first into two factions, and later on into three or more, only to disappear as fast as they had appeared. No one can blame the stranglehold of the Dravidian parties for their failure, which was what they had voluntarily and without any external help brought upon their own selves.

Around the time of 'Team Anna' initiatives and protests obtained ready traction all across the nation, the people were witness too, and also very much became a part of the 'Nirbhaya protests', again centred on and in political Delhi but with a reach that went into each and every drawing room and kitchen, street-corner and public place, even more than the anti-corruption drive. The crude and cruel gang-rape of an innocent migrant girl, in the heart of the national capital, in the middle of the night, sent out the kind of message or messages that nothing else had done in a long, long time.

It was more so, considering that the 'Nirbhaya episode' involved a solitary incident, as against gang-rapes and worse, whether it was in Delhi or any other corner of the country. In an earlier era, the 'Chopra children' murder case, which also involved the gang-rape of a teen-age daughter of a Navy officer, in Delhi, had shocked the nation into disbelief and worse. If people were shocked, then they were also numbed into not reacting as much. It did not, however, produce the kind of public revulsion, leading up to massive and weeks of protests, not just in Delhi, the venue of the gruesome incident, but also across the country, as the 'Nirbhaya episode' alone produced decades later. It is another matter that most participants in the 'Nirbhaya protests' had not even heard of the 'Chopra children' episode, even though the Government of India had instituted the annual 'Geeta Chopra' and 'Sanjay Chopra' bravery awards for children, as far back as 1978. The 'Nirbhaya' protestors were reacting to their times, their circumstances and social environment. Against this, participants at the 'Team Anna' protests quoted earlier instances of corruption in the country and outside, the law and practices, over a cup of tea, on the sidelines of the protest venues across the country, or in their own drawing rooms or clubs.

Mixed Record

Yet, neither the 'Team Anna' protests, nor the 'Nirbhaya revulsions' produced the kind of violence that was associated with the land take-over agitations in Singur and other parts of West Bengal. It was so in the case of other land take-over protests associated with the creation of Special Economic Zones (SEZ), as a part of the Centre's market-driven economic reforms agenda. Violence marked various protests against land take-over in different parts of the country, where new industries were to be set up or new coal-mining projects or power-generation units were to be set up. It was all in the name of protecting the environment and the locals, mainly tribal population, their interests and their own traditional and constitutionally-mandated rights and ownership. If there was political backing, and organisation behind some or many of these agitations, none cared to hide it from the public—though none of them claimed ownership of the various land agitations. The authorship(s) of most of these protests, almost always localised, were with the non-electoral, or anti-electoral centre-left organisations, in turn with a mixed record in terms of encouraging/eschewing violence. It was equally so in terms of the real authors giving a greater ideological identity than was possible for the so-called illiterate tribal population and their community leaders, who supposedly did not know their rights, nor had the means to enforce the same.

But in every such case where violence was involved and the law-enforcing authorities swung into action, the latter then became the target of political attacks, as their victims were 'innocent (tribal) people, seeking to protect their inherent rights'. In most cases, especially in terms of issues that had stalled development projects under the Centre, or where the Centre's decisions were involved, the 'innocent tribal population' did not have the knowledge and legal acumen to argue their case as well as was being done on their behalf. It was useful that Good Samaritans still existed and were ready to take the plunge—but their efforts did not go the way as would have been expected in the normal course.In many cases, the projects and schemes where there were protests and court cases only years ago, there has been great progress in implementation of the original 'developmental scheme'. Less said about the West Bengal and other cases where the respective State governments were involved the better.

As elsewhere in the country, in Tamil Nadu, too, the angst was there, and is still there. It might continue to be there for some more time, or years, to come. In a way, it was/is as much as it had been elsewhere in the country. There should thus be nothing more to the Jallikattu protests, if you recalled the likes of 'Team Anna protests', the 'Nirbhaya agitation', the Singur alienation and related issues of land acquisition and environmental degradation. Kudankulam might have shown the way, and later, there were similar protests against nuclear power-plants in places such as Jaitapurin Maharashtra. Not all of them turned violent, but most of them did succeed in the governments at the Centre and in the State concerned taking a re-look at the proposed developmental projects. That way, yes, Kudankulam protests started off quietly but turned violent in between, and sort of fizzled out ultimately. In comparison, the Jallikattu protests did produce results–and it might not have come this far, or helped re-commence the sport after the Apex Court had banned it, but for the protests. It too ended in violence, which was very much avoidable.

Not Episodic

'Angst' as an expression of a disturbed and disillusioned people's prevailing mood and mindset is not episodic or isolated. It is a collective, a sense of failure or betrayal flowing from a continuing or at least continual feeling and sentiment (justified or not-all-that justified). The youth in Tamil Nadu protested so very loudly and even more visibly on the Jallikattu ban. But they did not do so over something more immediate, if their divided political leadership(s) were to be believed. Both the

State government and almost all sections of the State's polity were opposed to NEET, but when push came to the shove, the former yielded, after all–and unlike in the case of Jallikattu, only months earlier.

The Supreme Court ordered it, and the Centre was tasked with conducting these examinations. Sections of the student community, especially medicos, too were/are opposed to what they say is the denial of 'equity' as may be different from 'equality', for students from poorer and rural sections, for reaching levels that only elitist schools offer elitist students from elite neighbourhoods—or, that was the argument. It was so, and remains so in a State where social equity and equality have been the *liet motif* of social reforms and political identity and being. For added cause, and also for added effect, the Tamil Nadu polity, always hyper-sensitive tothe 'State's rights' under the federal structure, saw it also as a Central initiative to hijack 'Education' from the Concurrent List of the Constitution, even though the Supreme Court alone had ordered it that way–and reiterated its resolve, too, to have it implemented or enforced.

No one asked the question loudly as to why the Centre was happily defying the Apex Court on the 'Aadhar Card' issue, but the Centre cited 'judicial direction' as the binding reason for implementing the Jallikattu ban andthe NEET implementation. On the reverse, no one wants to answer the often unasked question, why Tamil protestors cite 'federalism' to justify arguments on NEET but not give the Union of India room to decide on 'foreign and security policy issues' which was what the Sri Lankan ethnic dispute was/is all about in the internal Indian context(s).

From another angle to the same argument, the DMK's early political slogans centred on the theme '*Vadakku vaazhkirathu, therkku theikiradhu*' (North is prospering, South is suffering). The breakaway AIADMK, especially under the late Jayalalithaa, did not fall far behind, after party founder had begun by moving to the centre but could not hold there for long. But they were/are the ones who are opposed to every developmental project—big or small—in the name of 'environment' and 'livelihood' issues, terms that their political forebears had not heard. Rather, it was not on their agenda, then or now.However, the DMK-AIADMK have also acted and reacted irresponsibly over years and decades that they have handed over the serious business of agenda-setting to faceless peripheral parties and groups with deep pockets, and possible conviction that these smaller offshoots will never be in power, either to enforce their demands and promises, nor to consciously and continuously defy them with retrospective effect.

For their part, the organisers of the Jallikattu protests should explain, why they were so very focussed on a culture-oriented, non-livelihood issue like Jallikattu when NEET, for instance, was already a burning problem for their own younger brothers and sisters–and by extension the future of the State(assuming that most of the organisers were out of colleges and universities, and had gainful employment). NEET became a live issue only after the success of the Jallikattu protests and also after the restoration of the sport, and not when the 'sword' of a nation-wide common entrance test was hanging before the State's student community for years together, and when the generation of the Jallikattu protest-leaders' generation may have been getting admission to one engineering college or the other. That the issue blew up as big as it did only after Anita's suicide, and blew over when the Supreme Court, possibly wiser from the experience from the 'Jallikattu protests', acted tougher, and held the State government accountable for any law and order problem affecting this year's NEET examinations in Tamil Nadu.

Real Goals

Not that the organisation did not have its own weaklinks, especially in the current Indian context, but there is no explanation as to why PETA, the international NGO, suddenly became more or less the sole villain of the piece. It was evident from day one that the Animal Welfare Board of India (AWBI), constituted by the Centre under the law and whose members too are nominated by the Centre, was the main force behind the ban, at every turn. It cannot be blamed for getting the ban on the statute, as 'animal welfare' as the Board's members deemed fit was the mandate. The members of the Board were also chosen for their role as 'animal activists'. It was thus that the Board got into legal conflict with the MoEF on enforcing the ban. The PETA, yes, was another petitioner in the Supreme Court case, but could have only presented its representations and arguments only before the AWBI first, as the latter was the apex body in this regard. Did it mean that the late entrants to the protests and the social media scene on the 'revive Jallikattu' issue were trying to deflect criticism away from a public entity like the AWBI, towards a private NGO, with its own image and issue-related problems as a genre?

Reservations might exist about the constitution of PETA, or the larger issues regarding the Jallikattu ban, or even its funding and 'real goals', as is the case with most international NGOs, or INGOs, operating in Third World nations. Some of the related issues have been raising their heads wherever and whenever activist-induced protests in other parts of the State and the country take place. In the case of Kudankulam protests, for instance, then Prime Minister Manmohan Singh, known to be careful with his words in public, went on record that international NGOs were behind it. In other contexts too, both domestic and international NGOs were seen and believed to be using devious thinking and dubious means to hide their real goals and purposes and package their private and private sector concerns and interests as people's worries, or issues where people at large should be worried and protest.

Another after-thought mid-way through the Jallikattu protests was a self-imposed ban/denial of soft-drink brands identified by multi-trillion-dollar MNCs (multi-national corporations), from the West, incidentally the US in the two cases of Coke and Pepsi. There would soon come a verdict of the Madurai Bench of the Madras High Court, permitting State authorities to sell to the bottling-plants of the two MNCs, massive quantities of the Tamirabarani river waters in the southern districts, against local protests, when already there was a shortage of drinking and irrigation water locally, owing to a variety of reasons. The High Court verdict came only weeks after the Jallikattu protests, but the demand/decision against the two soft-drinks came earlier.

The issue also did not have any direct link or bearing on the Jallikattu ban, in whatever way one was to think. Did the Pepsi-Coke ban-demand have anything to do with other 'extraneous factors'? Why did some traders and their organisations in Tamil Nadu start identifying with the Jallikattu protests more than such other organisations and unions of other interest-groups? If they were the ones who distributed massive quantities of drinking water-bottles, and at times biscuits and other food items, to the protestors, was it all borne out of the goodness of heart alone, or identification with a larger causes of Jallikattu and the 'Tamil angst', or was there something more than met the eye? If it was an expression of the piling up of 'Tamil angst', it needs to be understood. If not, it needs deeper investigation.

Divine Rivers, Historic Waters

The Ganga is considered the holiest of all rivers in the country– and mostly just that. The Ganga is divinity, and is contextualised mostly to religious legends rather than its usefulness in irrigation, navigation and all other aspects of daily living and livelihood. The Indus has an equally important role in the North, or north-western India to be more precise. It is, however, related to its usefulness. It even lent its name to the landmass that we now call 'India'. In relatively recent times, it is once again involved in political issues on water-sharing between two adversarial nations in India and Pakistan. Water-sharing between Indian States on some of the Indus tributaries are a politico-economic issue, in which the Centre and the Supreme Court too have had their say. But it is not divine in the same sense and to the same extent as the Ganga.

The Aadi Perukku festivities are in the soul of the Tamil DNA, wherever he lives. The Cauvery is divinity for the average Tamil and is matched only by its proven usefulness– or, absence of it. Tamil history is a part of the folklore as the 'Grand Anicut' is a reality that has existed for centuries and generations now. The Cauvery is a part and parcel of Tamil literature, but was never ever a part of Tamils' great history of wars and victories, for them to have imagined that its denial could ever happen, and could ever hurt. But the denial of irrigation waters and the consequent discontinuance of education for children of hurts families and societies as much as all the direct consequences of such denial,has led up to farmers' suicides. Another factor is even less understood, for it to be acknowledged.

The denial of Cauvery waters has generally starved the tail-end where the river mingles with the sea, for decades now. Even without rain-shortage and other ways of water-shortages, agriculture is a seasonal and undependable phenomenon in terms of job and income securities. Thus tail-end farm labour has tended to look up to the sea for livelihood, which again is seasonal. They have taken to part-time fishing labour, adding to the pressures on the seas in those parts, contributing to the fishing dispute with neighbouring Sri Lanka.

In the Nagapattinam neighbourhood, it is fishing dispute, not fishers' dispute, as in the traditional Rameswaram area, where there is a history of 'traditional fishing' in 'historic waters'. The denial of Cauvery waters, for instance, hurts agriculture, family incomes, livelihoods and life-styles, which are not necessarily directly related to agriculture but flows from it all the same. In the era of industrialised India since Independence, social status has flowed more from education and fixed family incomes, going as far up to engineering education and overseas employment. There are other reasons, too, for the phenomenon, but farmers' suicides are new to, in and for Tamil Nadu.

Despite offering words and condolences, the Centre has not acknowledged these as yet in any serious manner. The State government is unable to and/or unwilling to handle the issue, because it does not understand it as yet. God forbid the day, but the rest of the nation will perhaps understand the Tamil feelings on the Cauvery water dispute if and only if the water-flow in the Ganga were to get reduced, and there are water-wars between the riparian States. There is already, for instance, talks of China damming the Brahmaputra, the only big Indian river to carry a 'manly' name. That is the kind of situation already prevailing between Karnataka and Tamil Nadu over the Cauvery water-sharing issues.

The more there was coalition politics at the Centre, the greater were the ways the Tamil Nadu polity and hence successive governments targeted Karnataka more than other institutions involved—institutions that were not direct stake-holders, but did have a definite role to play in resolving the dispute. The rest of the nation might not have known it, or cared to remember and recall it, but the Tamils as the affected community, polity and Tamil Nadu as a government do remember and recall the ping-pong game that the Centre and the higher judiciary too have been playing on the issue, playing the ball off to the other, whenever it finds itself stuck in the middle of a new knot in the problem that they had not visualised earlier, or not cared to visualise.

Duality of Purpose

The duality of purpose of the Centre in particular became even more visible and was observed with greater keenness than already when government ministers, both in the State and at the Centre, promised the agitating locals in Neduvasal that nothing would be taken forward on the hydrocarbon exploration scheme without their consent. But even as the protestors went back home, hesitantly, the Centre wentahead and signed the project agreement with the private promoters, again, in 'distant Delhi'.

Equally 'insincere' was the way the Centre as an institution sought to understand and under-estimate and under-appreciate the Tamil angst of the Jallikattu protests times. Even as the State was recovering from it, or trying to do so, and the Neduvasal protests were still on and the farmers' agitation too had reached the national capital, the authorities came up with another avoidable mis-step. Either they were blind to the core of 'Tamil sentiments' that had been flagged only during the very same time and space, or did not care the least. Despite the long history of the issue of 'Hindi imposition', the Centre went ahead and began re-writing the name-plates/mile-stones on some of the National Highways in the State, with the English part getting replaced by Hindi. It could have been the handiwork of an ignorant somebody somewhere, but the damage had been done.

The insensitivity of it all alone stood out even in the eyes of those that otherwise supported Hindi-learning and were not exactly convinced about the causes and issues of 'Tamil angst', *per se*. Not long after, the Centre would dust up an old parliamentary panel report on 'official language', for Hindi-knowing speakers, including the President of India, if applicable, and members, to speak only in that language, both inside the House and outside. Later, it would once again explain away, and this time as Prime Minister, it would be Narendra Modi's turn to talk about the greatness of Tamil language, at a meeting of chief ministers in Delhi, in April 2017.

The Jallikattu protests are a living and more immediate episode whose details can be more readily recalled. The question arises if the Tamil sentiments would have been hurt as much as it got portrayed and displayed on the streets (and across the nation and the world at large), had it not been for the casual way the Centre and the Supreme Court addressed the issue on the very eve of Pongal festivities in January 2017? The Centre was passing on the buck to the Supreme Court, which in turn told the nation and more intently-watching Tamil people that it could not be forced to act or react. The community was already preparing for a long, festival weekend, and were rudely shaken out of their wits, by the Apex Court's observation, that very 'Friday, the 13th'. So no one needed to give a call, and everyone was ready to heed a call that never really came–because the Centre and the courts did not heed the already flagged matter.

What thus makes the Jallikattu protests stand out was the very fact that there was no major organiser(s), at least anyone visible in the public, then or even later on. The spontaneity with which not just one section of the State's population of nearly 80-million responded (either by direct participation, or by expressing open sympathy, or by holding the peaceful conduct with some awe) too has been unprecedented—barring the 'Nirbhaya protests' in the collective national context of recent years and decades. There again, in the 'Nirbhaya protests', every woman student and worker, mother and mother-in-law, sister and sister-in-law directly identified with the cause, and rightly so. Then, there were fathers and brothers, husbands and friends, all male, who too could not but be shocked at the gruesome crime and were surprised into direct action, when the youth of Delhi, with girls in the vanguard, gave the call. There was something personal to it, a sense of personal deprivation and anxiety, the absence and the consequent need for security for the fairer sex in this world of unfairness and inequalities, still.

Stalled Self-education

This was not the case with the Jallikattu protests. For most of the Jallikattu protestors, say, possibly going up to 75 per cent of the participants and sympathisers, if not more, they were not exactly directly hit or hurt by the court ban on the martial sport from a forgotten past but being played out each year in some corner of the State, with its different packets of different cultures, or sub-cultures, to be more precise. Truth be acknowledged, they were not indirectly hit or hurt, by a ban of Jallikattu, either for a year or two, or forever. They were there because the protests represented a larger cause in their eyes and minds, in their thoughts and daily deeds.

Rather, the protest-call, when it gained a momentum and direction of its own, touched a raw nerve in each and every Tamil, to a greater or lesser degree. Many, if not most of them, did not even know such angst existed deep inside them in the first place. Nor would have any of them acknowledged that it was all just skin-deep, or had emerged from deep inside to the skin level, over the years and decades, as one episode after another, one politician after another, one government after another, ignored them as a people, overlooked their legitimate aspirations and natural expectations, and consequent demands, as citizens of a constitutional state as *'India, that's Bharat'*.

Does it mean that 'constitutional nationalism' as a remedy and replacement for what was essentially amorphous 'cultural nationalism', too, has failed the nation already? Or are there still some hopes of early correctives and ultimate retrieval?

The Indian state did not understand the angst of the people, when it was building up in pieces and stages, or later on. Nor did the Indian state as an institution, the Establishment as a deliverer, or the politico-bureaucratic set-up do anything about it, even when it was understood, the causes deciphered and the solutions too identified. In the case of Tamils and Tamil Nadu, as in the case of a few others like possibly Jammu and

Kashmir and the 'Seven Sisters of the North-East', the Indian State and the Establishment had begun the post-Independence approach on a rather negative note. Dravidian politics and the ideology were little understood elsewhere. Nor was any great effort made to understand it and acknowledge it. Whenever such understanding happened and acknowledgement came, it was long after they had become due–with retrospective effect. The State, its people and polity had moved far ahead of the space and time,by the time the rest of the nation woke up to acknowledge it. The acknowledgement thus made little or no sense to them.

But when ideology gave place to raw politics back in Tamil Nadu, and coalition compulsions caught up with them, too, as with their ever-changing and shifting national partners, the Indian state woke up. For the past 25 years especially, the nation stalled and stopped its self-education on States and regions, population and polity, as did Tamil Nadu in understanding the pan-Indian view. In the evolving political environment, increasing sense of mutual suspicions and fears replaced the self-confidence and self-assertion of the local polity, competitive as it was already.

All of it also owed to the seamless way that Tamil Nadu and the pan-Tamil Dravidian polity integrated itself into national politics and scheme, in stages and paces, each flowing from the previous one and setting the mood and methodology for the next. But down the line, it was beginning to fall apart, too, maybe because, Tamil Nadu once again was moving at a pace different from that of much of the rest of the nation. Maybe, it is easy to blame Tamil Nadu for the 'subsidy raj' of social welfare, or the attendant corruption, early on. But here again, as elsewhere in terms of social enlightenment and economic uplift, the State was ahead of its time, or ahead of the rest of the nation. Maybe, 'what Tamil Nadu does now, the rest of India does 30 years down the line' may have a great irony attaching to it.

Demographic Delineation

What then can be the way out? The government at the Centre, long ago invented an institution called the National Integration Council (NIC), where issues used to be thrashed out. It was a recommending body at best, yet, in times of nation-wide differences and national distress, people did look up to it, all the same. In the era of television media and social media, institutions such as the NIC can do a great service for sharing of ideas and for the evolution of newer angles and aspects to a possible solution. It is true that Jallikattu protestors (as only like the nation-wide Naxalite groups) did not have, or do not have even now, a group of leaders, or a simple set of demands, for the governments (at the Centre and/or in the State concerned) to negotiate with. But *institutions like the NIC, when duly-represented, and taken seriously by the governments concerned, can go a long way in convincing the affected people that someone hears and that someone possibly also listens.* Maybe, no consensus will emerge, but it can still go some way.

How things shape up from there, and how things can be guided from there, will be for the governments concerned to consider and take forward. But in situations where the governments and government leaderships are seen as deaf, but not mute, and where they are unidirectional, then divisions and disturbing trends like this can well become unavoidable—and repetitive. It is the kind of model that can get repeated, not just only in one State, but also elsewhere in the other States. The stress of all this collective on the Indian Nation and nationhood are both avoidable and possible....If and if only someone out there, high there, hears and is seen as hearing, listens and convinces others of the listening part, too.

Yet, none of it explains the periodicity of protests in Tamil Nadu over the past decade and more, their success-rates and issues that they have flagged. The justification may still be there, as is the case with the rest of the nation, and their individual and collective concerns and problems. But the reasoning for such frequency of protests has gone mostly unexplained. It is a proven part of the social history of various societies across the world that whenever youth constitute a fifth or more of the population, political revolution is on the cards. The various revolutions the world over through much of the twentieth century, including India's freedom movement, fitted the bill. It was/is thus far in the twenty-first century, too.

This apart, in Tamil Nadu, as per Census-2011, the rural-urban gap in Tamil Nadu is closing in fast, it was 51.6 per cent against 48.4 per cent in 2011. So is the gender ratio. In a population of 7.21 crores in 2011, the male female head-counts comprised 36,137,975 and 36,009,055, respectively—with a marginal gap of just 1.2 lakh. It has remained so for some time now and is closing in fast. In 2001, in a population of 62,405,679 the male-female numerical gap was 3.96 lakh. Yet, certain anomalies too seem to have crept in and needs to be addressed. Between 2001 and 2011, for instance, the population growth in Tamil Nadu was 15.61 per cent, as against 11.19 per cent in the previous decade. At the same time, to the national head-count, the State contributed 5.96 per cent in 2011 as against a higher 6.07 per cent. These figures trigger new aspirations and consequent assertiveness at the State-level, and contradictions and confusion at the national-level.

Multiplicity of Militancy

Keen observers of the emerging and evolving social patterns, the Bharatiya Janata Party (BJP), especially, was there in the right place, at the right time, to channel the energies of the country's youth in a more democratic manner than taking an anarchist turn, at the national-level. Once again, if a Narendra Modi had not been born, one would have been invented—just as Gandhiji and the nationalist movement in their times. Here again in Tamil Nadu, an Annadurai and his DMK got invented decades ahead of its time. It may have owed to the fact that much of the present-day Tamil Nadu had come under the yoke of the British East India Company in a single stroke, after they obtained revenue-collection rights from the Nawab of Arcot for most of the regions that constitute present-day Tamil Nadu. This meant, modern education, health care and non-agrarian job/labour opportunities, and consequent political enlightenment of the western model too had come to the region earlier than elsewhere in present-day India.

This alone does not explain the protests and the pattern that has been around in Tamil Nadu for so time—but without most people noticing it, and government authorities acknowledging it. Independent of whatever is said or written in defence of it all, there is no denying the fact that Tamil Nadu is also the citadel of every form of militancy known to the country. It is the kind of 'reputation' (if it is any) that no other State in the country can 'boast of' (!), either. Other States, including troubled land-border States, in the North and the North-East, have one or more form of militancy identified with one peripheral group or the other from within. That they may get 'external' encouragement, funds, arms and arms-training, cannot be overlooked. But Tamil Nadu is the only State where all of them do exist. Worse still, in each and every case, it is the peripheral groups that have dominated the political discourse, and dictated the course of and for the mainstream polity—hence the State government of the day, too.

The local media does understand it, but becomes a part of the periphery, either on specific issues or ideologies, or on the whole, and without a second thought. It is not 'sexy enough' for the national media, whose evening talk-shows got reduced to mutual name-calling very long ago, and has not changed gears. In a way, only one newspaper, and none from the TV media, focussed on the twin issues of the Tamil angst getting centred on the Jallikaatu issue, and the inevitability of violence that was being co-sponsored by individual sponsor organisations of the Marina protests. While all leading Tamil dailies like the *Dina Thanthi*, *Dinakaran* and *Dinamani* did not miss out on the details of the protests, the court cases and local mood, the *Dinamalar*, even while reiterating wholesome support for the larger cause, also kept alerting the readers (and the authorities, too?) to the emerging possibilities over the coming days—day on day. The newspaper kept reporting on the disquieting events being played out in the 'core' of the Marina gathering, by the core groups themselves. Each of them had earmarked an area for itself, and each of them had groups of young supporters gathering around them—and mostly around them. Their physical identities in some cases and the slogans that they shouted, the speeches that their 'leaders' (?) made, all betrayed their ideological identities and political purposes.

The very fact that none of them was ready to hear out peace-makers like retired High Court Justice D Hariparanthaman or issue-sympathetic actor Raghava Lawrence, and did not heed their sane suggestions, the former borne out of years of experience, both in the judiciary and in social causes, stood them out for what they actually were, and what their actual mood and methods were aimed at. In one word, it was 'anarchy', though at least some of them would not have understood that either, but their self-styled leaders did know and understand it all. Not that the governments at the Centre and in the State, and their various agencies, were/are totally unaware of the possibilities. Just as not addressing the Tamils' angst in any substantial manner, they seem to have done precious little to address the emerging mood and methods of militancy, not all of which has remained undocumented.

It is this that has been on display, where exceptional organisational skills are on display—be it in the ways that the Jallikattu protests came out of nowhere and remained everywhere, or in ways violence took over the successful conclusion of the protests, as if it was a part of the plans of the faceless organisers, and was neither an act of god or a pre-determined provocation of the police force in what still is considered a 'peaceful State' in the Union.

As with the end-game of the Jallikattu protests on the Marina, suddenly moving to the Tamil Nadu farmers' protests in distant Delhi, sympathy agitations nearer in the State have a visible and identifiable pattern to it. It is not that success breeds success, and successful methods seek to be aped. But in this case, as with the end-game of the Marina protests or the Jallikattu protests, youth supporting the farmers' cause, in Chennai, sought to attract media-attention and also provoke the police force, by entering the seas on the Marina, and shouting slogans on every pending, ongoing and upcoming issues that had formed the core cause of the Tamil angst over the past years, more so the past months and weeks. The pattern may be denied, but unmistakably it did exist. It might exist as much as the angst remains.

The question is whether the pattern of protest will outlive the angst, and if so to what ultimate end, *vis a vis* the rest of the State and its population, the rest of the Nation, the Constitution and the constitutional processes. For now, however, the Jallikattu protests have flagged the angst, but the revival of Jallikattu itself has not addressed the angst-issues, fully or even substantially. Why, even the continued revival and restoration of Jallikattu remains the main piece of the pending Supreme Court case. The evolving scenario is as nebulous as the addition of every other issue, including inevitability of growth and development, jobs and incomes, get pieced together as one, as a cause of the farmers and other individual sections of the State's population—without which, again, the State's youth cannot move forward, and does not want to be left out, either!

Epilogue

WHEN KASHMIR was burning and 'Kashmiriyat' was the issue, Tamils deep down south understood only the anti-national anxieties that were gripping the rest of the nation—better still, the ISI-sponsored terrorism part of it. When the 'body-bags' of the martyrs of the security forces arrived, they wept with the families, honoured the dead with the rest of the nation—a practice institutionalised with the Kargil War.

It was the case earlier with the 'Khalistan violence' in Punjab of the Eighties, against which there was only revulsion in 'Dravidian Tamil Nadu', which had smoothly dovetailed into the Indian Union in those years and decades after Independence. Even the politically-sensitive 'JP movement' did not cause ripples in the State, nor would the 'Team Anna' protests and the 'Nirbhaya cause' in more recent times—when compared to the much of rest of the nation. The elite and the NGOs came together and meet together on the very same Marina sands and closer to the Gandhiji statue, to express their own concerns against the growing menace of corruption, and solidarity with the 'Team Anna' cause, mostly without understanding the internal workings and dynamics of individuals posing as the sole voice and negotiator of the man in whose name they were galvanising public opinion.

It was unlike the freedom movement and more so like the JP movement, when the Sarvodaya leader was left out of the political manipulations, once his purpose had been served. In a way, Anna Hazare was used for the same purpose as JP in the Seventies, to mobilise multiplicity of divided political and public opinions under a common, apolitical and acceptable umbrella, only to be discarded the very same way.

In the Eighties in between, the 'Assam agitation' did not happen for most Tamils, and much of the rest of South India in particular, nor for most other parts of India, too. Considering that the youth were at the vanguard of the 'Assam agitation', with no political guide of the stature of Jaya Prakash Narayan, Acharya Kripalani, JP's comrade-at-arms in the Seventies, or even out-and-out political leaders like Morarji Desai and many others, and also given the greater fact that it was the most peaceful of all long drawn-out agitations anywhere in the nation, post-Independence, the 'foreigners movement' should have derived more media coverage and public attention than it actually did.

It does not mean that post-Jallikattu protests, the Tamils will be able to appreciate the angst of other sections of the nation's population better than most. It did not happen to the Assam or Nagaland, Punjab or Kashmiri protestors–the peaceful and non-militant groups within them especially. To 'em all, it was business as usual once their immediate goal had been met, or they had failed or had been proved wrong. It may remain so even in the case of the Tamils *vis a vis* other causes and other protests and protestors elsewhere in the country.

There is of course the contemporary global dictum that violence (too) unites. It was evident that those who were seen as being behind the end-game violence at the Marina protests had others fighting for similar (but not same) causes, with a profound local touch and localised participation, elsewhere in the country, elsewhere in the world. It is not that the causes and angst of any or all of these protestors were justified, and had been channel properly, as well.

The reverse may also be the truth. Like midway through the Neduvasal protests post-Jallikattu agitation, villagers across the State stalled drilling by the Central Ground Water Board (CGWB), based on wrong information and understanding that they were all for hydrocarbons. The work was suspended. The mapping of ground water resources was stalled in a State where drinking and irrigation water is a live issue for long and remains so still.

Post-Jallikattu protests, when the Archacological Survey of India (ASI), whose activities do not actually interest the common man or political parties, transferred a 'Superintending Archaeologist' from its otherwise promising Keezhadi/Keeladi site in Theni district of Tamil Nadu, an 'angst' angle got near-automatically added, with charges that the Centre was trying to shut down the site. Even as the transferred officer K Amarnath Ramakrishna contested his transfer from the Bengaluru Circle to Guwahati Circle, and the ASI argued that it was a routine transfer at the end of the usual two-year posting and also involved 26 others too, the protests only got louder and more frequent. The fact that the new officer taking over at Keezhadi, P S Sriraman, earlier Deputy SA in Jodhupur Circle, was a native of Tamil Nadu did not matter. The ASI's clarification that they undertake a project only for five seasons, or years, at a stretch, and the Keezhadi excavations had commenced in 2013 has also not had listeners in the State.

Yet, there is another side to the 'angst' story. Both before and after the Jallikattu protests, sporadic incidents of public protests were staged against liquor outlets run by the State government, called 'TASMAC shops' after the public sector corporation founded for the purpose. There were reports of left-wing fundamentalist groups provoking, penetrating or hijacking such protests. Considering that in the frontline of most such protests were local women, there were also suggestions that the brains behind those agitations were using women as 'human shields'. When the State government sought to frustrate the Supreme Court's direction to shut down all liquor shops located along National Highways and State highways across the country, women outnumbered men in most such protests that caught the imagination of the whole of Tamil Nadu. There were also media visuals of women attacking liquor vends, which were coming up in the interior, especially those located near temples, schools and bus-stops.

In the early years of the new millennia, the then Jayalalithaa government in Tamil Nadu, in a reformist mood and mode, sought to upturn a few social practices of local communities. This was apart from the Chief Minister's economic initiatives, which included 'denial' of pay and pension hikes for the 13-lakh government employees and another five-lakh pensioners, freezing procurement price and quantity of paddy, increasing the price of milk, rice, power-tariff and bus fares. On the societal front, the Jayalalithaa government passed legislation/orders, to end 'regressive practices' like animal sacrifice outside some temples, and parents burying their children in sand for a brief while, as part of a committed offering to the local deity.

The Mukkulathore community, whose name is now associated with the Jallikattu issue, was known to be among the followers of some such practices. They were also believed to be strong supporters of the Jayalalithaa leadership. The reason for this went beyond the community background of Sasikala, Jayalalithaa's live-in aide, now housed in Bengaluru's Paraparanagara Agraharam prison in a corruption case in which both of them were accused. Sasikala is now convicted and sentenced by the trial court, and this sentence has been confirmed by the Supreme Court after Jayalalithaa's death.

When Jayalalithaa's 'social reforms' came about, the Mukkulathore community promptly voted against her AIADMK in the 2004 parliamentary polls, along with other sections of the State's population. The ruling party lost all 39 Lok Sabha seats in the State, to a stronger alliance, and by huge margins. This forced the Jayalalithaa government to reconsider much of her social and economic agendas, and there is now electoral evidence that the Mukkulathore community has returned to the AIADMK fold, slowly but surely. What is true of the Mukkulathores and Tamil Nadu, is true of other communities and societies in the rest of Tamil Nadu and in other States, too.

All of it only means that the governments, policy-makers and the political class as a whole cannot still overlook the building up of socio-political sentiments, and continue to think that it is business as usual. The choice, in a way, is to arrest the drift all-round through continuing engagement with the State, its polity and society, rather than giving it a continual glance, from time to time, only when troubles of the Jallikattu protests kind brewed. The alternative can well be a complete drift, that none in the Indian state structure or in Establishment Tamil Nadu itself, seems to be noticing even as they happen and address them—instead, wake up in a trance, only when jolted out, not knowing what had happened and how to handle it, thus ending up holding up the wrong end of the stick, every now and again, and end up blaming the other for whatever had gone wrong in between.

All along, pre-Independence and post-Independence, present-day Tamil Nadu and the Tamil people have held a candle to the what's in store for the rest of India, starting with the all-embracing policy and politics of social justice, social uplift, education and employment, industrialisation and income-generation. What Tamil Nadu did pre-Independence, the rest of the nation observed over a period and absorbed the same and adopted it 30 or 60 years hence. It was so earlier, it is so at present. It can well be the same in future, too!